PERCEVAL

OR

THE STORY OF THE GRAIL

CHRÉTIEN DE TROYES

PERCEVAL

OR

THE STORY OF THE GRAIL

TRANSLATED BY

RUTH HARWOOD CLINE

THE UNIVERSITY OF GEORGIA PRESS

ATHENS

Published in 1985 by the University of Georgia Press
Athens, Georgia 30602

The paper in this book meets the guidelines for
permanence and durability of the Committee on
Production Guidelines for Book Longevity of the
Council on Library Resources.

Printed in the United States of America

5   4   3   2

Library of Congress Cataloging in Publication Data

Chrétien, de Troyes, 12th cent.
Perceval, or, The story of the grail.

Translation of: Perceval le Gallois.
Bibliography: p.
1. Perceval—Romances. 2. Grail—Legends.
3. Arthurian romances. I. Cline, Ruth Harwood.
II. Title. III. Title: Perceval. IV. Title:
Story of the grail.
[PQ1447.E5C5 1985]   841'.1   85-8600
ISBN 0-8203-0812-9 (pbk. : alk. paper)

CONTENTS

ACKNOWLEDGMENTS

In the preparation of this translation I am heavily indebted to the research and erudition of the great Arthurian scholars of the last 100 years. A translator is primarily concerned with what the author *said* and *meant*. In determining what Chrétien said, like all Old French readers since 1959, I am thankful for the existence of the Roach edition of B.N. Ms. Fr. 12576 of Chrétien de Troyes' *Conte du Graal*, with its clear text, extensive notes, and glossaries. I am indebted to the modern English and French prose translations listed in the bibliography for suggestions of felicitous modern renderings, but my ultimate source was always the Roach edition. Determining what Chrétien meant, literally and theoretically, was far more difficult. I was privileged to have the advice of William Roach of the University of Pennsylvania during the final stages of the preparation of this translation, and I thank him for his generosity in taking time to read the footnotes and guide me through the realms of studies on the *Conte du Graal*. As he advised, I have placed an emphasis on the classical scholarship of Alfons Hilka and Roger Sherman Loomis which is not intended to be limiting but to give modern readers enough information to attain a simple understanding of the *Conte du Graal*. Readers who are inspired to acquire a deeper understanding of the tale will find a wealth of material at their disposal; the extensive research and theoretical studies of recent years require the space of a library, not a bibliography.

The translation greatly benefitted from the encouragement and advice of other scholars. I am especially grateful to Julian Harris of the University of Wisconsin, Norris Lacy of the University of Kansas, and Edward Peters of the University of Pennsylvania for their careful readings of the translation and constructive criticism. Ruth Dean, Sally Fullman of Caldwell College, JoAnn Moran of Georgetown University, and Jo Radnor of American University gave me the benefit of their experience with Arthurian studies and the needs of their students. Sally Purcell of Oxford University was a skillful and knowledgable editor. Elizabeth Kennan of Mount Holyoke College deserves to be godmother to this verse translation because of her valiant efforts in bringing it to successful completion. I am deeply grateful to all of them, and, needless to say, the responsibility for any errors is exclusively my own.

I thank my husband, William R. Cline, for his steadfast encouragement and our daughters, Alison and Marian, for their forebearance, since their youthful years were intertwined with the translation. The

Story of the Grail requires an understanding of the human heart and Perceval's determination to persist in the pursuit of a goal pronounced unattainable, with the final realization that the key to the door of the inner room is the spirit of love and charity. I owe whatever appreciation of these qualities I possess to the persons to whom this translation is dedicated: my father, Burton H. Harwood, Jr. and my mother, Eleanor Cash Harwood.

Ruth Harwood Cline
Washington, D.C.

INTRODUCTION

Chrétien de Troyes was the celebrated 12th-century poet who created the Arthurian romance as a literary genre. When Chrétien began to write his last and perhaps most influential romance, *Perceval; or, the Story of the Grail*, he was a mature writer with a widespread literary reputation. The accepted information about his career is based more upon deduction and conjecture than upon fact, but probably Chrétien was born at Troyes in Champagne around 1135, where he received a classical education as part of his clerical training. Early in his career he composed verse adaptations of Ovid's *Art of Love* and *Remedy for Love* and of two tales from the *Metamorphoses*, "The Shoulder Bite" and "Philomela." He also wrote two love songs. Although Ovid was an enduring influence, Chrétien became fascinated with the Arthurian legends that were circulating in France. He composed a tale of King Mark and Iseut, which was lost, like all of his earlier works except the love songs and "Philomena."[1] Traditionally, it is thought that he wrote the first known Arthurian romance, *Erec and Enide*, between 1160 and 1170.[2] He signed this romance "Chrétien of Troyes," which implies that he was not living in Troyes at that time.[3] Chrétien returned to Troyes sometime after 1164 and wrote at least three other romances under the patronage of the cultivated Countess Mary of Champagne, who was the wife of Count Henry of Champagne and the daughter of Louis VII and Eleanor of Aquitaine. *Cligès*, written around 1176, was strongly influenced by the Tristan legend, despite its Byzantine setting. *Lancelot; or, the Knight in the Cart* relates the love story of Lancelot and Queen Guinevere. Countess Mary suggested its adulterous theme, which appealed so little to the moral Chrétien that he lost interest in the romance and left the last verses to be finished by a fellow cleric.[4] Chrétien turned to *Yvain; or, the Knight with the Lion*, a portrait of courtly love in marriage which is considered to be his finest completed work. Chrétien is believed to have written *Lancelot* and *Yvain* between 1177 and 1181. During this period there has been speculation, but no proof, that Chrétien traveled and was in holy orders.[5] He may have written another romance, *William of England*, but his authorship of that work is disputed.

In 1178 a change occurred in the political situation in France which had a direct effect upon Chrétien's career by bringing him under the influence of a new patron. Louis VII, seriously ill and paralyzed, authorized the coronation of Philip-Augustus, his 13-year-old son by his third wife, Adele of Champagne. Philip-Augustus's godfather, Philip of Alsace, Count of Flanders, was named first Councillor of the kingdom and tutor to the young prince, in which capacity Count Philip carried out the functions of regent from 1178 to 1181. During his period of authority Count Philip was on poor terms with the rival house of Blois-Champagne; in 1179 Count Henry of Champagne left France for the Holy Land and did not return to Troyes until 1181, one week before his death. At that time Chrétien's patroness, the widowed Countess Mary, retired from public life. Count Philip's period of authority also ended in 1181, when Philip-Augustus assumed control of his government. At that time Count Philip was officially reconciled with the members of the house of Blois-Champagne and joined a coalition with them against the young king. In 1182 Count Philip, recently widowed and residing in Troyes, sought a papal dispensation to marry Countess Mary, but the marriage never took place. In 1190 Count Philip left France during the Third Crusade and died of the plague in the Holy Land a year later, in June 1191. This is the latest possible date for the composition of the *Story of the Grail*, which Chrétien dedicated to him.[6]

It is not certain whether Chrétien composed the *Story of the Grail* between 1178 and 1181, when Count Philip was at the height of his influence and power at the royal court of Philip-Augustus, or between 1181 and 1183, when Count Philip had allied himself against the French king and was living in Troyes, or at a later date prior to Count Philip's death in 1191.[7] According to Chrétien's prologue, Count Philip gave Chrétien a book containing a "Story of the Grail," which the poet called the best story told to entertain the royal courts. At Count Philip's request that he write the story in verse, Chrétien began his last and longest romance, which was never completed. The prologue implies that the story existed in oral and written form, but Chrétien de Troyes' *Perceval; or, the Story of the Grail* is the earliest known version of the tale of a young knight's visit to the mysterious grail castle. Chrétien de Troyes' romance is the source of the masterpieces of the subsequent generations of composers and writers who have taken up the theme of the quest of the grail.

Chrétien de Troyes' *Perceval; or, the Story of the Grail* begins after a brief prologue in praise of Count Philip of Flanders and the virtue of Christian charity. A noble Welsh youth who had been raised in ignorance of chivalry left his grief-stricken widowed mother for dead to go to King Arthur's court to be knighted. On the way to the court, he unwittingly insulted a maiden in a tent and incurred her jealous knight's wrath. King Arthur recognized the youth's worth, despite his rough manners and Kay's jeering, and granted him the arms of an enemy Red Knight. Kay slapped a maiden and abused a fool who predicted that the rustic youth would become the best knight in the world. An older knight, Gornemant of Gohort, regularized the youth's situation by teaching him to use his new weapons. Gornemant gave the young man simple rules of behavior, one of which was not to talk too much, since his speech revealed his lack of education. The youth defended the besieged castle of Belrepeire and fell in love with its lady, Blancheflor. They spent a night together sleeping side by side. Despite his unconsummated love for Blancheflor, the youth left her to find his mother, if she was still alive.

At an impassable river, the youth saw a crippled nobleman fishing and was entertained magnificently at his manor. The Fisher King gave the youth a sword that would break in only one peril. During dinner the youth watched in silent amazement as a young man carrying a bleeding white lance, two young men with candelabra, a beautiful maiden bearing a gold, bejeweled grail (a large, somewhat deep, serving platter), and another maiden bearing a silver carving dish, passed in procession through the hall into an inner room. The youth longed to ask about the bleeding lance and the grail, but, mindful of Gornemant's admonition, remained silent. The next morning he awoke to a deserted castle and narrowly escaped injury when he left. Near the castle he met his cousin, who was mourning her slain lover, and who questioned him closely about his visit to the grail castle. She asked him his name, which he had never heard before, but he said intuitively was Perceval of Wales. His cousin informed him that his mother died of grief when he left, and that his sin against her prevented him from asking one of two questions: "Why does the lance bleed?" or "Whom are they serving with the grail?" which would have healed the crippled Fisher King and averted disaster.

Perceval avenged the death of his cousin's lover by overcoming his slayer. The defeated knight was the vengeful Proud Knight who had forced his maiden to follow him in rags since the day Perceval insulted her in the tent. Emissaries from King Arthur's court found Perceval in a forest clearing, contemplating three drops of blood on the snow and thinking of Blancheflor's glowing complexion. Perceval injured Kay, avenging Kay's churlish behavior, but the courteous Gawain persuaded him to appear before the king. Amidst their festivities an ugly maiden arrived at court and upbraided Perceval for his silence at the grail castle. She challenged King Arthur's knights to depart on many adventurous quests. Perceval chose a quest which the ugly maiden called impossible: to return to the Fisher King's castle and ask the correct questions about the lance and grail.

The story turns to the adventures of Gawain, King Arthur's nephew and the best knight in the world. Gawain was summoned to Escavalon to defend himself against the charge of unlawfully slaying its late king. Stopping at Tintagel, Gawain championed a child, the Maid with Little Sleeves. At Escavalon Gawain was warmly welcomed by the young king and his sister, who were unaware of his identity until they were enlightened by a rioting mob. To resolve his conflicting obligations toward a guest and his father's slayer, the king sent Gawain away to find the bleeding lance, which was revealed as the lance destined to destroy the realm of Logres (England).

Interrupting Gawain's adventures, the story returns to Perceval. For five years Perceval had been wandering, unmindful of God, until he met his Hermit Uncle in a forest on Good Friday. The hermit explained that Perceval's sin against his mother caused his silence at the grail castle, and that Perceval was closely related to the Fisher King. The man being served with the grail in the inner room was the Fisher King's father, a man so spiritual that he had been sustained for years by mass wafers brought to him in the grail, which the hermit declared to be a holy object. Perceval repented and received communion.

The story returns to Gawain. After a series of misadventures with a beautiful but evil maiden and a treacherous knight Greoreas, Gawain was ferried across a river to a splendid castle. Within this castle, a white-haired queen, her daughter, her granddaughter Clarissant, and five hundred youths and maidens were awaiting a perfect knight to free them from a spell. Gawain survived the perils of the Wondrous Bed and arose as their lord and deliverer. Challenged by the evil maiden, Gawain leaped the Perilous Ford and was informed by an enemy knight, the Guiromelant, that the ladies of the castle were Gawain's grandmother, Queen Ygerne (also King Arthur's mother), Gawain's mother, and Gawain's sister. After accepting the Guiromelant's challenge, Gawain returned to the castle and sent to King Arthur's court for witnesses to their combat. The text breaks off abruptly as Gawain's messenger arrived at court, and Gerbert de Montreuil explained why, in his continuation of the *Story of the Grail*: "Chrétien de Troyes, who began the story of Perceval, told all this, but death overtook him and did not let him bring it to an end."[8]

How Chrétien would have ended the romance is a fascinating question since, whatever the traditional ending of the "Story of the Grail" may have been, his version is the earliest one that has survived. It would be consistent with Chrétien's earlier romances for King Arthur to hasten with his court to witness his beloved nephew's combat with the Guiromelant and for Gawain to be victorious. The Guiromelant's love for the inaccessible Clarissant, symbolized by the emerald ring, brings to mind the emerald ring that the Proud Knight gave to the Maiden in the Tent. Perhaps these lovers also would have overcome the obstacles that separate them. Some scholars believe that Gawain's adventures are a counterpoint to Perceval's adventures, and when the text breaks off, King Arthur's court has assembled once again and seems about to displace itself to meet a triumphant hero who has visited an Otherworld castle. Perhaps the story would have returned to Perceval, who had become spiritually prepared to seek the grail. William Nitze speculates that Chrétien would have ended the story with an episode in which Perceval breaks the treacherous sword he received from the Fisher King, after which Perceval would return to the grail castle to ask the liberating questions and marry Blanche-flor.[9]

Chrétien's *Story of the Grail* is a controversial literary work, and one of many debates about the romance is whether its present form is authentic. The *Story of the Grail* has come down as a two-part romance featuring Perceval's adventures in the first half and Gawain's adventures in the second, which are briefly interrupted by Perceval's visit to his hermit uncle. This duality of action in itself is not atypical of Chrétien's works.[10] The unfinished *Story of the Grail*, however, is one-third longer than Chrétien's other completed romances and contains numerous discrepancies in its time sequence.[11] These irregularities made certain scholars question whether Chrétien had written the entire *Story of the Grail* in its present form. The prevailing opinion is that the entire text is authentic, and that any discrepancies may be attributed to the fact that Chrétien died before he had a chance to put the finishing touches to his romance.[12]

The greatest controversies about the *Story of the Grail* are centered on the *matière*, or source material; the *conjointure*, or organization and plot construction; and the *sens*, or overall meaning of the romance. Interest in Chrétien's romance is so intense, because its influence on European literature is so important, that new discoveries or theories are continuously appearing. Volumes have been written about the *Story of the Grail*, and it is impossible to cover the material adequately in the space of an introduction.

Before a specific discussion of the *Story of the Grail*, it may be helpful to recall that the three major sources of medieval literary material, including Chrétien's romances, were Rome, France, and Britain. From Rome, through his clerical training, Chrétien became familiar with the Bible and the teachings of the Christian church, and also with Greek and Roman mythology and the legends of the Trojan war. He was greatly influenced by Ovid and sometimes imitated his literary style. From France, Chrétien was familiar with the *Roman de Thèbes*, *Roman d'Alexandre*, *Roman de Troie*, and *Roman d'Enéas*, and he was one of the first to use this long romance form to write about King Arthur. Chrétien was also familiar with the French heroic epic traditions embodied in the *Chanson de Roland*. Chrétien seems to have been a critical listener when Breton storytellers, descendants of Britons who emigrated to Brittany in the 6th century, entertained the sophisticated Champagne court with tales of Celtic gods and heroes like King Arthur, Tristan, and Finn.[13] Chrétien was also familiar with written versions of stories about King Arthur through Wace's *Roman de Brut*, a French verse version of Geoffrey of Monmouth's

Latin *History of the Kings of Britain*.[14] Troyes was an important city on
several major trade routes,[15] and Chrétien might have been acquainted
with certain Byzantine legends and tales of the Holy Land which were
transmitted to France during the early Crusades. To a limited extent
Chrétien drew upon his earlier romances for material.[16] Proximity and
probability are the surest tests of source material, and speculation about
other sources of the *Story of the Grail* should be based on a review of
these well-proven sources of literary material before searching further
afield.

    In essence, Chrétien's *Story of the Grail* is a tale of a young knight
named Perceval who visited the grail castle and failed to ask the right
question. It is difficult to tell whether Chrétien was familiar with an ear-
lier lost version of the story, or whether he was the first to compose the
tale as we know it today. Certainly Chrétien was familiar with the name
"Perceval of Wales," for he listed him among King Arthur's knights in
Erec and Enide, but he did not indicate that the name "Perceval" was
connected with any particular story.[17] The prologue shows that Chrétien
was also familiar with an oral and a written version of a "Story of the
Grail," which was probably a tale of a young knight's visit to the grail cas-
tle. Chrétien may have been the first to combine the name "Perceval"
with the grail story. Alternatively, there has been unprovable specula-
tion that Chrétien might have known some lost English or Welsh version
of the story.[18] There has also been speculation that the elements of Per-
ceval's visit to the grail castle had been combined in some lost Provençal
source.[19] The facts are simply that Chrétien's *Perceval; or, the Story of
the Grail* is the earliest known version in existence.

    In the absence of a more immediate source for the *Story of the Grail*,
some scholars have sought its sources in mythology.[20] At the beginning
of the 20th century the grail castle episode was believed to be based upon
a Greek or Oriental vegetation or fertility rite. The prototype of the Fish-
er King was thought to be a fertility god, and the lance and grail were
thought to be sexual symbols. Perceval's visit to the grail castle was inter-
preted as a failed initiation into a fertility rite, in which a new young king
would replace a maimed fertility god whose impairment had brought
sterility upon the land.[21] This myth is essentially about the coming of
spring, and it can be found in virtually every part of the world. Perceval's
visit to the grail castle also bears certain resemblance to other tales which,
in Albert Pauphilet's words, express mankind's hope of overcoming death
by recounting a mortal's visit to the realm of the dead and failure to do
some trifling thing which would have restored their world to life.[22] Fur-
ther research in the middle of the 20th century showed that many ele-
ments of the *Story of the Grail* were much more obviously present in Celtic
myths and legends, which were transmitted to the French courts by pro-
fessional Breton storytellers.

Roger Sherman Loomis did extensive research on the Celtic sources of Chrétien's *Story of the Grail*. He pointed out that the form of Perceval's adventures resembled accounts of the boyhood adventures of Celtic heroes like Finn and Cuchulainn. One of these adventures is similar to a Celtic story of a mortal man's visit to the Otherworld castle of the god Lug. The Celts believed that the Otherworld was located in the physical world but apart from it, in another dimension outside of mortal time and space. Places like Avalon, heralded by the appearance of white fairy animals and often reached by a dangerous passage or over water, were worlds a mortal could enter and live in for centuries, surrounded by beautiful women in an atmosphere of perpetual youth and feasting, but returning was always difficult, if not impossible.[23] The grail castle and Queen Ygerne's castle of marvels resemble the Celtic Otherworld in many ways. The castle of the god Lug would have contained the treasures of the gods, among them a bloody lance, an inexhaustible drinking vessel, and an inexhaustible dish for serving food — all prototypes for the lance and grail.[24] The water deities, Bran and Nodens, are among the possible Celtic prototypes for the Fisher King.[25] The seriousness of the Fisher King's injury is related to the Celtic belief in the sacral nature of kingship: the king must be unblemished, or his incapacitation would bring sterility and devastation upon the land. The Celtic prototype for both the beautiful grailbearer and the ugly maiden who accuses Perceval of silence may be the legendary Sovranty of Ireland, who appeared in both beautiful and ugly forms. Like many Celtic tales, Perceval's boyhood adventures are concluded by the youth's recognition as a hero at a king's court.

In Chrétien's romance, these Celtic myths are slightly Christianized to suit the spirit of the age.[26] The bleeding lance, which makes so little impression on Perceval that when he sees another combination of blood and whiteness he thinks instead of his lady's face, is declared to be the destructive lance destined to destroy the realm of Logres. Yet its drops of blood are reminiscent of the Holy Lance of Longinus.[27] The grail, magical in its combination of light and jewels as Perceval first sees it, is later said to be a holy object in which a mass wafer is borne to the ascetic father of the Fisher King. Certainly the thread of Christian charity runs through the romance without being strong enough to unite it. Perceval's sin — his callousness and indifference to the suffering of others, exemplified by his failure to return to help his mother — is a lack of charity. His failure to ask the liberating question at the grail castle could be interpreted in religious terms as a lack of grace.[28]

Some scholars have sought the interpretation of the romance in the source material and have oversimplified it to a description of a fertility rite or the boyhood adventures of a Celtic hero. Yet Chrétien intended his romances to be more than collections of captivating stories and expressed his exasperation with professional storytellers who ruined a familiar story by transposing or omitting episodes that were essential to the development of the tale.[29] Chrétien insisted that his romances have an overall meaning conveyed by careful construction of the plot. The *Story of the Grail* suffers, as does any unfinished work, from the lack of final coordination and revision, but Chrétien did not compose his romances haphazardly and would have had a general design in mind.

Other scholars have superimposed the highly Christianized themes of the continuations and later versions on the far less religious *Story of the Grail*. The Christian theories about the romance are numerous. Perceval has been interpreted as a symbol of chastity, the Fisher King as a symbol of Christ, and the lovely grailbearer as a symbol of the church. The grail, a dish which Chrétien's hermit says might be expected to contain a large fish, has been said to be a communion vessel, a ciborium or chalice, or the dish of the Last Supper in which Joseph of Arimathea collected Christ's blood. The grail procession has been interpreted as a sick-bed communion service, a procession of a relic reminiscent of the Byzantine liturgy of St. John Chrysostomos,[30] or an elaborate allegory of the church.[31] Frappier, refuting these theories, thought it unlikely that Chrétien meant to Christianize the *Story of the Grail* to that extent.[32] Instead, the interpretation of the meaning of Chrétien's work must be drawn from the romance itself.

Among its other facets, Chrétien's *Story of the Grail* is a study of knighthood. In the first part of the romance Chrétien describes the education of a rough and selfish young man who resembles Count Philip's godson Philip-Augustus more closely than do Chrétien's other courteous and accomplished heroes.[33] The physical attributes of knighthood — courage and skill with weapons — come to Perceval by nature, and despite his many blunders, he is recognized at King Arthur's court as a fine knight. His psychological development is traced over a longer period. Callous and naive, Perceval memorizes the precepts of knightly behavior as he did his childhood prayers, but for a long time he is unable to grasp the spirit of chivalry. His indifference to suffering causes his failure to help his dying mother, his insolence to the Maiden in the Tent, his gauche behavior at King Arthur's court, and his failure to converse with the Fisher King and to ask the liberating questions at the grail castle. His love for Blancheflor and his introspection and delicacy of feeling in the blood-on-the-snow episode indicate great progress toward spiritual maturity. His decision to return to the grail castle and attempt to rectify his mistake, instead of accepting the consequences of his error and pursuing worldly glory, is a noble one, but five years of fighting bring him no closer to his goal. After his conversation with the hermit, Perceval is last seen embarking upon the road of penitence and faith.

In contrast to this rough and uneducated hero, Gawain is a mature, sophisticated bachelor and Chrétien's model of the best knight in the world. Gawain undergoes a series of adventures that seem to be a counterpoint to those of Perceval, but no knight at King Arthur's court could have confronted such adventures with greater courage and courtesy.[34] Gawain's perfect manners and resolute adherence to the code of chivalry might make him seem a model for Perceval. Gawain attends church regularly, settles his disputes with scrupulous fairness, assists the wounded, and honors and protects women of all ages and estates. Yet the triumphs of Chrétien's perfect worldly knight are all worldly ones and not unqualified when examined closely. Gawain is ridiculed at Tintagel for refusing to fight, causes a riot at Escavalon, heals the wounds of a knight who treacherously steals his horse, and becomes infatuated with an evil maiden who tricks and reviles him. His crossing of the Perilous Ford he owes to his extraordinary horse, and his triumph at Queen Ygerne's castle may result in life imprisonment. In comparison with Perceval's struggles and problems, Gawain seems static, unhesitating in courage and in his decisions. However adverse the circumstances or unworthy the object of his attention, Gawain knows that there is only one way for a knight to behave. In contrast with Gawain's more limited goals of worldly glory and fame, Perceval's concern for the Christian values of penitence and charity introduces a new chivalric ideal: the struggle for spiritual perfection and the desire to do great deeds, not for the love of a lady, but for the love of God. Perceval's desire to be worthy to search for the grail once again is the origin of an entire body of Arthurian literature, in which a knight without sin is rewarded with a vision of the Holy Grail, which symbolizes God's grace and love for mankind.

When Chrétien de Troyes died, leaving so fascinating a romance unfinished, other writers took up the story. Many continuations and versions of the *Story of the Grail* were written within 50 years after Chrétien's death, and these texts were translated into almost every European language. The themes of these writers were more religious than Chrétien's; as the grail story evolved, the grail became a sacred relic of Christ's suffering and death. The hero became a chaste knight who was sometimes Perceval and later, when Perceval began to seem unworthy of the vision of the grail, Lancelot's virgin son Galahad.

Some writers simply added to Chrétien's *Story of the Grail*.[35] Two prologues were written before 1200: the *Elucidation* told how the kingdom of Logres with its fairies became a wasteland; and the *Bliocadran* told about the death of Perceval's father during Perceval's childhood. The *First Continuation* told of Gawain's adventures at the grail castle, where he was served with food and wine from a rich grail, vainly attempted to unite the fragments of the sword that destroyed the realm of Logres, and asked the correct question about the bleeding lance that pierced Christ's side, thereby restoring the wasteland to greenness.[36] The *Second Continuation* related Perceval's love affairs and adventures, until he united the broken sword and became king of the grail castle.[37]

In the 13th centure two writers added to the *Second Continuation.* Manessier (1214–1227) concluded the story by returning Perceval to the grail castle, where he learned that the Fisher King was maimed by the broken sword and could not be cured until its owner was slain. Perceval found a smith to repair the sword, killed its owner, and became king.[38] Gerbert de Montreuil (1226–1230), writing independently of Manessier, added a broken sword episode and declared that the queen of the castle of maidens brought the grail to Britain before it was taken away by angels and entrusted to the Fisher King.[39]

Other writers continued to supply background material: two books relate the history of the grail from the time of Christ to King Arthur and account for its transportation from Jerusalem to Britain. In *Joseph d'Arimathie* (circa 1200), the Burgundian poet Robert de Boron described the grail as a Christian relic: a chalice at the Last Supper which Joseph of Arimathea used afterward to collect the blood that flowed from Christ's side. Joseph took the grail when he and his family were exiled. At Joseph's instruction, his brother-in-law Hebron (Bron) used the grail placed alongside a freshly caught fish as a chastity test for their followers, and thereafter Bron was known as the Rich Fisher. In the end Joseph entrusted Bron with the grail.[40] The *Estoire del Saint Graal* (circa 1200) repeated Robert de Boron's story in prose. As an evangelist, Joseph of Arimathea brought the grail to Britain, although the grail was once again a dish, not a chalice. Joseph of Arimathea's son Josephes became the first bishop. Eventually Joseph entrusted the grail to his nephew, Bron's son Alain, and it passed to a succession of British kings, ending with King Pelles in King Arthur's day. The *Estoire del Saint Graal* became the first member of the French *Vulgate Cycle*, a very long and popular prose work composed between 1215 and 1230.[41]

Other writers prior to 1230 were not content to add to Chrétien's romance and created their own versions of Perceval and the story of the grail. These versions often differed greatly from Chrétien's original work. The early 13th century *Peredur,* a Welsh prose account, tells how the hero, a young knight, saw the grail, the broken sword, and the bleeding spear assembled in the castle of a stately king who was Peredur's maternal uncle. Peredur's questions about these wonders would have restored the king's health and brought peace to his land. Yet there are marked differences from Chrétien's version: the broken sword symbolized Peredur's strength, and the grail was a platter containing a severed head swimming in blood.[42] In Wolfram von Eschenbach's German poem

Parzival (1200–1210), which inspired Wagner's opera *Parsifal*, the happily married hero left his wife to visit the castle of the dying Fisher King, Anfortas, where he saw the bleeding lance and received a sword. The grailbearer was a chaste queen, and the grail was a precious stone that provided food and drink and had youth-preserving qualities. Parzival failed to ask the questions and was rebuked by an ugly maiden for his callousness. At the end, Parzival fought incognito with Gawain, whose feud with Gramoflanz (the Guiromelant) came to an end as Gramoflanz married Gawain's sister. Parzival was reunited with his wife, healed Anfortas by asking the questions, and became king of the grail.[43] In the French prose romance known as the *Didot Perceval* (circa 1202) the quest of the grail began when Perceval took an inappropriate seat at the Round Table. The seat cracked, and a voice declared that disaster would fall upon Britain until a knight found Bron, the Fisher King, and asked about the grail. Perceval failed at his first visit, but, with Merlin's advice, he managed to ask the right questions. Bron was healed of his wound and died in peace after giving the grail to Perceval.[44]

Manessier's continuation shows that he was familiar with another French prose romance, *Perlesvaus* (1191–1212). Its author made the dubious claim that his source was a Latin book in Glastonbury Abbey, which became associated with Joseph of Arimathea and the grail legends and is mentioned frequently in grail literature. In *Perlesvaus*, three heroes searched for the grail, which was holy and had youth-preserving qualities. Gawain saw the wonders of the invalid Fisher King's castle, which included a bleeding lance and a bloody sword that had slain John the Baptist. The grail seemed to contain a chalice; first it was borne by a maiden, and later it hovered in the air during Gawain's vision of Christ. Lancelot was not permitted to see the grail because he refused to renounce his sinful love for Guinevere. Perlesvaus, a virgin hero, was urged on the quest by a bald maiden, formerly the beautiful grailbearer, who became ugly when Perlesvaus failed to ask the questions. Perlesvaus made his confession to a hermit king named Pelles, the Fisher King's brother. At last, Perlesvaus saw the grail and reconquered and ruled the grail castle after the Fisher King's death.[45]

Two other books in the French *Vulgate Cycle* contain accounts of the grail story in which Perceval was not the hero and introduce a new virtuous knight named Bors. In the *Prose Lancelot*, Gawain, Lancelot, and Bors made separate visits to the grail castle. In accordance with a rival tradition that the Fisher King was not invariably maimed, the custodian of the grail was a healthy king, Pelles, and the beautiful grailbearer was Pelles' daughter Elaine, who never appeared in an ugly form.[46] The rich grail was shaped like a chalice, and it had the powers of healing, serving food, and discriminating between the worthy and the unworthy. Gawain was expelled from the castle. King Pelles deceived Lancelot into believing that Elaine was Queen Guinevere, a union that resulted in the birth of Galahad. Bors visited the grail castle twice, more successfully than Lancelot. Lancelot, insane because of Guinevere's anger about Elaine, wandered back to the grail castle and was cured by the grail.[47]

The second book, the *Queste del Saint Graal*, followed the *Prose Lancelot* in the *Vulgate Cycle*. The hero was Galahad, the virgin son of Lancelot and Elaine, and a happy fusion of two popular Arthurian themes: Lancelot's love for Guinevere and the quest of the grail. In the *Queste del Saint Graal* King Pelles was wounded through the thighs with a sword, and there is no grailbearer. The grail appeared to King Arthur's court covered with white samite cloth. It floated through the hall dispensing food and drink and was declared to be a holy relic: the dish from which Christ ate the Passover lamb at the Last Supper.[48] Gawain failed to attain the grail; Lancelot had a vision of the grail but was struck down for attempting to see it. Three more spiritual knights — Perceval, Bors, and Galahad — did see the grail as part of a vision of transubstantiation in which Bishop Josephes elevated the host with the Christ child's body incorporated in the bread, which he placed in the grail. Galahad united the broken sword and healed the maimed king's wound. Galahad died in ecstasy shortly thereafter, followed a year later by Perceval. The *Queste del Saint Graal* was translated into English in the late 15th century by Sir Thomas Malory as books XIII through XVII of *Le Morte d'Arthur*.[49]

In this way, within 50 years after Chrétien de Troyes' death sometime after 1181, the elements of the modern versions of the grail story had appeared in literature. The prototype of the grail was a Celtic vessel dispensing food and drink in an Otherworld atmosphere of perpetual youth and feasting. The grail appeared in Chrétien de Troyes' romance as a gold, bejeweled serving dish, large enough to contain a fish, but which was also a holy object and contained a single mass wafer. In the versions of Chrétien's continuators and successors, the grail became a eucharistic vessel dispensing the spiritual nourishment of the sacraments and, through redemption, offering eternal life.

Since that time, Chrétien de Troyes' romances, particularly the "best one" about the grail, have struck such responsive chords that they have been retold with the style and emphasis popular in each generation for eight centuries. It is not possible to study the 14th-century *Gawain and the Green Knight* or the works of Malory and Chaucer without discovering their indebtedness to Chrétien de Troyes. Modern readers may understandably be more familiar with Chrétien's successors. Their impression of the grail story may be a composite of the tragic grandeur of Malory's *Le Morte d'Arthur,* the heroic music of Wagner's *Parsifal,* the delicate sentiments of Tennyson's *Idylls of the King*, the poignancy of T. S. Eliot's "The Wasteland," and the elegant wit of T. H. White's *The Once and Future King*, and Chrétien's romance possesses all these qualities.

Nonetheless, the literary fashions of the 12th century were not like those of the 14th, 19th, or 20th centuries. Readers who expect to find languishing lily maids may be unprepared for Chrétien's vibrantly beautiful blonde heroines, who are usually virtuous and inclined toward marriage, but retain the ardor, charm, and adroitness of their distant fairy prototypes. Readers who expect to find in Perceval a pure knight leading a life of fasting and prayer in hope of becoming worthy of a glimpse of the grail may be momentarily disconcerted. The original Perceval is Chrétien's clumsy adolescent hero, who spent the night with his girlfriend and never went to church. In this state of unworthiness he stumbled upon the grail, which was carried back and forth in front of him in the vain hope that he might ask about it, while he was feasting in a Welsh castle on his way home to confirm a sinking feeling that he had finally managed to break his poor mother's heart. Readers who are familiar with the successors may be surprised by Chrétien de Troyes, but not as much as Chrétien would have been surprised by his successors.

The *Story of the Grail* should be considered in the light of its author's personality. Chrétien de Troyes was a court poet of high reputation who won and retained the support of powerful royal patrons throughout his 20-year career. His vast knowledge of human nature is expressed through realistic characters whose personalities and motivations are as recognizable today as they were in the 12th century. His romances are enlivened by a keen sense of the ridiculous as he slides his characters back and forth across chessboard squares of reality interlocked with fantasy. As his romances reveal, Chrétien de Troyes was a well-educated man with a very moral outlook on life, but there is no evidence that he was a religious mystic. He displays no idealistic views of Perceval's chastity, no overwhelming cynicism about life, and no violent hatred of women. His anti-Semitic passages, few in number and unique to the *Story of the Grail*, are distasteful to the modern reader, but they suited the tastes of his medieval audiences as well as did the lengthy love debates of his previous romances. Above all else, Chrétien meant to be entertaining, and unquestionably he succeeded. The *Story of the Grail* should be read and enjoyed with Chrétien's balanced and humorous spirit.

Branches of the wide river of Arthurian literature have flowed through many countries, and a common human aspiration is the desire to follow a river to its source. In life and in literature, sometimes the source is not impressive and has little to commend it besides its antiquity. In the case of Chrétien's *Story of the Grail*, the reader is like Yvain who rode for days through Brocéliande Forest to find a storm-making spring. Yvain found not damp and leaf-covered ground but a 12th-century fountain, bubbling with clear water and embellished with gold and jewels, undoubtedly fed by lost subterranean sources, and conveying the impression that an unknown earlier craftsman had been there before. The storm greatly exceeded his expectations. Like Yvain and Perceval, readers find adventure, fierce knights, great animals, and beautiful ladies in the 12th-century Arthurian world; they find marriage, fame, heartbreak, repentance, and reconciliation. It is a clear and colorful world — witty, erudite, and passionately human. If Chrétien's *Story of the Grail* were not the earliest known version of the grail story and the source of the subsequent versions, it would still be ranked among the masterpieces of Arthurian literature.

Note on Numbering

This translation is numbered to coincide with William Roach's 1959 edition of B.N. Ms. Fr. 12576 (ms. T), which in turn is numbered to coincide with Alfons Hilka's 1932 edition of B.N. Ms. Fr. 794 (ms. A). As Roach notes on pages xi and xii of his introduction, verses in ms. T that are not included in ms. A are indicated by lower case letters (a, b, . . .), and verses in ms. A that do not occur in ms. T are omitted (130, 133). The only difference is that this translation is numbered by 10; not by 4, and there is a close, but not always line-by-line, correspondence between the Old French passages and their verse translation.

Notes

1. Chrétien introduces himself at the beginning of his second romance, *Cligès*, as

> The one who wrote of *Erec and Enide,*
> translated the *Commandments of Ovid,*
> the *Art of Love* in French did write,
> and wrote about "The Shoulder Bite,"
> about King Mark and blonde Isolde,
> the metamorphosis retold
> of the "Hoopoe, Swallow, and Nightingale,"
> is now beginning a new tale . . .

(Chrétien de Troyes, *Cligès*, edited by Alexandre Micha [Paris: Champion, 1957], p. 1). *Erec and Enide* was the first Arthurian romance. The Commandments of Ovid were probably *Remedy for Love.* "The Shoulder Bite" was a version of the Pelops legend, in which Tantalus served up his son Pelops as a dish for the gods. The gods restored Pelops to life, but since one of the gods had taken a bite out of his shoulder, the gods were obliged to replace his bitten shoulder with an ivory one. The metamorphosis of the Hoopoe, the Swallow, and the Nightingale, also known as "Philomena," is the account of the affair of Tereus, Procne, and Philomena, who were changed into the forms of these birds as a punishment for their crimes. Chrétien's two songs are entitled, "Amors tançon et bataille" and D'amors qui m'a tolu a moi." See also Jean Frappier, *Chrétien de Troyes* (Paris: Hatier, 1968), pp. 7-9 and 63-68.

2. The dates of Chrétien de Troyes' romances are disputed. William A. Nitze proposes the earliest range of dates: after 1158 for *Erec and Enide*, the date of the investiture at Nantes of Henry II's brother Godefroy as Duke of Brittany, because of the reference to Erec and Enide's coronation at Nantes; after 1164 for *Lancelot*, the date of Mary's marriage to the Count of Champagne; around 1170 for *Yvain*, owing to its reference to Sultan Nureddin, who died in 1174; and before 1181 for *Perceval*, the year when Count Philip of Flanders signed the pact at Gisors against King Philip-Augustus, in *Perceval and the Holy Grail* (University of California Publications in Modern Philology, vol. 28, no. 5 [Berkeley and Los Angeles: University of California Press, 1949], pp. 284-285). The dates in the introduction are the widely accepted ones given by Frappier in *Chrétien de Troyes*, p. 9. C. A. Luttrell proposes that Chrétien's romances were written during a shorter and later period between 1184 and 1190, in *The Creation of the First Arthurian Romance: A Quest* (London: Edward Arnold, 1974).

3. Urban T. Holmes, Jr. speculated that Chrétien might have visited England in connection with Count Henry of Champagne's uncle, Henry of Blois, who became Abbot of Glastonbury and Bishop of Winchester (in *Chrétien de Troyes* [New York: Twayne Publishers, 1970], p. 24.) Holmes speculated that Chrétien might have visited Nantes in Brittany for the investiture of Godefroy, brother of Henry II, as Duke of Brittany, in 1158. In *Erec and Enide*, Chrétien describes in detail the coronation ceremony and festivities that take place in the palace and cathedral of Nantes when King Arthur crowns the royal couple (Chrétien de Troyes, *Perceval ou le Roman du Graal*, translated by Jean-Pierre Foucher and André Ortais [Paris: Gallimard, 1974], p. 363). The precise geographical information about the location of such English towns as Canterbury, London, Oxford, Dover, Wallingford, Winchester, Windsor, and Southampton, which Chrétien includes in *Cligès*, has been offered to substantiate the theory that he visited England. There is no proof to support these speculations, and Chrétien's information could have been acquired second-hand.

4. Chrétien de Troyes, *Lancelot (Le Chevalier de la Charrete)*, edited by Mario Roques (Paris: Champion, 1958), p. 216, vs. 7098-7112.

> My lords, should I more words employ
> they would appear as an intrusion,
> so I am reaching the conclusion.

> This is the ending of the work.
> Geoffrey de Lagney, the clerk,
> has put the last hand to *The Cart*,
> but let nobody blame inpart
> that he wrote more than Chrétien meant,
> because he worked with the consent
> of Chrétien, who wrote the start:
> he took the tale up at the part
> where Lancelot was walled up fast,
> and he stayed with it to the last.
> He wrote so much, no more, no less,
> lest it be spoiled by awkwardness.

5. Gustave Cohen notes that the exceptional knowledge of tournaments and escutcheons that Chrétien displays in *Lancelot* is the only basis of Gaston Paris' speculation that Chrétien might have served at court as a herald, in *Chrétien de Troyes, Oeuvres Choisies* (Paris: Classiques Larousse, 1936), p. 9. There has been speculation, but no proof, that Chrétien de Troyes might have been in holy orders: Nitze and Holmes note that in 1172 the Count and Countess of Champagne awarded the benefice of Saint Maclou to a Chrétien who may have been the poet, and there is also a record of a Chrétien who was a canon of the Abbey of Saint-Loup in Troyes, in Holmes, *Chrétien de Troyes*, pp. 22-23, and Nitze, *Perceval and the Holy Grail*, p. 282. In addition to the possibility of travel in Nantes and England mentioned in note 3, it is possible that Chrétien de Troyes accompanied Count Philip to Flanders. Jean Frappier, *Chrétien de Troyes et le Mythe du Graal* (Paris: Société d'Edition d'Enseignement Supérieur, 1972), pp. 51-52, cites Maurice Wilmotte's observation in *Le Poème du Graal et ses auteurs* (Paris: Droz, 1930), pp. 99-101, that the seaport of Escavalon with its great market and the burghers' riot, which is similar to uprisings that took place in Flanders between the 12th and 15th centuries, are described so realistically in the *Story of the Grail* that Wilmotte, a Belgian himself, stated that he felt himself to be in Belgium. Frappier observes that such speculations go from hypothesis to hypothesis, and that it is not possible to come to firm conclusions (p. 51).

6. Rita Lejeune, "La date du *Conte du Graal* de Chrétien de Troyes" in *Le Moyen Age 60* (1954): 53-58.

7. Frappier. *Chrétien de Troyes et le Mythe du Graal*, p. 51, thinks it likely that the date of composition of Chrétien's *Story of the Grail* was closer to 1180 than 1190. In a footnote, Frappier summarizes the debate about the date of composition that took place between Rita Lejeune and Anthime Fourrier during 1954 to 1958. Frappier states that Fourrier believed that the *Story of the Grail* was written between May 1182, and autumn 1183, whereas Lejeune believed that the romance was written between 1178 and 1181.

8. Gerbert Continuation, vs. 6984-6987, in Holmes, *Chrétien de Troyes*, p. 133.

9. Nitze, *Perceval and the Holy Grail*, p. 300. Frappier raises the questions about the love between the Guiromelant and Clarissant and the arrival of King Arthur's court in *Chrétien de Troyes*, p. 209. Frappier quotes Lucien Foulet ("Sire-Messire" in *Romania 71* [1951]: 21) as saying that Perceval is the hero of the book and the conquest of the grail would have been reserved for him, in *Chrétien de Troyes et le Mythe du Graal*, p. 73, and observes on pp. 106–107 that marriage between the hero and heroine takes place in all of Chrétien's romances except *Lancelot*.

10. Frappier notes that a similar duality of action occurs in *Erec and Enide* and *Cligès*, which are two-part romances, and that *Lancelot* and *Yvain* introduce Gawain as a symbol of the perfect worldly knight whose adventures are a counterpoint to the adventures of the hero, in *Chrétien de Troyes et le Mythe du Graal*, pp. 60–61.

11. Perceval's adventures, from his arrival at King Arthur's court to his breaking Kay's arm in combat, are supposed to have taken place within two weeks (see the fool's prediction, v. 1265), and Gawain's adventures within one year. The most noticeable discrepancies in the time sequence are snow and frost following shortly after spring and Pentecost, two celebrations of Pentecost within the same year, and Perceval's meeting with the hermit, after five years of wandering, in the middle of Gawain's single year of adventures, as is noted by Jean Frappier, "Note complémentaire sur la composition du *Conte du Graal*" in *Romania 81* (1960): 314–315, and Félix Lecoy, review of "La composición de *Li Contes del Graal* y el 'Guiromelant'" by Martin de Riquer, in *Romania 80* (1959): 269, and review of "La Lanza de Pellés," "Perceval y las gotas de sangre en la nieve," "Perceval y Gauvain en *Li Contes del Graal*" by Martín de Riquer, in *Romania 78* (1957): 410–412.

12. Frappier notes that Ph. A. Becker (*Zeitschrift für Romanische Philologie 55* [1935]: 385) believed that Chrétien wrote Perceval's adventures only through the visit to the grail castle; that Stefan Hofer (Chrétien de Troyes, *Leben und Werke des altfranzösischen Epikers* [Gras-Köln: 1954]), believed that Chrétien wrote all of Perceval's adventures but attributed Gawain's adventures to a continuator; and that E. Hoepffner, (*Romania 65* [1939]: 412) believed that the adventures of Perceval and Gawain constituted independent, unfinished romances by Chrétien which an editor united after his death.

Frappier concludes that there is no evidence to support the theory that the *Story of the Grail* was not written in its present form entirely by Chrétien de Troyes. The manuscript tradition supports the authenticity of the romance, and so, indirectly, does the *Parzival* of Wolfram von Eschenbach, which was written shortly after Chrétien's romance in 1200–1210 and which shows that Wolfram knew of only one text of the *Story of the Grail* that united Perceval's and Gawain's adventures. Furthermore, Gawain's adventures are thought to be written in Chrétien's most recognizable style. Frappier, *Chrétien de Troyes*, pp. 171–172, and "Note Complémentaire," pp. 314, 326, 332–333.

13. Roger Sherman Loomis, *Arthurian Tradition and Chrétien de Troyes* (New York: Columbia University Press, 1949), pp. 18–24.

14. W. Wistar Comfort, in Chrétien de Troyes, *Arthurian Romances* (London: Dent and Sons, Everyman's Library, rept. 1970), pp. viii and xiv.

15. Loomis, *Arthurian Tradition*, p. 7.

16. In addition to certain reworked literary conceits, the *Story of the Grail* has a knight who treats his sweetheart harshly (*Erec and Enide*) a knight in a tower and a wondrous bed (*Lancelot*), a hermit, two quarreling sisters, a lion, and a helpful animal (*Yvain*), all skillfully transformed and adapted to the plot of the *Story of the Grail*.

17. Frappier notes, in *Chrétien de Troyes et le Mythe du Graal*, pp. 53-54, that Perceval le Gallois is listed as one of King Arthur's knights in *Erec and Enide* (v. 1506, Roques edition) as is Gornemant of Gohort (v. 1675, Roques edition), and that Perceval is also mentioned as a knight of great renown in *Cligès* (v. 4774, Micha edition).

18. Frappier notes, in *Chrétien de Troyes et le Mythe du Graal*, p. 54, that the 14th-century English romance, *Sir Perceval of Galles*, agrees with Chrétien's earlier romance in many ways but says nothing of the Fisher King and Grail. Frappier thought it possible that the English romance was derived partly from an adventure story in which the story of Perceval was not combined with the story of the Grail.

    Likewise, the 13th-century Welsh *Peredur* has many parallels with Chrétien's romance, but also many differences. Frappier noted, in *Chrétien de Troyes et le Mythe du Graal*, p. 19, that it is difficult to decide whether *Peredur* is entirely derived from the *Story of the Grail*, or whether it is also partly derived from some Welsh tale that preceded Chrétien's romance. Frappier thought the second hypothesis more likely.

19. There are other hints at a Provençal source for the *Story of the Grail* besides Wolfram von Eschenbach's dubious claim that the real story of the grail came to Germany from Provence (see Roger Sherman Loomis, *The Grail: From Celtic Myth to Christian Symbol* ([New York: Columbia University Press, 1963], pp. 197-198). Rita Lejeune states that the troubadour Rigaut de Barbezieux wrote before 1160, "Just as Perceval, when he was alive, was lost in wonderment at the sight, so that he could never ask what purpose the lance and grail served, so I likewise, *Mielhs de Domna* (possibly Eleanor of Aquitaine), for I forget all when I gaze on you," in "The Troubadours," *Arthurian Literature in the Middle Ages*, edited by Roger Sherman Loomis (London: Oxford University Press, 1969), pp. 396-397. Frappier, when discussing the derivation and various forms of the word "graal," noted that the "a" in Chrétien's form of the word is closer to the Provençal *grazal* and the variations in the langue d'oc regions than to the langue d'öil form *greel*, in *Chrétien de Troyes et le Mythe du Graal*, pp. 9-10.

20. See J. D. Bruce, *The Evolution of Arthurian Romance*, Vol. I (Baltimore: Johns Hopkins University Press, 1928), pp. 240-289; Frappier, *Chrétien de Troyes et le Mythe du Graal*, pp. 163-212; Holmes, *Chrétien de Troyes*, pp. 137-167; and Nitze, *Perceval and the Holy Grail*, pp. 281-325, for summaries of the Christian, Celtic, and Ritual theories of the *Story of the Grail*. For a summary and criticism of more recent theories, see Frappier, *Chrétien de Troyes et le Mythe du Graal*, pp. 25-40, and also Frappier, "Le Graal et ses feux divergents," in *Romance Philology* 24 (1970-71):373-440.

21. Frappier notes (*Chrétien de Troyes et le Mythe du Graal*, pp. 178-180) that Jessie Weston formulated the Ritual theory that the grail legend had its origins in the ancient mysteries of the cults of Atys, Osiris, and Adonis. While Weston's theory is no longer widely accepted, her book *From Ritual to Romance* (1920) was influential in its day and inspired T. S. Eliot's poem, "The Wasteland."

22. Mario Roques, in his preface to *Perceval le Gallois ou le Conte du Graal* by Chrétien de Troyes, translated by Lucien Foulet (Paris: A. G. Nizet, 1970), pp. xii-xxiv, shares this sentiment and cites Pauphilet's resumés of two such tales: one of a sailor who discovers the underwater Cathedral of Ys, and another of a woman who comes upon a marine city with streets filled with shops. The sailor fails to offer to serve at mass, and the woman has no money with which to buy a penny's worth of cloth, and so the cathedral and the city remain submerged.

23. A. C. L. Brown, *Iwain: Studies in the Origins of Arthurian Romance.* (New York: Haskell House, 1968), pp. 30 and 58.

24. Loomis, *The Grail: From Celtic Myth to Christian Symbol*, pp. 47-54 and 77-78. Loomis believes that Perceval's visit to the Grail castle has a source in the Celtic tale, "The Prophetic Ecstasy of the Phantom," which related King Conn's visit to the god Lug's castle: a young woman called the Sovranty of Ireland, after asking Lug the question, "To whom shall this cup be given?" and receiving the answer "Pour it for Conn," served Conn with meat and with ale from a golden cup, while Lug, in a trance, named each of Conn's royal descendants. Then Lug and his dwelling vanished, but the cup remained with Conn. Loomis also mentions another tale of a fairy king of a land under a spell who dismisses with mockery a mortal who fails to obtain great wealth by not asking the right question, and a related Celtic tale, included in a prose romance called the *Suite de Merlin*, dated around 1230, of Balaain (Balin) who, when seeking a weapon in King Pellehan's castle, came into a room that contained a silver and gold vessel on a silver table and a lance, standing upright unsupported. Balaain wounded King Pellehan in the thighs with the lance and fled, with Merlin's help. Outside he found the crops destroyed and the inhabitants dead, and the kingdom was afterward called the Waste Land.

25. Frappier, *Chrétien de Troyes et le Mythe du Graal*, pp. 190ff.

26. Frappier notes that the logical direction in the Middle Ages was to moralize pagan myths, and not to paganize Christian ideas, in *Chrétien de Troyes et le Mythe du Graal*, p. 211.

27. Frappier relates the legend of Longinus in *Chrétien de Troyes et le Mythe du Graal*, p. 165. Longinus was said to be a blind centurion who thrust his lance into Christ's side at the crucifixion. The blood and water ran down the lance onto his hand and, wiping his hand across his eyes, Longinus recovered his sight. It was said that as a result of this experience Longinus was baptized and became so devoted to the Christian faith that he died a martyr.

28. Frappier, *Chrétien de Troyes et le Mythe du Graal*, pp. 69-70.

29. Chrétien de Troyes, *Erec and Enide*, edited by Mario Roques (Paris: Champion, 1966), p. 1, vs. 19-22:

> The tale of Erec, son of Lac,
> which those who live by stories hack,
> or spoil, or often cut too short
> before the kings and counts at court.

30. Nitze states, in *Perceval and the Holy Grail*, pp. 307–309, that the lance of Longinus was discovered at Antioch in 1098 and was incorporated into the Byzantine liturgy of St. John Chrysostomos. In Konrad Burdach's description of the mass, the priest strikes the host with the Holy Lance while saying, "One of the soldiers pierced His side with a spear, and at once there came out blood and water" (John 19:34). The priest lays the host on the *diskos*, a broad and deep vessel supported by a single pedestal. In the procession, first come lictors carrying lighted candles, then the priest with the *diskos*, then one celebrant with the lance, another with the sponge, and finally others with gospels and relics.

31. Holmes, *Chrétien de Troyes*, pp. 137–141 and 157.

32. Frappier, *Chrétien de Troyes et le Mythe du Graal*, pp. 164ff., refutes some of the more Christianized theories about the grail. He notes that there was no evidence of a religious ceremony taking place at the grail castle. The grail and the carving dish were not of the same metals, as communion vessels would have been, and they were being carried by women, which was forbidden except for sickbed communion services. The Fisher King's father was not sick; he was an ascetic eating a meal of mass wafers. As for the Byzantine liturgy, Frappier notes that the Holy Lance of Longinus was much shorter and (unlike the Celtic lance) was not known for bleeding continuously, and that there were no women in the Byzantine procession.

33. Lejeune, "La date du *Conte du Graal*," pp. 54–55.

34. Frappier, *Chrétien de Troyes et le Mythe du Graal*, p. 73.

35. Albert Wilder Thompson, "Additions to Chrétien's Perceval — Prologues and Continuations," in *Arthurian Literature in the Middle Ages*, pp. 206–217. See also Loomis, *The Grail: From Celtic Myth to Christian Symbol*; and Frappier, *Chrétien de Troyes et le Mythe du Graal*, pp. 13–20 and 41–45.

     Thompson and Frappier note that the *Elucidation* contains 484 verses and the *Bliocadran* contains 800 verses. The *First Continuation*, formerly called the Pseudo-Wauchier, contains between 9,500 and 19,000 verses about Gawain. The *Second Continuation*, formerly thought to be by Wauchier de Denain, adds 13,000 verses about Perceval. Manessier added about 10,000 verses to the *Second Continuation*, and Gerbert de Montreuil added 17,000 verses to it.

36. Loomis, *The Grail: From Celtic Myth to Christian Symbol*, pp. 65–71.

37. Loomis, *The Grail: From Celtic Myth to Christian Symbol*, p. 82.

38. Loomis, *The Grail: From Celtic Myth to Christian Symbol*, pp. 82–83.

39. Loomis, *The Grail: From Celtic Myth to Christian Symbol*, p. 215.

40. Loomis, *The Grail: From Celtic Myth to Christian Symbol*, pp.229–232.

41. Loomis, *The Grail: From Celtic Myth to Christian Symbol*, pp. 146,

235-236 and 248. Loomis notes (pp. 134-144) that a much later poem, *Sone de Nansai*, written in the second half of the 13th century, equated the maimed Fisher King with Joseph of Arimathea and linked his health with the fertility of the land. The hero Sone visited the Grail castle in Norway and therein found the grail, described as Joseph's vessel, and Longinus' bleeding spearhead.

42. There has been disagreement about whether *Peredur* is based entirely upon Chrétien's romance or shares a common source with it in some earlier work. See Frappier, *Chrétien de Troyes et le Mythe du Graal*, pp. 18-19; and Loomis, *The Grail: From Celtic Myth to Christian Symbol*, pp. 87-96.

43. Wolfram von Eschenbach's German poem *Parzival* is based upon Chrétien's *Story of the Grail*, the *Bliocadron* prologue, and the *First Continuation*. Wolfram accounted for his deviations from Chrétien's text by citing an unknown and possibly fictitious source: Kyot the Provençal. See Loomis, *The Grail: From Celtic Myth to Christian Symbol*, pp. 196-222.

Another German poem by Heinrich von dem Turlin, *Diu Krône*, has Gawain as the hero who visits the Grail castle, as Frappier notes in *Chrétien de Troyes et le Mythe du Graal*, p. 18.

44. W. T. H. Jackson, *Medieval Literature* (New York: Collier Books [Macmillan, Inc.], 1966), pp. 89-90.

45. Jackson, *Medieval Literature*, pp. 89-90, and Loomis, *The Grail: From Celtic Myth to Christian Symbol*, pp. 97-134.

46. Loomis, *The Grail: From Celtic Myth to Christian Symbol*, pp. 158-159.

47. Loomis, *The Grail: From Celtic Myth to Christian Symbol*, pp. 147-148.

48. Loomis, *The Grail: From Celtic Myth to Christian Symbol*, p. 174.

49. Frappier, *Chrétien de Troyes et le Mythe du Graal*, pp. 16-17; and Loomis, *The Grail: From Celtic Myth to Christian Symbol*, pp. 165-195.

PERCEVAL
OR
THE STORY OF THE GRAIL

PROLOGUE

He little reaps who little sows.*
The man who wants good harvests strows
his seeds on such a kind of field,
God grants a hundredfold in yield;*
on barren ground good seeds but lie
until they shrivel up and die.
So Chrétien sows, disseminating
this story he's initiating,
and sows it in such fertile soil,
he can but profit by his toil,   10
when toiling for the finest man
within the Roman Empire's span.
That man is Philip, Count of Flanders,*

v. 1. Alfons Hilka notes in his footnotes to Chrétien de Troyes, *Der Percevalroman (Li Contes del Graal)*, edited by Alfons Hilka ("Christian von Troyes sämtliche erhaltene Werke," ed. Wendelin Foerster; Vol. 5) (Halle [Salle]: Max Niemeyer Verlag, 1932), p. 615, that this proverb is included in J. Morawski, *Proverbes français antérieurs au X X Ve siècle* (CFMA, 1925), no. 2074: "Qui petit seme petit queut."

v. 4. Hilka notes (*Der Percevalroman*, pp. 615-616) that this passage is from Luke 8: 5-8: "A sower went out to sow his seed, and as he sowed, some fell by the wayside . . . and some fell upon a rock; and as soon as it was sprung up, it withered away because it lacked moisture . . . and other fell on good ground, and sprang up, and bare fruit a hundredfold." The parable is repeated in Matthew 13:8 and 13:23. Chrétien uses expressions similar to "a hundredfold" in *Cligès* (Micha edition), vs. 211 and 832.

v. 13. Philip of Alsace, Count of Flanders, was born circa 1143, the elder son of Count Thierry of Alsace and his second wife, Sibylle of Anjou, the daughter of Count Foulques V of Anjou and the sister of Geoffrey Plantagenet, who was the father of Henry II of England. Thierry of Alsace had been rewarded for his services in the Second Crusade by a gift of a phial of the Holy Blood (still at Bruges). Count Philip was married to a niece of Eleanor of Aquitaine, Elisabeth of Vermandois, whose lands bordered on Champagne. Count Philip became the ruler of Flanders in 1168. He was appointed the tutor of his godson, Philip-Augustus, King of France, and in that capacity exercised the functions of regent between 1178 and 1181. Childless himself, the count had such influence over the young Philip-Augustus that he persuaded the king to marry his niece, the Countess of Hainaut. Count Philip fell out of favor and allied himself against the king by signing the pact made at Gisors on May 14, 1181, with the rival house of Blois-Champagne. Count Philip was twice in the Holy Land, once in 1177, when he negotiated with Greek envoys from Constantinople on a projected military campaign against Saladin, and once in 1190. He died of the plague at Acre on June 1, 1191. Lejeune, "La date du *Conte du Graal*," pp. 53-58, and Nitze, *Perceval and the Holy Grail*, pp. 285, 307-308.

whose worth surpasses Alexander's,*
of whom they give such good account.
I'll prove that we should count the count
a better man, who has surpassed
great Alexander, who amassed
all sorts of vice and frailty
of which the count is pure and free.   20
The count won't hear or pay attention
to vulgar jokes and vain pretension.
If slanderers say something bad
of anyone, it makes him sad.
The count loves justice, equity,
the Holy Church, and loyalty;
all low behavior he detests.
Though generous with his bequests,
the count, no cunning hypocrite,*
gives in accord with Holy Writ,*   30
which says, "Let not thy left hand know
the good thy right hand doth bestow."
The man may know when he receives,
and God, who secret things perceives
and hidden thoughts of every kind
that lie within the heart and mind.
Why does the Gospel so command,
"Hide thy good deeds from thy left hand,"?
Because, according to the story,
the left hand signifies vainglory,   40
which comes from false hypocrisy.
The right hand stands for charity,
which does good, seeking to conceal it,
instead of boasting to reveal it,

---

v. 14. Hilka notes (*Der Percevalroman*, p. 616) that Chrétien de Troyes mentions the wealth and generosity of Alexander the Great, the hero of the *Roman d'Alexandre*, in *Erec and Enide* (Roques edition), vs. 1967, 2214, 6611, and 6622.

vs. 30-31. Hilka notes (*Der Percevalroman*, p. 617) that the reference to hypocrites comes from Matthew 6:2 and the reference to the left and right hands from Matthew 6:3: "But when thou doest alms, let not thy left hand know what thy right hand doeth."

so no one knows of it but He
whose name is God and Charity,
for God is Charity. I've read
the text in which Saint Paul has said,
"Who lives in charity shall dwell*
in God and God in him as well."　　　　50
Let truth be known: the large amount
of gifts presented by the count,
good Philip, are from charity.
None counsels generosity
except his good and noble heart
which teaches him this virtuous art.
So is he not of greater worth
than Alexander, with his dearth
of charity and works devout?
Yes, there cannot be any doubt.　　　　60
Chrétien shall gain, since he has striven
at the command the count has given　　　　64
and made endeavors manifold
to rhyme the best tale ever told*　　　　63

v. 49. Hilka notes (*Der Percevalroman*, p. 617) that Chrétien has made an error, un-usual in the light of his extensive knowledge of the Bible. This passage is from I John 4:16: "God is love [caritas], and he that dwelleth in love dwelleth in God and God in him." Saint Paul's famous passage on charity is in I Corinthians 13 and begins: "Though I speak with the tongues of men and of angels and have not charity, I am become as sound-ing brass or a tinkling cymbal."

v. 63. Frappier says that the common meaning of *rimoüer*, "to rhyme," is "to compose in verse," in *Chrétien de Troyes et le Mythe du Graal*, p. 53, whereas Roger Sherman Loomis thought that it meant "to versify prose," in *Arthurian Tradition and Chrétien de Troyes* (New York: Columbia University Press, 1949), pp. 10–11.

v. 67. "the book." Frappier notes, in *Chrétien de Troyes et le Mythe du Graal*, p. 53, that we know from this line that Chrétien did not invent the entire "story of the grail," and that he was working from a written source. There has been much debate about Count Philip's lost book. Roger Sherman Loomis believed that it was a prose narrative of a medley of Celtic tales ("Grail Problems" in *Romanic Review* 45[1954]:17), but it must be noted in contradiction that the earliest known French prose narratives were not writ-ten until the end of the century. William A. Nitze and Harry F. Williams believed that by

in any royal court: this tale
is called the *Story of the Grail*.
The count has given him the book;*
now judge what Chrétien undertook.

"book," Chrétien meant a Latin treatise, as he did in his earlier romances: in *Erec and Enide*, "livre" (v. 6680, Roques edition) refers to Macrobius's commentary on the *Dream of Scipio*, and in *Cligès*, "livre" (v. 20, Micha edition) refers to the book of St. Pierre at Beauvais (in *Arthurian Names in the Perceval of Chrétien de Troyes*, University of California Publications in Modern Philology. vol. 38, no. 33 [Berkeley and Los Angeles: University of California Press, 1955], p. 288). In contradiction, Helinand of Froidmont declared early in the 13th century that he could not discover any Latin version of the grail story, as Bruce noted in *The Evolution of Arthurian Romance*, pp. 246-247. The theory that the book was a simple prose account of the Byzantine liturgy of St. John Chrysostomos does not account adequately for Chrétien's other references to the book throughout the romance (Nitze, *Perceval and the Holy Grail*, p. 308). Furthermore, Holmes notes that a great fire at Troyes in 1188, which spread to Count Philip's library, probably destroyed many documents that would have helped to settle some of these questions about Chrétien's sources for the *Story of the Grail*, in *Chrétien de Troyes*, p. 161.

THE MEETING WITH THE KNIGHTS

Once, in the season of the year*
    when fields grow green, and leaves appear,   70
and birds, in their own idioms,
sing sweetly when the morning comes,
and all things are aflame with joy,
at daybreak there arose a boy*
who was a widowed lady's child.
Deep in her forest lone and wild
he saddled up his hunter, and
he took three javelins in his hand
So armed with this accoutrement
out of his mother's manse he went.   80
He planned to visit, where he rode,
his mother's harrowers, who sowed
the fields of oats by light of dawn:
six harrows by twelve oxen drawn.

v. 69 ff. Frappier notes, in *Chrétien de Troyes et le Mythe du Graal*, p. 75, that this poetic passage about dawn in springtime is in the best tradition of the songs of the troubadours and minstrels. Hilka notes (*Der Percevalroman*, p. 618) that there is a similar passage in *Cligès*, vs. 6263-6265 (Micha edition).

v. 74. There are many Celtic prototypes for the young hero of the romance, whom Chrétien will not name until v. 3575. Loomis noted that Perceval's early history, his father's injury in battle, his upbringing in a forest, his skill with javelins, and his departure to a king's court, are very similar to the sagas of the boyhood adventures of Finn, son of Cumal. Moreover, like Perceval, Finn visited a hermit uncle (*The Grail: From Celtic Myth to Christian Symbol*, p. 62.)

Nitze, in *Perceval and the Holy Grail*, p. 313, noted similarities between Perceval's early adventures and those of three other Celtic heroes: Kulhwch, Lug, and Cuchulainn.

Kulhwch was sent to Arthur's court to be recognized as kin. He carried two spears and was refused admittance because the court was feasting. When he was admitted, he rode into the hall without dismounting (see v. 904), as Perceval does.

The god Lug was reared by a foster mother far from the king's court but made his way to Nuadu's (Noden's) palace at Tara. Lug slew Balar of the Evil Eye by hurling a sling-stone in his eye (see v. 1113); Perceval kills the Red Knight by throwing his javelin through his eye.

Cuchulainn was reared in his parents's home and was related, on his mother's side, to Conchobar mac Nessa. He learned of Conchobar's court at Emain and went there, despite his mother's urging him to remain with her. He was awkward and rude in Concho-

He went into the forest glade.
The sweetness of the season made
the heart within his breast rejoice,
and in the trees he heard the voice
of birds who filled the air with joy:
these things gave pleasure to the boy.   90
Due to the mildness of the weather,
the youth removed the bit and tether
and let his hunter go and eat
new green grass growing at his feet.
Meanwhile the lad, who truly knew
the way to cast his javelins, threw
the javelins as he walked around:
at times behind him on the ground,
and then before, then high, then low,
until he heard five armed knights go   100
through the deep forest in a band.
The knights were in full armor, and
their arms and weapons, drawing near,
made crashing noises, dread to hear,
as mighty oak and hornbeam branches
thumped on the weapons, and the lances
were knocked against the shields and clattered.
The hauberk meshes clinked and chattered;
the wooden shield frames clunked and banged;
the iron armor clanked and clanged.   110
The young man heard, but did not see,

---

bar's presence. Like Finn and Perceval, Cuchulainn received his name only after passing
through an important exploit.

Searching for a more immediate model for Perceval, Lejeune noted many similarities
between Perceval and Count Philip's godson, the young king Philip-Augustus. Both
were adolescents with incapacitated fathers (like Perceval's father and the Fisher King,
Louis VII was paralyzed in his last years and had to be carried in a litter). Both were
somewhat hostile to their mothers, whose influence had predominated in their youth.
Both spent their early years in the country riding and hunting; both showed little interest
in clothes; neither one was formally educated. Both were tutored by an older man whose
niece they loved or married. In personality, both were direct, unheeding of consequences,
selfish, and indifferent to culture, refinement, or gallantry ("La date du *Conte du Graal*,"
pp. 61–67). Frappier, *Chrétien de Troyes et le Mythe du Graal*, pp. 71–72, agreed that
these similarities were valid but warned against using them to support a limited view of
the *Story of the Grail* as an educational novel for the young prince, a sort of 12th-century
Telemachus, in Frappier's words.

the knights approaching rapidly.
"Upon my soul," exclaimed the youth,
"my lady mother spoke the truth
that day she taught me devils are
the vilest things on earth, by far,
and said I would be doing right
to cross myself against their might.
Her counsel's no concern of mine;
I'll never make the cross's sign!   120
I'll use one of my javelins three
to strike the strongest fiend I see.
None of the other devil-men
will ever come near me again!"
He told himself what he would do
before the knights had come in view.
Yet, when he saw the knights with ease
as they came riding through the trees,
he saw the jingling hauberks and
the shining helmets of the band,   130
and the vermilion and the white   133
that glistened in the morning light,
the silver and the blue and gold
that was so splendid to behold,
"Sir God, be merciful to me,
for here are angels that I see!
Now I have done a dreadful sin:
how terrible I must have been   140
to call them devils I despise.
My mother did not tell me lies;
for angels are, she did insist,
the fairest beings that exist,
except for God, who is most fair.
The Lord God have me in His care,
for I see God here in this place.
One has so fair a form and face,
the other ones could never be
one tenth as beautiful as he.   150
My mother said herself the Lord,
above all else, should be adored:
so I will pray to him foremost
and then to all the angel host."
That very moment, with one bound,
he flung himself upon the ground,

and he recited the Creed through
and every other prayer he knew,
his mother taught him to recite.
The leader of the knights caught sight.   160
"Stay back! A youth who saw us here
collapsed upon the ground in fear.
If five of us rush to his side,
he would become so terrified,
it seems to me that he would die
and be unable to reply
to any question that I chanced."
They halted there while he advanced
and rode as quickly as he might.
He hailed the youth to calm his fright,   170
"See here, young man, don't be afraid."
"I'm not," was the reply he made,
"for by the Saviour whom I trust,
are you not God?" The knight, nonplussed,
said, "No, my word, that is not right."
"Who are you then?" "I am a knight."
"I haven't met a knight before,"
the youth replied, "nor seen one, nor
heard talk about them, which is odd,
but you are handsomer than God.   180
If only I could look so fine,
and be as strong as you, and shine!"
The youth drew near. "Lad, did you see
five knights today with maidens three?"
he asked for those he wished to find.
The youth had other things in mind,
and he continued to advance.
He put his hand upon the lance.
"My dear sir, you whose name is 'knight',
what is this thing you hold so tight?"   190
"Now I have all my information!
Although I came in expectation
of learning things from you instead,"
the leader of the riders said,
"my good friend, you appear to be
intent on learning things from me!
I'll tell you, since you want to know it:
it is my lance." "Sir, do you throw it
the way I make my javelins go?"

"It's used to strike a sudden blow!   200
Young man, you are an utter fool!"
"One javelin is a better tool,
for I have three, and when I choose
to kill wild beasts or birds, I use
my javelins from as far away
as crossbows could be drawn to slay."
"My lad, that isn't my concern.
The knights: that's what I came to learn.
Now do you know where they may be,
and have you seen the maidens three?"   210
The youth had grasped the shield he bore.
"What's this? What do you use it for?"
he asked in all sincerity.
"You're tricking and distracting me!
You change the subject as you go
to things I didn't want to know.
So help me God, I truly thought
you would instruct me as I sought
about the knights whom I pursue;
you have me here instructing you!   220
But I will tell you all the same
the way you use it and its name,
because I like you," he revealed.
"The thing I'm holding is a shield."
"A shield?" The leader answered, "Yes,
it's shown me such devotedness,
I must not treat it scornfully.
Should someone cast or shoot at me,
instead my shield receives the blows.
This is the service it bestows."   230
The knights who'd stayed behind their master
came up now riding all the faster.
When they had made their way to him,
the knights began to say to him,
"Sir, what's this Welshman telling you?"
"His manners are extremely few.
God love me, he did not supply
one answer or one straight reply
to any question since I came.
Whatever he sees, he asks its name   240
and then the use to which it's turned!"
"By now, my lord, you must have learned

all Welshmen are inherently*
more dumb than grazing beasts could be:
this one is simple as a sheep.
Fool he who stops, unless to keep
himself amused with idle play,
or else to while his time away!"
"I do not know, but in God's sight,
before I leave," replied the knight,   250
"I'll tell him all he wants to know;
until I have, I will not go."
The leader questioned him anew.
"Young man, if I'm not troubling you,
five knights with maids are in this land;
did you see them or meet their band?"
But by this time the youth had grasped
his hauberk's mail, and held him fast,
and tugged the hauberk while declaring,
"Now tell me, sir, what you are wearing."   260
"Lad, don't you know?" the knight exclaimed.
"No." "Hauberk, lad, is what it's named.
It weighs on me as heavily
as iron, which it is, you see."
The youth replied, "I did not know,
but God preserve me, it is so
extremely beautiful!" he swore.
"How is it used? What is is for?"
"That's easy, lad. Were you to throw
a javelin or to bend a bow,   270
you could not harm me if you chose."
"Sir knight, God keep the stags and does
from wearing hauberks, for I could
not chase the wild deer through the wood
and kill them, if they ever did."
"God keep you, lad, and God forbid!
But now, can you put me to rights
and tell about the maids and knights?"

v. 243. Hilka notes (*Der Percevalroman*, p. 620) other references to the stupidity of
the Britons and the Welsh, among them Geoffrey of Monmouth's *History of the Kings of
Britain* (Faral edition, pp. 213 and 303). This concept was characteristic of the Norman-
French ruling class in England during Chrétien 's time. See vs. 320ff for an example of
frequent linguistic difficulties, as Perceval translates the knight's questions into Welsh
and the harrower's replies into French (Nitze, *Perceval and the Holy Grail*, p. 292).

The young man questioned him, however,
for he was anything but clever,   280
"Sir, were you born as you are now?"
"No, lad, that cannot be, I vow.
No man is ever armed at birth."
The youth continued, "Who on earth
has given all these things to you?"
"I will be glad to tell you who."
"Then tell." "Lad, I will have you know
that less than five full years ago
King Arthur dubbed me; then and there
he gave me all these arms I bear.   290
Once more, please tell me what's become
of those knights who came riding from
this wood escorting maidens three.
Did they ride slowly? Did they flee?"
He said, "Sir, see the upper bounds
of the high forest which surrounds
that mountain rising in the sky?
that's where Mount Snowdon's passes lie."*
He asked, "And what of it, dear brother?"
"The harrowers there work for Mother.   300
They sow and work her fields today,
and if those people went that way,
they'd see them and could tell you so."
The knights replied that they would go,
if he would lead the way, and bring
their band to those out harrowing
the fields of oats. The young man rode
his hunter where the workers sowed
plowed fields with oats and harrowed ground.
But when they saw their lord around,   310
the harrowers all shook with fright,
and do you know why? At the sight
of knights in armor coming too,
because the harrowers well knew
if he had talked with knights like these
and learned of their activities

v. 298. Loomis notes that the locality of Mount Snowdon, an accepted reading for
Valbone, harmonizes perfectly with Helaine Newstead's evidence that Perceval's father
was a king of North Wales (in *Romanic Review 36*, [1946] pp. 3–31), in *Arthurian Tradi-
tion*, p. 490.

and way of life, as well he might,
the youth would want to be a knight,
and then his mother would go mad.
She'd wanted to prevent the lad   320
from seeing knights and to forbid
his hearing of the deeds they did.
He asked the drivers, "Did you see
five knights escorting maidens three
pass by your fields or go this way?"
"They've ridden through this pass all day,"
the ox-drivers said in reply.
"The knights and maidens did pass by;"
the youth repeated to the knight
who talked so long to set him right,   330
"They went this way when traveling.
Sir, tell me more about the king
who makes the knights and also say
where he is likeliest to stay."
The knight said, "Yes, lad, I shall tell.
The king sojourns at Carduel;*
in all five days have not yet passed
since he was in that city last,
for I was there and saw the king.
If not, someone in town will bring   340
the news of where the courtiers are;
he won't have traveled very far."*   342
He rode off at a gallop great   361
to join the others, being late;

v. 336. Nitze and Williams note, in *Arthurian Names*, pp. 268-269, that Carduel,
one of the seats of King Arthur's court, is the modern Carlisle.

v. 342. In a disputed passage to which Reto R. Bezzola attaches symbolical impor-
tance, because it shows that until now Perceval has no sense of his own personality and
has existed only in relation to others (*Le Sens de l'Aventure et de l'Amour* [*Chrétien de
Troyes*] [Paris: Champion, 1968], pp. 51-52), the leader of the knights asks Perceval his
name at this point. Perceval replies that it is "dear son." The leader asks him if he hasn't
another name, and Perceval replies "dear brother." The leader asks him for his real
name, and Perceval replies "dear sir." The leader comments that they are "endearing"
names, but hasn't he another one? Perceval replies that he doesn't think so, because he
has never heard anyone call him anything else, and the knight is utterly astounded. Peter
Haidu notes, in *Aesthetic Distance and Chrétien de Troyes* (Geneva: Droz, 1968), p.
126, that only two manuscripts, including Paris B.N. manuscrit français 794, contain
this passage, and that Hilka had commented that, as Baist had recommended, it should
be eliminated from a definitive critical edition.

they went ahead some time ago.
The youth was anything but slow
to ride back to his manor, where
his mother's heart was dark with care.
But once the widow saw her boy,
she felt the greatest sense of joy
and was not able to conceal
the joy the sight had made her feel.   370
A loving mother, at a run
she called out, "Son, dear son, dear son,"
at least one hundred times, no less.
"My heart has suffered great distress
because you were away so long.
My pain and sorrow were so strong,
I nearly died of my dismay.
Where you have been so long today?"
"Where, lady? Yes, I shall reply
and never tell you any lie,   380
since I have felt a joy so keen
because of something I have seen.
Did you not frequently declare
the angels and Our Lord so fair,
that nothing Nature has created
could be so lovely, and you stated
no fairer things are seen on earth?"
"Dear son, I did. To show its worth
I shall repeat that it's the truth."
"Be quiet, Mother," said the youth,   390
"have I not seen, this very day,
the fairest beings on their way
through the wild forest? Fairer far
than God and all His angels are."
His mother clasped him in her arms.
"God keep you safe from all that harms,
my dearest son! I greatly dread
that you have seen," his mother said,
"those angels of whom we complain.
All people whom they meet are slain."   400
"I haven't, Mother, it's the truth!
They say they're knights," replied the youth.
As he said "knights," his mother heard
and fainted at the very word,
and afterwards, when she came to,

she wailed, as angry women do,
"Ah, woe is me! I had expected,
sweet son, that you could be protected
so perfectly from chivalry
that you would never hear or see   410
one thing about it, for by right,
dear son, you would have been a knight,
if God had let your father and other
friends live to raise you, not your mother.
No knight was ever so revered,
so greatly honored, and so feared,
as was your father, dearest son.
His name was known to everyone
throughout the islands of the sea.*
You may well boast your family,   420
your father's household and his line
will not disgrace you, nor will mine.
I am descended from the best
knights of this land, and they attest
in the sea's isles, no line has shown
itself more noble than my own,
but now the best have been brought low.
As many instances will show,
misfortunes overtake the bold
and noble warriors who uphold   430
the codes of honor: wickedness
must flourish, shame and idleness,
and yet the good must be brought low.
Your father, for you do not know,
was wounded through the thighs and maimed.
The property that he had claimed
and won through valor beyond measure:
his vast lands and enormous treasure,
was lost in its entirety:
he had to live in poverty.   440
All these impoverished noblemen
lost their inheritances when
the late king, Uther Pendragon,
met with his death. King Uther's son*

---

v. 419. Hilka notes (*Der Percevalroman*, p. 623) that these islands are the Hebrides.
There are other references to the islands in King Rion of the Isles (v. 851) and Clamadeu
of the Isles (v. 2776).

is good King Arthur. They were banned,
unjustly banished from their land,
for which they had no restitution:
the poor were left in destitution.
All people who could flee here, fled.
Your father could not flee; instead,   450
he knew one refuge in his need
and had a litter made with speed.
By litter bearers he was brought
to the sole refuge that he sought:
his manor in the forest wild.
Then you were just a little child,
not more than two, and nursing still.
You had two handsome brothers, till
your father felt, when they were grown,
that each of them should go alone   460
to join a king's court and receive
a horse and weapons. By his leave,
at his advice, the older one
served with the king of Escavalon*
till he was dubbed; the younger met
and served King Ban of Gomoret.*
The two young brothers knights were made,
and they received the accolade
on the same day, and they departed.
They left their courts that day and started   470
their journeys home, because each boy

v. 444. Hilka notes (*Der Percevalroman*, p. 624) that Geoffrey of Monmouth (Faral edition, p. 227) relates the death of Uther Pendragon, who was treacherously poisoned by the Saxons. This passage echoes Wace's description of the ensuing confusion:

> You would have seen lands laid to waste. . . .
> Who could flee promptly fled in haste.
> The poor fled, and the affluent;
> the burgers and the farmers went;
> the peasants fled, and the enfeoffed;
> most of the barons also left. . . .

Brut, vs. 13893 ff (Arnold edition).
v. 464 (463, Roach edition). The king of Escavalon (Cavalon) is the father of the young king mentioned in v. 4791.
v. 466 (467, Roach edition). Hilka notes (*Der Percevalroman*, pp. 624–625) that King Ban of Gormoret is mentioned in *Erec and Enide* v. 1923 (Roques edition).

would bring me and his father joy.
He never saw his sons again,
for they were overcome and slain
in knightly combat on the way,
and I have mourned them to this day.
The elder had a foul demise:
the rooks and crows pecked out his eyes.*
That's how he was when they were found.
Their father's grief was so profound,   480
he died of it, and I have led
a bitter life since he was dead
and suffered greatly. You, my lad,
were all the comfort that I had,
for I was utterly bereft.
Of all my family, God left
no more to me except one boy
to gladden me and bring me joy."
The youth was hardly listening.
He told his mother, "Go and bring   490
some food to me and set it out!
I don't know what you're talking about!
I'll go and search until I find
the king who makes knights; never mind
what people think!" His mother tried
to keep the young man at her side.
His mother, as befitted him,
attired and outfitted him*
in a coarse hempen shirt and breeches
made in the Welsh style, that one which is   500
to make the breeches and the hose
attached together, I suppose,
a hood and coat of buckskin leather
which wrapped around and clasped together.
His mother dressed him in such ways.
He stayed there only three more days,

---

v. 478. Nitze and Williams note that Cuchulainn was attacked by the Morrigan, who then flew away in the form of a crow. The Celts had a particular horror of the carrion crow, for it was supposed to be frequently the guise of the war goddess Morrigan, who with her companions incited the warriors to the madness of battle and revelled among the bodies of the slain (*Arthurian Names*, p. 281.).

v. 498 ff. Hilka includes detailed references to the short buckskin coat and long breeches of the Welsh peasant, in *Der Percevalroman*, pp. 625-626.

and afterwards, although she pleaded,
her tears and coaxing went unheeded.
Then through his mother strange pain crept;
she kissed and hugged her son, and wept.   510
She said, "How terribly I grieve,
my handsome son, to see you leave.
Go to the royal court; declare
the king must give you arms to bear:
I know that he will not refuse.
The time will come when you must use
those arms, and what will happen, son?
To do a thing you've never done
and seen nobody go about!
You won't know how! I have no doubt   520
you will be awkward and will blunder.
And yet I think it is no wonder
you would be clumsy, when in fact
no one has taught you how to act.
Not learning what one's seen and heard
time and again seems more absurd.
Son, I've a lesson I must tell:
you would be wise to listen well,
and if my teaching you retain,
you will have everything to gain.   530
My son, soon you will be a knight,
God willing; I am sure I'm right.
If you find, near or at a distance,
a lady who requires assistance,
or a distressed and troubled maid
who tells you she has need of aid,
with her request you must concur:
all honor lies in helping her.
The man who does not honor women
shows honor must be dead within him.   540
Serve ladies and serve maids, dear son;
you'll be admired by everyone.
And, if a favor you desire,
do nothing to provoke her ire.
He who receives a maiden's kiss
has much, and if she grants you this,
there is no more that you may take,
if you will leave off for my sake.
But if she wears a finger ring

or, on the belt encircling   550
her waist, an almspurse, and for prayer
or love she gives you it to wear,
you've my approval and permission
to take and wear, on that condition,
the maiden's almspurse or her ring.
Dear son, I'll say another thing:
on roads or at an inn, it's wrong
to be with someone very long*
without first asking him his name.
When all is said and done, they claim   560
that by the name you know the man.
Dear son, as often as you can,
converse with gentlemen and be
found often in their company.
A gentleman gives counsel sane
to those he numbers in his train.
Above all else I recommend
that church and chapel you attend.
Pray to Our Lord, that He may give
great honor to you while you live   570
and in such deeds your life expend
that you may come to a good end."
"What's a church, Mother?" "Son, it is*
a place where they hold services
to God, who Heaven and earth created
with men and women populated."
"What is a chapel?" "Son, the same:
a fine and holy house, a frame
for sacred relics, treasures godly,

v. 558 ff. Hilka cites (*Der Percevalroman*, p. 627) the *Disciplina clericalis* by Petrus Alphonsi (Hilka edition, Sammlung mittellateinischer Texte [Heidelberg: C. Winter, 1920] 27, 33) as a reference for this passage: "The Philosopher says 'Do not travel with anyone with whom you have not previously become acquainted.'" Frappier notes in *Chrétien de Troyes et le Mythe du Graal*, pp. 120 ff., that the saying, "by the name you know the man," expresses a concept of medieval symbolism that there was a relationship between the name and the person; the name was a consecration of the personality.

v. 573. Frappier notes, in *Chrétien de Troyes et le Mythe du Graal*, pp. 82-83, that Perceval's question, "What's a church?" shows as incredible a lack of knowledge as the fact that Perceval doesn't know his own name and that his mother has forgotten to tell him. Frappier believes that Chrétien intended to portray Perceval as almost a pagan in order to trace his religious development more fully.

wherein they sacrifice the body　　　　　　　　　　　580
of Jesus Christ, the prophet holy*
toward whom the Jews behaved so lowly.*
He was betrayed, judged wrongfully,
and He endured the agony
of death for women and for men,
whose souls went down to Hell's depths when
they left their bodies, there to dwell,
and Christ delivered them from Hell.
Against a pillar He was tied,
and He was scourged and crucified,　　　　　　　　　590
a crown of thorns upon his head.
Pray to that Lord, as I have said,
at any church that you may pass
and hear the matins and the mass."　　　　　　　　594
He'd wait no longer by her side.　　　　　　　　　　599
He took his leave. His mother cried.　　　　　　　　600
His horse was saddled as required;
he was appareled and attired
in fashions that the Welshmen use,
and he was shod in rawhide shoes.
He always, everywhere he went,
took his three javelins, and he meant
to take them with him on that day.
His mother, though, took two away,
because he seemed too Welsh to her;
to leave all three was seemlier,　　　　　　　　　　610
could she have made him understand.
He held a switch in his right hand
to whip his hunter on the ride.
His mother kissed her son, and cried,
and said her prayers that the Lord
would keep the son whom she adored.

v. 581. Hilka notes (*Der Percevalroman*, p. 627) that the description of Jesus Christ as "the prophet holy" is reminiscent of Matthew 21:11, Luke 24:19, and John 4:19, 6:14, 7:40, and 9:17.

v. 582. The virulent anti-Semitism of v. 582 and vs. 6292 ff is atypical of Chrétien's works; Lejeune notes in "La date du *Conte du Graal*," pp. 75–76, that Chrétien never mentioned the Jews in his previous romances. These passages may reflect an intensification of the anti-Semitic spirit of the times. Early in 1180 Philip-Augustus signed the first edicts of persecution of the Jews at a time when some Jews were actually put to death in the vicinity of Paris.

"God grant to you, wherever you go,
more joy than I can ever know!"
The youth rode off, but looked around
a stone's throw off, and on the ground   620
in the short time that had elapsed,
he saw his mother had collapsed
beside the drawbridge, where she lay
unconscious, and in such a way
it seemed to him that she had slipped
and fallen dead. The young man whipped
his hunter's croup with his small switch.
Without a stumble or a hitch
the horse shot forward, bearing him
into the forest dark and grim.   630
He rode as fast as he could ride
from morning until eventide
and slept within the woods that night
until the day dawned clear and bright.

THE MAIDEN IN THE TENT

The youth arose, to birds' sweet song.
He mounted, and he rode along
until his traveling revealed
a tent pitched in a pretty field
beside a fountain's flowing stream.
He saw its beauty was extreme,*   640
for one part of the tent was red,
the other trimmed with golden thread,
with a gilt eagle at the summit.
The bright red sunbeams glanced off from it
and lit the field, so the entire
field glittered in the brilliant fire
the eagle and the tent reflected.
Welsh lodges, too, had been erected,
and leafy arbors all around,
the finest tent that could be found.   650
He rode toward it across the lea.
"Oh, God, this is your house I see,
and what an error I would do
not to go in and worship You.
My mother told the truth for sure
the day she told me chapels were
more beautiful than any dwelling.
I can remember Mother telling,
that if I found one on my way,
I ought to go inside and pray   660
to the Creator, as I must,
the one in whom I place my trust.
I'll enter, worship, and entreat
the Lord to give me food to eat:
I badly need some nourishment."
The young man came up to the tent

v. 640 ff. Hilka (*Der Percevalroman*, pp. 630–631) cites references to similar tents in the *Roman d'Alexandre*, the *Roman de Thèbes*, the *Eneas*, the *Roman de Troie*, among others, and especially to the fairy tent in Marie de France's *Lanval*, which was also pitched in a field and topped by a golden eagle.

and found that it was open wide,
and when the young man looked inside,
there in the center was a bed
with a brocaded, silken spread.   670
A maiden slept there all alone,
because handmaidens of her own
had gone away into the wood
to pick fresh flowers, so they could
strew flowers on the tent's hard floor,
which was their custom heretofore.
But when the young man had gone in,
his horse neighed loudly, and the din
startled the sleeping girl awake.
In terror she began to shake.   680
The youth said, for he was naive,
"I greet you, maid, as I believe
my mother taught: wherever I meet them,
if I find maidens, I must greet them."
The maiden, trembling with fear
of the young man, who did appear
to be a fool, thought she had shown
herself a fool, to stay alone
and let herself be caught off guard.
She said to him, "Don't disregard   690
my warning, lest my sweetheart see!
Go on your way, young man, and flee!"
"First I will kiss you, by my head,
no matter who's annoyed," he said,
"as Mother taught me I should do."
"I'll never give a kiss to you,"
the maiden said, "of my free will!
Flee, lest my sweetheart find you still,
for if he finds you, you are dead!"
The young man had strong arms; instead   700
he crushed the maid in his embrace,
not knowing how to act with grace.
He stretched her out beneath him, lying
upon her, and she struggled, trying
to fend him off and to get loose,
but her best efforts were no use.
The youth kissed her, will she or no,
the story says that it was so,
without pause seven times, before

he caught sight of the ring she wore.*   710
It had an emerald, very bright.
He said, "My mother said I might
take the ring from your finger too,
but to do nothing else to you,
so, maid, give me that ring and stone;
I want to have it for my own."
"You'll never have it, on my word!"
the maiden told him, "Rest assured,
unless you force it off my finger!"
Of course the young man didn't linger;   720
he seized her hand by force, extended
her finger, and, as he'd intended,
he put her ring upon his hand.
"Farewell, maid, I am feeling grand.
I like the kisses that you give
more than the chambermaids' who live
at Mother's house, those I've embraced,
for your mouth has no bitter taste."
She wept as she began to say,
"Young man, don't take my ring away,   730
I'll suffer for it if you do.
Eventually, I promise you,
you'll lose your life to pay for it."
The young man did not care a whit
for anything the maiden said.
He'd fasted till he felt half dead
and found a cask, not far from him,
filled full of wine up to the brim,
a silver goblet at its side,
and on a bunch of rushes spied   740
a towel lying, clean and white.
He lifted it: to his delight
he found three pasties, venison.
At once the youth broke open one;
with hunger goading him and teasing,
this meal was not at all displeasing.
He ate the whole meat pasty up,

v. 710. Nitze notes (in *Perceval and the Holy Grail*, p. 312) that a Celtic source for this episode may be an episode in the Finn saga in which Finn overtakes three fairy women outside the green mound of Slieve Slanga and snatches a magic brooch from one of them.

and then he filled the silver cup
with wine, which was not hard to taste,
and drank it in great gulps in haste.   750
He said, "Maid, I won't find a way
to eat three pasties in one day.
Do come and eat; they're nicely done.
In fact, if each of us eats one,
another whole one would be left."
The maiden cried as if bereft;
though he entreated her and urged,
the maiden answered not a word.
She wrung her hands, and sobbed, and wept.
The youth ate all he pleased and kept   760
imbibing till he wished no more.
He covered what he left before
he took his leave and turned to go,
commending her to God, although
the words of parting that he gave her
brought no ease. Asking God to save her,
he said to her, "Now for God's sake,
dear friend, because I'm going to take
your ring away, you must not cry:
I'll pay you back before I die.   770
Now I am going, by your leave."
She did not cease to cry and grieve.
She'd not commend him to God's care,
she told him, she would have to bear
disgrace and misery, far more
than any wretch had borne before,
and what was worse, she felt assured
that never, while her life endured,
would he consent to help or aid her,
so let him know he had betrayed her.   780
The maid remained to weep and cry.
When a few minutes had gone by,
her sweetheart came back from the wood.*

v. 783. Frappier notes, in *Chrétien de Troyes et le Mythe du Graal*, p. 127, that the knight's name, "the Proud Knight of the Glade," is mentioned in *Erec and Enide*, v. 2121 (Roques edition) as a knight overthrown by Erec at the tournament at Tenebroe. Frappier notes (p. 84) that the Proud Knight's harsh treatment of the maiden in the tent is a reworking of Erec's abruptness to Enide; Erec tells Enide, however, to dress in her most beautiful gown and to ride her finest horse when they go in search of adventure.

He saw tracks where the horse had stood,
although the youth had gone away,
and his love weeping with dismay.
He sternly said, "It seems to me
that, judging from these signs I see,
a knight has been here, maiden fair."
"He was no knight, my lord, I swear,   790
but just a young Welsh fool, a clown,
an oaf, who started gulping down
your wine, enjoyed it thoroughly,
and ate some of your pasties three."
"But lovely one, please tell me why
so small a thing should make you cry?
For if he had consumed the rest,
I would not be at all distressed."
"My lord, but that is not the whole.
My ring's involved, because he stole   800
my ring and carried it away.
I wish that I had died today
than have him take your ring with him."
The knight's heart filled with feelings grim.
"That was outrageous," said the knight,
"but since he took the ring, he might
as well keep it; but I've begun
to think what else he might have done.
If there is more, don't try to hide."
"My lord, he kissed me," she replied.   810
"He kissed you!" "Yes, it's true, but still
he did so much against my will."
"No, you enjoyed it, when he kissed,
and never once did you resist!"
Distraught, he made this jealous vow.
"Don't you believe I know you now?
How well I know you! You will find
I'm not so one-eyed or so blind*
to falseness in that episode.
You've started down a wicked road,   820
you've started on a wicked path.

v. 818. Hilka speculated (*Der Percevalroman*, p. 634) that Chrétien might have been
influenced by the passage in the *Disciplina clericalis* about the deceived husband and the
one-eyed vintner (15, 6, Hilka edition).

Your horse shall not eat oats," in wrath
he vowed, "and he shall not be bled
until I am avenged," he said,
"and if your horse should lose a shoe,
he never will be shod anew,
and you will follow me on foot
if he should die. You will not put
new clothes on till I have his head.
You'll follow me on foot," he said,   830
"and naked; I will not consent
to any other punishment."
And then the knight sat down and ate.

THE RED KNIGHT

The youth rode at a steady rate,
until a charcoal burner hove*
in sight behind the ass he drove.
The youth said, as it came to pass,
"My noble man who drives an ass,
give me directions now, and tell
the quickest way to Carduel.   840
I want to see King Arthur there,
for he makes knights, so they declare."
"In that direction, lad," said he,
"there is a castle by the sea.
Dear friend, if you will go that way,
you'll find King Arthur sad and gay."
"Now tell me what I want to know:
why does the king feel joy and woe?"
"I'll tell you quickly that the king
and all his host were battling   850
and beat King Rion of the Isles,*
and that is why King Arthur smiles.
But he is angry with the men
who fought beside him: they have been

v. 835. Lejeune notes, in "La date du *Conte du Graal*," pp. 65–67 and 75, that this verse contains the only reference to a charcoal seller in the entire works of Chrétien and links the story to an episode in the youth of Philip-Augustus. On August 15, 1179, Philip-Augustus was going to be crowned at Compiègne, at his father's request. Two days before the ceremony, Philip-Augustus became separated from his companions while hunting and spent the night and most of the next day wandering lost in the forest, until at twilight he met a blackened and terrifying-looking charcoal seller. The peasant took Philip-Augustus back to the right road to Compiègne, where the court was agonizing over the loss of the heir to the throne. The experience shattered Philip-Augustus's nerves, and despite his own illness Louis VII made a pilgrimage to Thomas Beckett's tomb in England to pray for his son's recovery. He was accompanied by Count Philip of Flanders.

v. 851. Nitze and Williams (in *Arthurian Names*, pp. 289–290) note that King Rion of the Isles was probably the giant Ritho mentioned by Geoffrey of Monmouth (Faral edition, p. 257); the giant Rithon of Wace's *Brut*, vs. 11,587 ff. Ritho was dressed in the beards of the kings he had slain, and when he ordered King Arthur to send him his beard, King Arthur defeated the giant.

returning to their towns, where they*
find it more comfortable to stay.
What they have done he doesn't know;
that's why the king is filled with woe."
The youth cared not a penny for
the burner's news about the war,   860
except he traveled down the road,
the one the charcoal burner showed,
until he saw, above the sea,
a castle, strong and beautifully
designed and placed. Then he beheld
a warrior in arms, who held
a gold cup, coming through the gate.
In his left hand he held his great
long lance, his shield and bridle, and
he held the cup in his right hand.   870
The knight was armed and helmeted
in handsome arms of scarlet red,*
becoming and entirely new.
The youth admired his weapons too.
"My word, I'll ask the king for these,"
he told himself. "If he agrees
to give them to me, I shall be
extremely pleased, and cursed be he
who wants arms of another sort!"
He hurried on toward Arthur's court   880
to reach the castle at long last.
The red knight, as the youth went past,
detained him momentarily.
"Where are you going? Answer me."
"To court, where I shall ask the king
for those red weapons." "Just the thing!
Go on, young man, you're doing right,
and come back quickly," said the knight.
"Inform the coward king if he
will not hold his domain from me   890

v. 855. Hilka notes (*Der Percevalroman*, p. 635) that Gawain is one of the absent
knights, and that on vs. 4086 ff, King Arthur has to tell him about Perceval's arrival at
court.

v. 872. Loomis notes (*The Grail: From Celtic Myth to Christian Symbol*, p. 84) that
the color red associated with the knight whom Perceval slays links the story to the Finn
saga, since Finn's hereditary enemies were the sons of Daire the Red.

and be my vassal, to surrender
or send someone as its defender,
for I proclaim his lands are mine.
Let him believe you by this sign:
Right to his face, I have snatched up
and carried off his golden cup
filled with his wine!" He might prefer
to send another messenger,
for this one had not heard one word!
The young man rode on undeterred   900
to reach the king's court, where he found
the great hall, level with the ground.
The king and knights were at the table.
Although on horseback, he was able
to enter; it was paved inside
and was as long as it was wide.
The king sat at the table's head
lost in his thoughts. High-spirited,
the warriors around the king
were laughing loud and bantering;   910
he brooded silently withal.
The youth proceeded through the hall,
but did not know which man to greet,
nor know the king he came to meet,
till Yvonet came over, and
he held a sharp knife in his hand.*
"Show me the king," the young man told
the squire, "you who've a knife to hold."
Said Yvonet, whose words were fair,
"See, friend, the king is over there."   920
Then the young man, as best he knew,
rode up to greet King Arthur, who
was thinking and did not reply.
The young man made another try;
King Arthur's thoughts were so profound,
he did not utter any sound.
"Upon my word," the young man swore,
"this king has not made knights before.   928
How could he make knights? It's absurd;   930

v. 916. Hilka notes (*Der Percevalroman*, p. 638) that Yvonet has a knife in hand be-
cause he is carving the meat.

He can't be made to say one word!   929
The young man started to return
and forced his hunter's head to turn.
The hunter ridden by the youth,
who acted like a fool, in truth,
was so close to King Arthur, that
it actually knocked his hat
upon the table. Then the king
turned toward the youth, abandoning
his thoughts, and raised his head to meet
the youth he was about to greet.   940
"Be welcome; do not take it ill
that, at your greeting, I was still;
I was too angry to reply.
The worst of foes with whom I vie,
the enemy I hate and fear
above all others, came in here
and claimed my land, and he is so
outrageous that, will I or no,
he wants the lands wherein I reign.
He is the Red Knight; his domain*   950
is called the Forest of Quinqueroi.
The queen sat with me, bringing joy
to these brave wounded knights you see.
The knight would not have angered me,
whatever he said, but he came up
in front of me and seized my cup,
raised it so recklessly, he spilled
the wine with which the cup was filled
upon the queen. That was, in fact,
a boorish and insulting act!   960
At once the queen withdrew, aflame
with sorrow, rage, distress, and shame.
She went back to her room thereby,
and I am certain she will die
of indignation and of grief.
So help me God, it's my belief
she is not going to survive."

v. 950. Hilka notes (*Der Percevalroman*, p. 638) that the Red Knight from the Forest
of Quinqueroi may be the youth of Quintareus mentioned in *Erec and Enide* v. 1693
(Roques edition).

The young man did not care a chive
for anything the king related,
and in no way commiserated   970
with his wife, shame, or suffering.
"Make me a knight, my lord the king,"*
was what the youth was heard to say,
"I'm eager to be on my way."
The eyes of this young savage-bred
were sparkling within his head.
No people present thought he seemed
intelligent, and yet they deemed
the fine youth someone of account.
The king replied, "My friend, dismount   980
and give your hunter to a squire
who'll care for it as you desire.
You'll soon be knighted; it's your due.
It honors me and betters you."
"The other knight," the youth replied,
"whom I met in the field outside
had not dismounted from his steed
the way you've asked me to proceed.
I will not do so, I believe;
just knight me quickly and I'll leave."   990
"Ah, my dear friend, most willingly.
It betters you and honors me."
the king replied. "My lord king, no,
but rather, by the faith I owe
to my Creator," the youth said,
"if I can't be a knight in red.
I'll wait for long until I can!
Give me the weapons of the man
who stole your golden cup away.   999
I met him by the gate today."   1000
The seneschal, whose wounds were sore,
was angered by this speech and swore,

v. 972. Perceval's bold demand, "Make me a knight," is absurd; his only qualification is his noble birth. In the normal course of events, a young man wishing to be knighted would have served a long apprenticeship away from home at another lord's court. During his youth he would have received instruction in arms and in the code of chivalric and courteous behavior. When eligible, at a great and infrequently held ceremony, he would have been given a ritual bath and, after spending a night standing vigil in a church, would have received his arms and the accolade from the lord.

"My friend, you're absolutely right.
Go seize the weapons of that knight!
Now they belong to you, and you'll
discover that you were no fool
to come here for his armor red."
The king heard and in anger said,
"Kay, you are very wrong to jeer.
No gentleman should taunt and sneer.   1010
As for the young man, you may find,
although he has a simple mind,
he is of noble family still,
and though he has been trained so ill
by a rough master, yet he can
become a valiant nobleman.
It's rude of you to jeer and make
a promise you intend to break.*
You know a gentleman must not
thus promise to another what   1020
he can or will not give, for he
will earn that person's enmity
who would have been his friend, except
he feels the promise should be kept
if once the promise has been made.
This is the reason I'm afraid
it's better to refuse him plainly
than to keep someone hoping vainly.
Were anyone the truth to tell,
the man deceives himself as well   1030
who makes a pledge he won't fulfill,*
for he will lose his friend's good will."*
Thus did the king admonish Kay.
The youth, already on his way,
beheld a lovely, noble maid.
He greeted her and was repaid;
she greeted him and then began
to laugh, and laughing, said, "Young man,

v. 1018. Hilka notes (*Der Percevalroman*, p. 640) that among other references for "et de prometre sanz doner" is Morawski, *Proverbes français* no. 230: "Bel prometre e nient doner fait fol conforter."

vs. 1031-1032. Hilka notes (*Der Percevalroman*, p. 640) that this proverb is listed in Morawski, *Proverbs français* no. 2106: "Qui promest et riens ne solt le cuer de son ami se tolt."

if you have long enough to live,
deep in my heart I'm positive 1040
no knight will be acclaimed or found
in any land the world around
to be a better knight than you,
and I feel certain it is true."
She had not laughed at least six years.
The maiden's words had reached all ears;
she spoke so loudly that they were
heard by the court. Kay sprang at her,
the prophecy had hurt him so,
and gave the maiden such a blow 1050
that when his palm struck her soft face,
he stretched her out flat by her place.
When he had slapped her, Kay, returning,
walked past a fire that was burning.
A fool stood there, and in his ire
Kay kicked the fool into the fire,
because the fool was wont to say:
"This maid won't laugh until the day
she sees the man to whom will be*
awarded knighthood's sovereignty." 1060
The fool was screaming, and the maid
was crying, and the youth delayed
no longer, and despite his lack
of counsel, started riding back
out of the castle to pursue
the red knight. Yvonet, who knew
the shortest paths and byways there,
and who was always glad to bear
news back to court, went out alone,
without companions of his own, 1070
into an orchard by the hall,

v. 1059. The *geis*, a magical prohibition or injunction, such as not laughing for six years, is often a stimulus to the action in Celtic tales. Frappier notes in *Chrétien de Troyes et le Mythe du Graal*, p. 89, that with a French storyteller the Celtic *geis*, such as "You will not laugh until you have seen the best knight in the world," becomes a prediction, and explains that "Since the *geis* imposes extraordinary trials which are always religiously performed by the hero, it is natural to see in it the realization of a prophecy by a predestined being." Hilka notes (*Der Percevalroman*, p. 642) that the fool's prophetic gift is one of the magical elements of the romance, and that in the *Prose Tristan* a fool prophesied Morholt's death at Tristan's hand.

descended through a postern small,
and came out on the thoroughfare.
The knight was waiting for his fair
adventure and his knightly deed.
The youth went riding at high speed
toward him whose arms he meant to claim.
The knight, before the young man came,
had set the cup he called his own
upon a block of dark brown stone.   1080
The youth called, when he'd ridden near
enough to him so each could hear,
"Lay down your weapons heretofore;
you shall not bear them anymore,
King Arthur is commanding you."
The knight said, "Lad, can it be true
King Arthur hasn't any knights
who dare to come uphold his rights?
If no one's coming, do be frank."
"The devil, what is this, a prank?   1090
Come on, sir knight, why is it you've
not done my bidding? You remove
your weapons now, as I desired."
"Young man," he answered, "I inquired
if any of King Arthur's staff
are coming here on his behalf
to fight with me?" "This minute, doff
your arms, knight, or I'll take them off!
I am not going to allow
your wearing arms. Remove them now!   1100
You understand me, I will hit,
if you make me say more of it."
At that the red knight's anger blazed.*
With his two hands, his lance he raised,
and gave the youth so hard a blow
across the shoulder blades (although
he used the butt, not iron) that
he made the youth crouch over flat

---

v. 1113 (1115, Roach edition). Nitze and Williams note (*Arthurian Names*, p. 292)
that in Irish legend, Balar lost his evil eye when Lug cast a sling-stone at him, and in
Welsh legend; Kulhwch strikes Yspaddaden Penkawr with a weapon that pierces his eye.
Hilka notes (*Der Percevalroman*, p. 643) that knights are killed through the eye in *Erec
and Enide*, v. 4418 (Roques edition), and in *Lancelot*, v. 2386 (Roques edition).

on his steed's neck. Bruised and aflame,
the angry youth took careful aim, 1110
as best he could, at his foe's eye,*
and then he let his javelin fly
and struck the knight through eye and brain.
He never saw nor heard again.
The youth saw brains and blood escape
above the shoulders at the nape.
In agony, the knight's heart stopped;
full length upon the ground he dropped.
The youth dismounted on the field,
put down the lance, removed the shield 1120
from the knight's neck, but found that he'd
no knowledge of how helms were freed.
The young man struggled to unclasp it,
but did not know the way to grasp it.
Then he attempted to ungird
the sword, but he had never heard
or seen how it was done beneath,
and could not draw it from the sheath.
He grasped the sword and pulled and jerked.
When Yvonet saw how he worked, 1130
he started laughing. "My dear friend,
just what is it that you intend?"
The youth replied, "I do not know.
I thought your king meant to bestow
these arms on me! To make them mine,
I'll have to cut this corpse up fine
in chops and slices, for the knight
wore armor made to fit so tight,
his body and the armor stick
so close together, by some trick, 1140
they seem to be all of one piece."
Said Yvonet, "I can release
and separate them in a hurry
if you desire, so do not worry."
"Then separate them right away;
give me the arms without delay,
and work as quickly as you can,"
the youth said. Yvonet began
to strip the body to the toes
and left no hauberk, mail, nor hose, 1150
nor arms, nor helm upon his head.

But Yvonet, for all he said,
discovered that he could not make
the youth remove his clothes and take
the padded tunic, made of rich
soft woven silken fabric, which
the red knight, when alive and hale,
had worn beneath his hauberk's mail,
nor part him from his brogues of hide.
To his advice the youth replied,   1160
"The devil, what is this, a jest?
Exchange the clothes in which I'm dressed,
ones Mother made the other morn,
for poorer clothes which he has worn?
The fine, thick hempen shirt I'm in
for his shirt, which is soft and thin?
My coat for his? My coat can stop
the rain, and his lets in each drop.
Shame on the fool who'd ever trade
good clothes for clothes that are ill-made!"   1170
Ah yes, they say that as a rule
it's very hard to teach a fool.*
He took the arms, no more, no less,
although beseeched to change his dress.
So Yvonet at long last laced
the young man in the armor, placed
the spurs upon the brogues the lad
was wearing, fastened them, and clad
the young man in the hauberk's chain
(no one will look so fine again)   1180
and on the headcap placed the helmet,
which was becoming, very well set,
showed him how swords are girded, so
his would swing loosely to and fro,
led up the war horse, and then put
the youth upon it with his foot
inside the stirrup, which the lad
had never seen, nor had he had
with spurs the least acquaintanceship,
but just the willow switch or whip.   1190

v. 1172 (1173, Roach edition). Among other references for this saying, Hilka cites
(*Der Percevalroman*, p. 645) Morawski, *Proverbes français* no. 367: "Chastier fol est
cous en yaue."

Then Yvonet fetched lance and shield.
He had not left the battlefield
before the youth began to say,
"My hunter you may lead away.
I'm giving you a worthy steed
of which I have no further need.
Take back the golden cup and bring
my greeting with it to the king.
Inform the maid of whom I speak,
the one whom Kay struck on the cheek,   1200
I hope, before my dying day,
to have such reckoning with Kay,
she'll think the scores are evened up."
The squire said he would take the cup
back to King Arthur and relay
the message in a truthful way.
The youth rode off. There was a stir
in the hall where the barons were,
as Yvonet went through the door
and brought the king his cup once more.   1210
"Rejoice now, sire," they heard him say,
"because your knight who came today
restores to you your cup of gold."
"Which knight is it of whom you've told?"   1214
"The one," said Yvonet, "who started   1217
from court and only just departed."
"What, the Welsh youth," King Arthur said,
"who asked me for the armor red   1220
belonging to that knight, the one
who has insulted me and done
his very best to cause me shame?"
"Indeed yes, sire, he is the same."
"How was my golden cup restored?
The red knight, of his own accord,
gave the young man my cup of gold?"
"My lord, no, it was dearly sold.
The young man took the red knight's life."
"My friend, what brought about the strife?"   1230
the king asked. "I'm not positive,
but sire, I saw the warrior give
the youth a lance blow on the back
and hurt the youth, who hit him back.
He put a javelin through his eye,

so brains and blood began to dye
his neck and back; the knight was downed
and stretched out dead upon the ground."
King Arthur told the seneschal,
"See all the harm that did befall   1240
from idle banter that has sprung
unhindered from your wicked tongue!
Oh, Kay, you drove a youth away
who served me notably today."
"Sire," Yvonet said to the king,
"he sent a message I must bring
and give the queen's handmaiden, whom
Kay struck in jealousy and gloom.
The maid will be avenged, said he,
at his first opportunity."   1250
The king's fool heard; he had been keeping
his fireside seat, and he came leaping
onto his feet and left his place
to seek King Arthur on the dais.
The fool was overjoyed; he pranced,
and skipped across the room, and danced.
"God save me, King," the fool said, grinning,
"for our adventures are beginning,
and often ones you will regard
as dangerous to bear and hard.   1260
This is the pledge that I shall give:
Kay can be wholly positive
he will regret his hands and feet
and hateful tongue, without deceit.
Before a fortnight's passed away,
the knight will cap my kick from Kay;
the slap Kay gave the queen's handmaid
will be sold dear and well repaid,
for Kay will break his arm," he told her,
"his right arm, just below his shoulder.   1270
Slung from his neck, this boorish knight
will bear it six months, serves him right;
he can't escape, for all his trying,
not any more than he can dying."
The evil tidings he foreboded
stung Kay, who practically exploded
with rage and spite. In front of all
Kay nearly went across the hall

to kill the fool, but such a measure
would have incurred the king's displeasure, 1280
and therefore Kay did not attack.
King Arthur said, "Ah, Kay, alack!
You make me angry. Had we trained
the youth a little, or explained
the use of armor, shield, and lance,
so that he would have had some chance
of self defense, or helped him out,
he'd be a worthy knight, no doubt.
Yet he knows nothing or next to it
of fighting and the way to do it: 1290
he could not draw his sword at need.
He's sitting armed upon his steed,
and he is bound to meet some knight
who will not hesitate to fight
and wound him for the horse he's claimed.
The youth will soon be dead or maimed,
for he has such a simple mind
and is so clumsy, he will find
he won't know what defense to make.
Soon he'll have placed his final stake." 1300
And so King Arthur mourned for him,
lamented, and looked very grim,
but there was nothing to be gained;
the king fell still and so remained.

GORNEMANT OF GOHORT

Meanwhile the youth, without a rest,
went riding through the wood and pressed
until he reached, in open land,
a river which could not be spanned
by crossbow shot, it was so wide.
The waters that the land supplied   1310
were drawn into the river bed.
He crossed a field and went ahead
toward the river rushing in its track
but shunned the water, wild and black.
The river Loire was not so deep.
The young man much preferred to keep
close to the bank and opposite
a towering rocky cliff, for it
was on the bank that lay in face,
and water beat against its base.   1320
Upon the cliff side, sloping down
the ocean side, a castled town,
extremely rich and mighty, lay,
and where the river joined the bay
the youth turned to the left, and caught
sight of the castle's towers, and thought
the towers looked exactly if
they'd sprouted from the rocky cliff,
were born of the embankment steep.
He saw a huge and mighty keep   1330
square in the castle's center, placed
near ramparts, strong and high, which faced
upon the wide bay, where the ocean
and river fought with pounding motion;
the tides beat on the rampart's foot.
Four lower turrets had been put
upon four corners of the wall,
of hard stone blocks, strong, handsome all.
The castle was well situated,
and was, within, well decorated.   1340
The castle's outerwork was round.
In front of it the young man found

a strong high bridge was built, which spanned
the river, made of sandstone and
of limestone, and well fortified
with crenelation on each side,
a tower midway and at one end
a drawbridge, fitted for its end,
which was to be, for the estate,
by day a bridge, by night a gate.   1350
On toward the drawbridge rode the lad.
A nobleman paced on it, clad
in silks of purple; in this way
he paced and whiled his time away
while waiting for the newcomer.
Two squires who wore no mantles were
accompanying their master, and
he held a short staff in his hand,
which lent an air of dignity.
The youth remembered perfectly   1360
his mother's lessons, for he bowed
and afterward observed aloud,
"Sir, I was taught that by my mother."
The lord replied, "God bless you, brother,"
for by his speech he knew the youth
was simple, awkward, and uncouth,
"from where, dear brother, have you come?"
"King Arthur's court is where I'm from."
"What were you doing there?" "The king
made me a knight, and may it bring   1370
good luck to him!" "A knight! I vow,
I wouldn't have supposed that now
he would make knights, nor that the king
would turn his thoughts to such a thing;
his mind would be on something other.
And now, please tell me, gentle brother,
who's given you those arms of red?"
"The king gave them to me," he said.
"He gave them? How?" As it occurred,
the youth retold the tale you've heard.   1380
To tell the tale once more to you
would be too tiresome — pointless too —
no tale improves with repetition.
The nobleman asked in addition
just what the youth did with his horse.

"I make him run, the way I'd force
my hunter once, the one I had
at Mother's house," replied the lad,
"I run him over hill and vale."
"Now, dear friend, tell me without fail   1390
the way you use your arms and bear them?"
"I take them on and off and wear them
the way the squire taught me to do.
He took them off the knight I slew
and stripped the body of the knight.
The arms and armor are so light,
they don't tire me or interfere!"
The lord said, "I am glad to hear.
That's news I must say I enjoyed.
Now tell me, if you're not annoyed,   1400
what purpose brings you to my dwelling?"
"Sir, I remember Mother telling
that I should go with gentlemen
wherever I find them again,
and I should do as they advise:
for taking their advice is wise."
The nobleman said, "My dear brother,
may there be blessings on your mother;
she gave you sound advice that day.
Now have you something more to say?"   1410
"Yes." "What is it?" "This and no more:
tonight please lodge me at your door."
"With pleasure," said the lord, "in kind
do me a favor you will find
to your advantage." "Which might be?"
"Take counsel both from her and me."
"I will," he answered, "Yes, of course."
"Dismount." The youth got off his horse.
One squire took it in his care;
the other squire of the pair   1420
helped take the armor off the lad.
The young man stood there, rudely clad,
dressed in his coat of buckskin leather,
ill-fitting, roughly sewn together,
with rawhide brogues, the ones he wore;
his mother had given him before.
The sharpened steel spurs that the lad
had brought with him, the great lord had

put on his feet. He mounted, hung
the shield on by a strap he flung   1430
around his neck, and grasped the lance.
He said, "My friend, here is a chance
to learn to use your arms and see
how to hold lances properly,
and I will show you the correct
way that a horse is spurred and checked."
The nobleman unfurled the banner
and taught the youth the proper manner
for holding shields, by holding it
in front of him a little bit,   1440
touching the horse's neck, and laid
the lance in rest. With spurs to aid,
he pricked the horse, a charger worth
a hundred marks. No horse on earth
could match his spirit, strength, and speed.
The lord was excellent indeed
at using lance and horse and shield,
equipment he had learned to wield
in boyhood, and the youth was thrilled,
because the lord was highly skilled.   1450
When finished with the exercise
performed before the young man's eyes,
a drill at which the lord excelled,
he rode back to the youth and held
his lance raised, coming to inquire,
"Tell me, my friend, if you desire
to learn to check and spur a steed
and use a lance and sword at need?"
At once the youth began to say
he would not live another day   1460
or have great wealth and lands to claim
until he learned to do the same.
"You can learn any lesson new
that you are willing to pursue.
So, my dear friend, to make a start
in all professions, you need heart,
hard work, and practice; you will see*

v. 1467. Among other references for this saying, Hilka cites (*Der Percevalroman*, p. 649) Morawski, *Proverbes français* no. 1069: "Li cuers fet l'euvre."

we gain all knowledge by those three.
But since you've never tilted nor
seen others use their arms before,   1470
your ignorance cannot be blamed,
nor need you feel the least ashamed."
He told the lad to mount, and he
bore lance and shield as skillfully
as if, throughout his life, he'd spent
his time at war and tournament,
had gone to every land and sought
for great adventures where he fought,
because it came to him by nature.
When Nature's lessons are made greater   1480
by heartfelt effort, the result
is nothing is too difficult,
when Nature and the heart have striven.
The fine performance he had given
was so outstanding, when he ceased,
the nobleman was highly pleased.
Deep in his heart he contemplated
that if the youth had dedicated
his life to arms and drilled with them,
he would be very skilled with them.   1490
After the youth had had his turn,
he circled back on his return,
proceeding with his lance upraised,
just like the lord, who stood and gazed.
"Did I do well, sir, and will I
learn tilting, if I try and try?
I've never laid eyes on or seen
a thing that I have felt so keen
a wish to learn. I wish I knew
as much about the arms as you."   1500
"Friend, if your heart is truly set,"
the lord said, "you will learn it yet,
so have no fears upon that score."
The lord remounted three times more,
and three more times the great lord taught
all he could teach, until he thought
each time the lesson would suffice,
and then the youth remounted thrice.
The lord asked, at the final set,
"Tell me, my friend, what if you met   1510

a knight who gave you a hard thwack:
what would you do?" "I'd hit him back."
"What if you broke your lance in two?"
"There would be nothing else to do
but fall upon him with my fist."
"Friend, never do that, I insist."
"What should I do then?" "Fence, instead,
and use your sword on him," he said.
He took the lance back from the knight
and set it in the ground, upright,   1520
in front of him, because he thought
the youth should be shown more and taught
to use a sword in self defense
or to attack with it and fence
as circumstances might demand.
He picked the sword up in his hand
and, grasping it, he said, "My friend,
this is the way you must defend
yourself, if someone strikes at you."
"No one hits better than I do;   1530
I've often practiced with a stick
on bucklers and on cushions thick
at Mother's manor house, God's name,
until I was worn out and lame!"
"Let's go inside the castle, brother,
for I don't know of any other.
We'll have, and think it wrong who might,
Saint Julian's bed and board tonight!"*
And then they entered side by side.
"My lord, my mother once advised,"   1540
the young man told the nobleman,
"that I not go with any man,
nor be long in his company,
and not learn what his name might be.
As Mother taught before I came,
sir, I would like to know your name."
"It's Gornemant of Gohort," said*

v. 1538. See Hilka, *Der Percevalroman*, p. 650, for other references to Saint Julian the
Hospitaller, the patron saint of boatmen, innkeepers, and travellers.

v. 1547 (1548, Roach edition). Hilka notes (*Der Percevalroman*, p. 650) that the
nobleman Gornemant of Gohort is mentioned in *Erec and Enide*, v. 1675 (Roques edi-
tion).

the nobleman. They went ahead
Inside the castle, as the pair
were walking up the castle stair   1550
with hands clasped, of his own accord
a squire met the guest and lord.
He brought a short cloak, and he ran
to cover up the younger man,
so that he would not catch a chill
after the heat of his hard drill.
The lord's abode was rich and spacious
with many servants, quick and gracious,
who'd cooked a meal, well seasoned, fair,
and served it smoothly to the pair.   1560
The knights washed and sat down to eat.
The lord gave the young man a seat
next to his side, and at his wish
the two of them ate from one dish.
I won't say what the courses were
or number them, but do be sure
they had enough to eat and drink,
which is the reason I don't think
I need say more about the meal.
The gracious lord tried to appeal   1570
to his young guest, when they arose,
to stay a month, and if he chose
the young man seated at his side
could stay a whole year and reside
and learn some skills, if he desired,
which very well might be required
or useful in an hour of need.
The young man answered, "Sir, indeed,
although it isn't very clear
that I am any place that's near   1580
the manor where my mother lives,
I pray God such good guidance gives
that I shall see my mother soon.
I saw her fall down in a swoon
beside the drawbridge at her gate.
I do not know what's been her fate
or if she lives, but I am sure
her sorrow at my leaving her
was what brought on the fainting spell.
I must find out if she is well;   1590
I cannot stay and must be leaving

at dawn tomorrow." So, perceiving
it would be useless to implore,
the lord fell still and said no more.
They went to bed without debating.
The beds were ready and were waiting.
At dawn the nobleman arose
and brought the youth a gift of clothes.
He found him lying in his bed.
He brought the young man hose dyed red,   1600
some breeches and a shirt to wear,
both made of linen, fine and fair,
a silk coat, indigo in shade,
from India, woven there and made.
The nobleman informed his guest
that it was time that he was dressed.
"Friend, if you've confidence in me,
put on this clothing that you see."
The young man answered, "I am sure
you can advise me better, sir.   1610
Are not the garments Mother sewed me
much better than the ones you've showed me?
Why wear these newer clothes instead?"
"Young man, I tell you, by my head,
and by my two eyes, as I've sworn,   a
they're better than the clothes you've worn."   b
"No, they are worse," the youth replied   1615
"My friend, when I brought you inside,
you promised me you would obey
whatever counsel I might say."
"I'll wear the clothes, for that's the truth.
I shall not fail," replied the youth,   1620
in any way to do your bidding."
He donned the new clothes quickly, ridding
himself of those his mother fashioned.
The nobleman bent down and fastened
the right spur on the young man's foot,
as was the custom: he must put
the spur on the new knight who made him.
The squires were there as well to aid him
while he was arming the new knight
at any need, however slight.   1630
The lord attached the sword in place.
He gave the young knight an embrace
and said he'd given with the sword

the highest honor of Our Lord,
an order made by God's decree,
and it was knighthood, chivalry:
that such an order must remain
without deceit, without a stain
"Dear brother, bear my words in mind.
If it should happen that you find   1640
you're fighting with another knight
who proves unequal to your might,
I want to urge you and command,
once that you have the upper hand,
and he no longer holds his own
and pleads that mercy now be shown,*
then you must show him clemency:
don't slay the knight intentionally.
You must not talk too freely, for
no one can talk too long before   1650
he makes a statement lacking sense,
or which is rude and gives offense.
The wise man's saying's always been
that 'Too much talking is a sin.'*
So I forbid excessive speech.
Friend, also do as I beseech:
if you find men or women, maybe
an orphan or a noble lady
who seem in any way distressed,
give help and counsel, do your best,   1660
if your assistance will suffice,
and if you have some good advice.
One more thing you should realize,
a lesson you must not despise

v. 1646. Hilka notes (*Der Percevalroman*, 652) that there is a similar passage about showing mercy to a defeated foe in *Yvain*, vs. 5674 ff (Roques edition) and in *Lancelot*, vs. 902 ff (Roques edition).

v. 1654. Frappier notes, in *Chrétien de Troyes et le Mythe du Graal*, p. 93, that the wise man's saying was the wisdom of the Proverbs which the Middle Ages attributed to Solomon: Proverbs 10:19: "When words are many, transgression is not lacking." In addition, Hilka cites (*Der Percevalroman*, p. 652) the *Disciplina clericalis*, 8, 11: "Be silent until it is necessary for you to speak. The Philosopher says, 'Silence is a sign of wisdom and loquaciousness a sign of foolishness,'" and also Morawski, *Proverbes français* no. 125: "A saige homme afiert pou de parole," no. 2278: "Sovant est blamez qui trop est emparlez," and no. 2428: "Trop parlet nuist."

or ridicule in any way:
go frequently to church and pray
to Him who made creation whole,
so He'll have mercy on your soul,
and in this temporal condition,
so He will keep you as His Christian." 1670
To which replied the lord's young guest,
"Oh, my dear sir, may you be blessed*
by all the Popes that dwelt in Rome!
My mother said the same at home."
"Hereafter, never say, dear brother,
that you learned something from your mother,"
the lord said. "You are not to blame
for what you've quoted since you came,
but now I ask you to correct
your speech, if you do not object, 1680
because if you continue you'll
be thought and treated like a fool,
so do avoid it, lad, I pray."
"In that case, sir, what shall I say?"
"You may explain, as I prefer,
the lord who buckled on your spur
once similarly instructed you."
He promised that was what he'd do,
that never, while his life endured,
would he repeat another word 1690
his mother said, because he found
the nobleman's instruction sound.
The lord then made, above his head,
the sign of the cross, and after said
with hand upraised, "Since I perceive
that you would like to take your leave
and are annoyed by the delay,
may Heaven guide you on your way."

v. 1672. Hilka (*Der Percevalroman*, p. 653) cites G. Baist's note that they are chiefly
Saints Peter and Paul, and notes that there is a similar expression, "Par toz les sainz qu'an
prie a Rome" in *Lancelot*, v. 2480 (Roques edition).

BLANCHEFLOR, ANGUINGUERON,
AND CLAMADEU

The new-created knight departed,*
   for he was eager to get started,   1700
to find his mother, and to learn
that she was well on his return.
He rode into the forest wild —
familiar since he was a child,
far more so than a heath or moor —
and made his way to a secure
walled castle, finely situated.
Without there were uncultivated
fields, river, sea, and nothing more.
He hurried toward the castle door   1710
and came before the bridge, but he
was forced to cross so rickety
a bridge before he reached the gate,
he thought it might not bear his weight.
He rode upon the bridge and came
across it with no harm, or shame,
or other mishap as his fate.
The youth arrived before the gate,
but with a key he found it locked.
Do not believe he gently knocked   1720
or softly called to be let in;
he banged so hard, at last a thin
pale maiden came and leaned her head
out the hall window, and she said,
"Who's calling? Who is it outside?"
The youth looked up and then replied,
"Friend, I'm a knight, and I request
your leave to enter as your guest
and to have lodging for the night."

v. 1699. Gornemant of Gohort knights Perceval in order to regularize the situation caused by Kay's jest about giving him the arms of the Red Knight. Hilka notes (*Der Percevalroman*, p. 653) that Chrétien begins to refer to Perceval more consistently as "the knight" rather than as "the youth" after this point.

She said, "Sir, you will not delight   1730
in entertainments we provide,
though we will lodge you; come inside.
You have my promise we shall do
our very best to honor you."
The maid withdrew. The youth remained
and feared he would be long detained.
He pounded once again and yelled.
Four men-at-arms appeared, who held
huge axes, and fine swords they wore.
The men-at-arms unlocked the door,   1740
and opened up the gate, and said
to the young man, "Please come ahead."
They would have been attractive men,
if times were easier than then
and had not forced them to endure
such great misfortunes, that they were
much weakened and could hardly keep
upright for lack of food and sleep.
For if, without, the youth had found
the fields were barren, empty ground,   1750
within there was impoverishment;
he found, no matter where he went,
the streets were empty in the town.
He saw the houses tumbled down
without a man or woman there.
Within the town there was a pair
of churches: they were abbeys once;
and one was filled with frightened nuns
and one with helpless monks and wary.
The youth found neither sanctuary   1760
attractive and in good repair.
The walls were broken, cracked, and bare
with roofless towers. The building lay
open by night as well as day.
No mill was grinding, oven baking,
in any street that he was taking
throughout the town, and furthermore,
there was no wine nor sweet cakes nor
another thing for sale, not any,
not even goods which cost a penny.   1770
There was no bread for sale, no fine
baked pastries, cider, beer, nor wine:

the town was wholly desolate.
On toward a palace roofed with slate
the four men led him through the town,
disarmed him when they'd helped him down.
At once a squire came down the stair
with a gray cloak for him to wear,
and he attached this gray attire
around his neck. Another squire   1780
put his horse in a stable stall.
They had no wheat, no oats at all,
and very little straw and hay
within the house upon that day.
The squires brought him up a flight
of stairs and walked behind the knight.
A maiden and two noblemen
advanced to meet the young man when
he reached the hall, which was most fair.
The noblemen had graying hair,   1790
but it was not yet white with time;
both men would have been in their prime
and at the peak of strength and skill,
had they not suffered grief and ill.
The maiden started to advance:
her gracefulness and elegance
could not be equaled by the walk
of parrot or of sparrow hawk.*
Her black silk dress and mantle were
gold-starred and trimmed with ermine fur.   1800
The collar of her cloak, they say,
was made of sable, black and gray,
not cut too long nor yet too wide.
Now, if I ever have described
the loveliness that Heaven's grace
can give a woman's form and face,*

v. 1798. Hilka notes (*Der Percevalroman*, p. 657) that there are descriptions of dresses similar to the one Blancheflor is wearing in *Erec and Enide*, vs. 1587 ff (Roques edition), and also in the *Roman de Thèbes*, the *Eneas*, and the *Roman de Troie* and other references.

v. 1806 ff. Hilka notes (*Der Percevalroman*, p. 657) that a similar description of feminine beauty as the creation of Nature, personified as an artist, whose handwork can be surpassed only by God, appears in *Yvain*, vs. 1497-1510 (Roques edition), among other references.

I'm happy to begin anew
and change no word of what is true.
The hair with which her head was crowned*
fell freely, since it was unbound.   1810
Onlookers would indeed have thought,
if it could be, her hair was wrought
of gold entirely, pure and fine,
so luminously did it shine.
Her forehead was white, smooth, and high,
as if it had been sculpted by
an artist's hand, as best he could,
of stone or ivory or wood,
with eyebrows wide apart, beguiling,
and blue-gray eyes, large, bright, and smiling.   1820
Her nose was straight and regular;
the crimson over white was far
more beautiful upon her face
than scarlet on a silver base.
The Lord created her a wonder
to steal men's hearts away as plunder,
and never, since that time or later,
has He bestowed a beauty greater
on any girl to be her rival.
The knight saw her on his arrival   1830
and greeted her, and she replied,
as did the warriors at her side.
With grace and perfect self command
the maiden took him by the hand.
She said, "Tonight, sir, you will find
your lodging place is not the kind
that would befit a man of rank.
If I began by being frank
and told you of our sad condition,
my words might give you the suspicion   1840
that my description of your stay

vs. 1809 ff (1811 ff, Roach edition). Hilka notes (*Der Percevalroman*, p. 658) that the description of Blancheflor is typical, and that there are similar descriptions in *Erec and Enide*, vs. 411 ff (Roques edition), *Cligès*, vs. 780 ff (Micha edition), and *Yvain*, vs. 1465 ff (Roques edition), as well as in the *Roman de Thèbes*, the *Eneas*, the *Roman de Troie*, and other references. The vivid red and white complexion, unusual for blondes with blue-gray eyes, is taken from classical descriptions of Greek maidens blushing in the presence of warriors (see v. 4199).

was meant to make you go away.
Accept what lodging we extend:
tomorrow morn may Heaven send
a better place than mine has been."
She took his hand and led him in
a spacious room, in handsome state;
its vaulted ceiling was ornate.
There they sat down upon a bed;
its cover was a samite spread.   1850
Into the room came warriors
in groups of sixes, fives, and fours.
They sat and did not say a thing.
They watched the young man visiting
their lady, but the youth refrained
from conversation and remained
completely silent, for he thought
about the lesson he was taught
so firmly by the nobleman.
Before too long the knights began   1860
some conversations of their own.
The men said in an undertone,
"Do you suppose this knight is dumb?
A shame, no fairer knight has come
in being of a mortal mother.
How well they look beside each other,
the way he's sitting next to her
and she to him, but we'd prefer
that they did not remain so still!
He's handsome and she's beautiful;   1870
there never were a knight and maid
so nicely matched, as if God made
each for the other, with foresighted
plans that the two would be united."
While everyone was whispering,
the maid awaited anything
her guest might care to say to her.
As minutes passed, the maid felt sure
the young knight who was now her guest
would not speak till he was addressed.   1880
The maiden, gracious and polite,
spoke first by saying to the knight,
"From where, sir, have you come today?"
He said, "Last night, fair maid, I lay

within the castle of a lord,
and I enjoyed his bed and board.
It had five mighty towers: one tall
whereas the other four were small.
I can describe it; all the same
I do not know the castle's name.   1890
As for the lord, my noble cohort,
his name is Gornemant of Gohort."
"Dear friend, how right you are," said she.
"You've spoken with such courtesy!
May God our King give you reward
for calling him a noble lord;
there is no truer thing you'll say.
The lord is, by Saint Richier,*
a very noble man indeed,
and I could vouch for it at need,   1900
for you should know I am his niece,
though weeks have passed without surcease
since I have seen my uncle's face.
Why, since you left your dwelling place
you've met no nobler man than he.
He welcomed you most joyously,
as gaily as my uncle can.
He is a noble, courtly man,
and mighty, prosperous, and rich,
whereas I have five white rolls which,   1910
with one small flask of boiled wine,
were sent here by an uncle of mine,
a saintly and religious prior,
for me to eat when I retire.
So if my servant did not go
to shoot a roebuck with his bow,
there would be nothing else but bread."
The tables should be set, she said,
and supper laid; then everyone
sat down to eat when it was done.   1920
They did not linger at the meal
but ate it with tremendous zeal,
and after supper left the keep,
except the men who were to sleep,

v. 1898 (1899, Roach edition). Hilka (*Der Percevalroman*, p. 660) cites Baist's note
that Saint Richier, a folk hero, is rarely evoked in the courtly epics.

since they had watched the previous night.
The men-at-arms prepared to fight:
it was their turn and obligation
to keep the castle watch and station
the fifty knights and men on guard.
The other men were working hard   1930
to please their houseguest while he stayed.
The servants saw his bed was made
with white sheets and a costly spread
and placed a pillow at the head.
And so the youth enjoyed that night
all kinds of comfort and delight
in bed that one can bring to mind,
save only the delight he'd find
beside a maiden, if he would,
or by a lady, if he could.   1940
The young knight, though, knew nothing of
our worldly ways, including love,
so there was not a thing to keep
the youth from falling fast asleep.
The young man's hostess could not rest,
shut in her room, and while her guest
slept peacefully, the maid was tense,
because she could find no defense
against the thoughts that marred her rest.
The maid was troubled and distressed,   1950
and tossed, and turned, quite ill at ease.
Then she threw over her chemise
a cloak of crimson silk and started
on her adventure, a stouthearted
courageous maiden, bold and daring.
It was no trifle: she was faring
forth from her room to find her guest.
What thoughts had brought about her quest
she'd tell the youth, at least in part.
The maiden left her bed to start   1960
in tears to go in search of him,
and trembling in every limb;
she shook with terror and perspired.
She left the room where she'd retired
and came to where the young knight slept.
The maid sighed deeply, and she wept,
and knelt beside his bed, and bent

across him so her tears went
upon his face and made it wet.
She dared not be more forward, yet   1970
she cried so hard and with such art,
the knight awakened with a start.
He was astonished when he felt
his face was wet and saw she knelt
beside him with her two arms clasped
around his neck and held him fast.
He had the courtesy and taste
to put both arms around her waist
and draw her closer to inquire,
"Fair maiden, what do you desire?   1980
Why have you come to me tonight?"
"Oh, please have mercy, noble knight!
For God's sake, for His Son's dear sake,
I beg of you, do not mistake
my meaning and believe me shamed
for coming here," the maid proclaimed.
"Although I may be nearly nude,
my thoughts were never bold nor lewd.
For you must know, the world around,
no living creature can be found,   1990
however sad and miserable,
but that I am not sadder still,
for each day is a grief to me,
and nothing brings relief to me.
I shall not see, such is my sorrow,
another day except tomorrow
or night except tonight; I've planned
to take my life with my own hand.
Of the three hundred knights and ten
who manned this castle, fifty men   2000
are all, at present, who remain,
for sixty minus twelve were slain
or captured by the wicked wiles
of one knight: Clamadeu of the Isles'
cruel seneschal Anguingueron.
I grieve as much for those who've gone
to prison as for those he slew.
I'm sure he'll kill the prisoners too;
they can't escape, and I believe
that I have every right to grieve,   2010

so many men courageously
have met their deaths because of me.
We've been besieged one winter and one
whole summer by Anguingueron,
and could not budge him in the least.
His troops and forces have increased,
while ours have dwindled; our food store
has grown so low, we have no more
than one man's rations in supplies.
Unless God chooses otherwise,   2020
we're so weak, once this night is ended,
this castle cannot be defended,
and so it must be handed over,
and I along with it, moreover,
as a poor, wretched prisoner.
He won't take me alive, for sure;
I'll kill myself; when I am dead,
I won't care if I'm caught and led
to Clamadeu. Though he desires me,
he won't have me till he acquires me   2030
devoid of spirit and of life,
because I keep a fine steel knife
within my jewelry box, and I
shall plunge it in my heart and die.
I've told you why I am distressed.
I shall withdraw so you can rest;
I've said enough," the maid declared.
Here was a chance, if the knight dared,
to garner some renown and fame!
She wept upon his face and came   2040
to him with only one intent.
No matter what she said, she meant
her story to inspire the knight
enough to undertake the fight,
provided he would dare defend
her lands and person. "Dearest friend,
be comforted," he answered her,
"tonight you must be happier
and weep no more about your fears.
Come closer, wipe away your tears.   2050
If God is willing, furthermore,
He will have better things in store
tomorrow morn than you have said.

Come lie beside me in this bed;
it's wide enough for you to stay.
Don't leave me any more today."
The maid replied, "If you prefer,
I shall do so." The knight kissed her;
within his arms he held her clasped,
and gently, tenderly, he grasped   2060
and wrapped them in the coverlet,
and what is more, the maiden let
the knight kiss her; I cannot say
that it displeased her! So they lay*
the night together, side by side
and mouth to mouth till morningtide.
The knight was filled with joy, embracing
with mouth on mouth, arms interlacing,
and sleeping till the break of day.
At dawn the maiden made her way   2070
back to her room; without the aid
of handmaiden or chambermaid,
she sought her garments out and dressed,
since everyone was still at rest.
The guards who watched throughout the night,
when they could see the morning light,
went in to wake the sleepy heads,
insisting that they leave their beds.
So everyone arose in haste.
At the same time, the maid retraced   2080

v. 2064 ff. Perceval's chastity has been the subject of considerable and sometimes amusing debate, most notably when Sister Amelia Klenke, who interpreted Perceval as a symbol of chastity, was challenged by Roger Sherman Loomis, who believed that Perceval remained a virgin, technically, but that his conduct was far from chaste. Frappier notes (*Chrétien de Troyes et le Mythe du Graal*, pp. 98 ff) that Chrétien emphasizes that it was Perceval's naiveté, not any penchant for chastity, that prevented him from obtaining what Chrétien calls the *soreplus*. Neither his mother and her chambermaids nor the maiden in the tent had any illusions about his inclinations. Yet Chrétien says that the couple spent the night sleeping, and Perceval asked Blancheflor for her love the next morning, which would make little sense if he had already received it. Frappier points out that the most important aspect of this episode is that its incompleteness enables Perceval to pursue his adventures and his personal development unconstrained by marital and social responsibilities. Frappier quotes Jean Marx's comment in *La Légende Arthurienne et le Graal*, p. 211, that the most important of the Simpleton's virtues is not his chastity, but his lack of attachments, his ability to take risks in the pursuit of the quest (p. 107).

her steps and went back to her knight.
Her words were gracious and polite.
"Sir, may God give you a good day.
I'm well aware you will not stay,
for were you longer to remain
it would be utterly in vain.
I would not mind if you should leave;
I'd be discourteous to grieve
or to be angered in the least.
We have done nothing that increased   2090
your comfort or that gave you ease.
But I shall pray to God to please
send you a better house than mine,
where there's more salt and bread and wine
and provender than I possess."
He answered, "Lovely one, unless
I have restored your lands today,
I'll seek no other place to stay
until I've brought you peace or tried.
If I should find your foe outside,   2100
and if his presence caused you pain,
I won't allow him to remain.
If I defeat or kill the lord,
I'll seek your love as a reward;
it shall be mine; please realize
I will accept no other prize."
She answered with great courtesy,
"Sir knight, what you have asked of me
is such a little thing to choose;
were I, however, to refuse,   2110
you'd think me cold and arrogant,
so your petition I shall grant.
But all the same, do not contend
that I am to become your friend
on one condition, which would be
that you go forth to die for me,
because it would be such a shame.
You may be sure you cannot claim
that you could hold your own in war
against that knight, because you are   2120
not strong enough and old enough
to face a warrior as tough
as that great knight who waits outside."

"Soon you will see," the youth replied,
"for I shall fight with him this morning
and will not stop for any warning."
She blamed his plans, expressed her doubt,
and hoped they would be carried out.
We often know how to conceal
a heartfelt wish that we may feel,   2130
when we see someone else ambitious
to carry out our private wishes,
to make him more ambitious yet.
The clever maiden made him set
his heart and mind on undertaking
the project for which she was making
such stern rebukes. He said they'd best
bring him his arms: at his request
the people brought the arms he sought
and armed him fully; then they brought   2140
and had him mount a saddled steed
that they had harnessed for his need
within the middle of the square.
Then everybody who was there
looked mournful and began to say,
"Sir knight, God give you help today,
and cause misfortune to befall
Anguingueron, the seneschal,
who has laid waste to this estate."
They prayed and walked him to the gate.   2150
Both men and women watched him start
to leave the castle and depart,
and with one voice they cried aloud,
"Sir, the true cross, where God allowed
His son to suffer, grant protection
from mortal peril, and subjection,
imprisonment, and injury,
and bring you in security
to someplace you may be at leisure
and may have every joy and pleasure."   2160
They prayed for him, and off he went.
Anguingueron sat by his tent,
and as the young man came in sight,
his soldiers pointed out the knight.
He thought his army would compel
the town, before that evening fell,

to send somebody out to yield
or meet him on the battlefield,
and had his mail hose laced already.
His men rejoiced and thought it heady   2170
the town and land were finally won.
As he arrived, Anguingueron   2172
went riding toward the youth with speed   2175
upon a strong and heavy steed
and said, "Who sent you; what's his name?
Tell me the reason why you came:
have you come seeking peace or war?"
"First you must tell me why you are   2180
within this land and must explain
why you have had the warriors slain
and laid the countryside to waste?"
Anguingueron replied in haste,
aggressively and haughtily,
"This very day the keep must be
relinquished and the town vacated;
you have held out too long," he stated.
"My master means to have the maid."
The youth said, "Cursed the man who made   2190
such plans, which I as well denounce!
All claims to her you must renounce;
you'd better not pursue the matter!"
"You're giving me much idle chatter,
Saint Peter!" said Anguingueron,
"and many a man who's never done*
the wrong has paid the penalty!"
The youth was stirring restively.
He laid his lance in rest, held low,
and each knight spurred against his foe   2200
as fast as horse could carry him.   2215
The rage that made their faces grim
increased the force their arms obtained
and sent the splinters that remained
of each lance flying through the air.
Anguingueron had fallen there,   2220
a lance thrust through the shield he bore,

vs. 2196-2197. Hilka notes (*Der Percevalroman*, p. 663) that this proverb appears in
Cligès, vs. 550-551 (Micha edition).

so that his arms and sides were sore
with cuts and bruises. In due course,
not knowing what to do on horse,
the youth dismounted; and he drew
his sword to fight. I wish I knew
the best way to describe the fight,
to tell what happened to each knight,
how each one fought, and to recount
a detailed, blow by blow account,   2230
but since both knights were very strong,
the blows were hard, the fight was long.
At last Anguingueron fell back.
The young man made a fierce attack,
until the seneschal was pleading
for mercy, but the youth, unheeding,
said mercy he would not accord.
Then he remembered how the lord
instructed him, upon that day,
that he should not elect to slay   2240
a knight whom he had conquered and
with whom he'd gained the upper hand.
The seneschal cried out, "Kind friend,
don't be so cruel as to contend
you won't be merciful to me,
for I concede most willingly
you have the best of me this fight
and proved you are a splendid knight,
but anyone who knew us both
and had not seen it would be loath   2250
to think you killed me on the field
with no help but the arms you wield.
I'll be your witness: in fair fight
you overcame me in the sight
of my own men, before my tent.
They'll take my word without dissent,
for people will believe my story,
and you shall have more fame and glory
than any knight has ever known.
Think, if you have a lord who's shown   2260
his favor and benevolence
and has received no recompense,
send me to him, and I shall go
on your behalf to let him know

you conquered me in battle, sir.
I shall become his prisoner
to treat as he sees fit," he swore.
"Then cursed be he who asks for more!
Now you will go — do you know where?
to that town. Tell the maiden fair,   2270
who is my love, your whole life long,*
you'll never do her any wrong
or cause her any controversy
but be entirely at her mercy."
"When she learns she can have me killed,
her dearest wish will be fulfilled,
so you may kill me in that case.
She seeks my death and my disgrace
above all else," the knight replied.
"I was there when her father died,   2280
and I have greatly angered her;
I've killed or taken prisoner
all of her knights throughout this year.
You would be very cruel, I fear,
to send me to a jail of hers.
You could not find another worse,
so if you have no other friend,
no man or woman, you should send
to somebody who bears no grudge,
for if this maiden were my judge,   2290
she would not fail to have my head."
The young man ordered him, instead,
to find a certain nobleman:
he gave his name and castle's plan.
In all the world there was no mason
who could describe its situation
and structure better, for he praised
the river and the bridge they raised,
the little towers and the keep,
the walls and outworks, high and steep,   2300
until the warrior realized
he would be sent a captive prized
to where he was most deeply hated.

v. 2271. Hilka notes (*Der Percevalroman*, p. 664) that a similar situation in which a defeated knight is sent to be a lady's prisoner occurs in *Erec and Enide*, vs. 1024 ff.

"I'll be no safer there," he stated.
"You're sending me down fatal roads
to evil hands at both abodes.
God help me, in this wartime strife,
I took one of his brothers' life.
You mean to kill me, dearest friend,
if he's the one I must attend,   2310
and if you drive me there, you'll see
that it will be the death of me."
The youth said, "Then you shall go farther.
Go as a prisoner to King Arthur,
greet him, and ask on my behalf
to see the maid who had to laugh
when she saw me, the maid whom Kay
the seneschal had slapped that day,
and when he introduces her,
you will become her prisoner.   2320
And, if you please, tell her thereby
I pray God will not let me die
before I have avenged that blow."
Anguingueron said he would go
upon this mission with delight,
and then the young victorious knight
turned toward the castle, and his foe
went toward the prison he must know.
His army bore his flag away.
The siege was lifted on that day;   2330
no foes remained, blond-haired or brown.
The lady's warriors left the town
to meet the knight when he returned,
but they were sorry when they learned
that he had not decapitated
the knight whom he had subjugated.
The men rejoiced on his account,
and helped the young knight to dismount
beside the block and to disarm.
They asked, "When you were threatening harm   2340
to that Anguingueron, instead
why didn't you cut off his head?"
The knight said, "By the faith I trust,
I think that would have been unjust.
He killed so many of your kin,
what guarantee could I begin

to give of his security?
You'd have killed him in spite of me.
I would not be of much account,
once I managed to surmount   2350
the knight, if I were merciless.
You know the form of his redress?
He'll be King Arthur's prisoner,
if he is of good character."
The maiden hailed the young man, whom
she led with joy into her room
to be at leisure there and rest.
Nor did the lovely maid protest
when kissed and hugged by the young lad.
They did not eat or drink but had   2360
their kisses, hugs, and talk for fare.
But Clamadeu, all unaware,
made senseless plans, for he supposed
he'd have the castle unopposed.
Lamenting at this episode,
a squire met him on the road;
he went to seek his master out
and bring the sorry news about
Anguingueron the seneschal.
"Bad news, my lord, God help us all!"   2370
the young man cried, in such despair,
with his two fists he tore his hair.
Then Clamadeu stopped to inquire,
"What's happened?" "Sir," replied the squire,
"your steward, on the battlefield,
was beaten and has gone to yield
to good King Arthur." "Squire, tell
who conquered him, how it befell!
How could he have been overcome?
From what place could the knight have come   2380
who proved so valiant a defender,
he made so brave a knight surrender?"
The squire said, "I don't know his name.
I only know, sir, that he came
out of the town of Belrepeire,*

---

v. 2385 (2386, Roach edition). Hilka notes (*Der Percevalroman*, p. 664) that Belre-
peire is the name of the castle of Gawain's mother, Morcadés, in the *Enfances Gauvain*.

and that he had red arms to wear."
"What do you think that I should do?
Advise me, squire," said Clamadeu,
who was beside himself with fury.
"Sir, you should turn back in a hurry,   2390
for even if you go ahead,
you won't gain anything," he said.
At this the graying knight who trained
the youthful Clamadeu, maintained,
"Young man, no, it would not be wise
for him to do as you advise,
for he needs wiser counsellors;
more sensible advice than yours.
He'd be an idiot to heed
your warnings: no, he should proceed."   2400
He added, "Sir, how would you care
to take the knight and Belrepeire?
For I can tell you how to do it,
and you will find there's nothing to it.
Within the castle's walls, I think,
there's nothing left to eat or drink.
The knights have fasted for so long,
that they are weak, while we are strong,
unplagued by hunger or by thirst,
and able to withstand their worst.   2410
If any of the warriors from
the town grow bold enough to come
out by the gate and start to group
their forces, we will send a troop
of twenty knights there, rallying
the red knight, who is dallying
with his dear friend, the fair Blancheflor.*
He wants to do great deeds of war
and will be captured then or slain.
He can't fight twenty, and it's plain   2420
his friends will offer no resistance;
they are too weak to give assistance.

---

v. 2417. Loomis notes (*Arthurian Tradition*, p. 479) that Blancheflor was a common name in Old French literature, and that possibly it was attached to the heroine since somewhat similar stories were told of Floree in the *Livre d'Artus* and of Florence in *Artus de la Petite Bretagne*.

Our twenty will retreat and leave them,
still fighting hard, which will deceive them,
and lure them from the castle wall.
We'll burst through and surround them all
by coming on them through this vale."
"My word, you've shown me in detail
a splendid scheme of false retreat,
because our army's an elite   2430
corps of four hundred knights, and then
we have on foot a thousand men,
well armed and well equipped," he said.
"We'll catch them as if they were dead."
So he sent twenty disciplined
men to the gate, who, in the wind,
unfurled gonfalons, flags, and banners,
which were designed in different manners.
The castle's knights saw them outside
and opened up the town gates wide,   2440
because the young man wished it so.
With all the rest, he left to go
and meet the warriors. Bold and proud,
the young man fell upon the crowd,
and he attacked them; all of those
who met the youth did not suppose
that he was an apprentice knight,
for he was expert in the fight.
His lance blows disemboweled the best,
one in the nipple, one the chest.   2450
He broke an arm, a collarbone,
killed one man, hurt one, knocked one prone,
took one man prisoner, gave each steed
he caught to knights who were in need,
until the men who had ascended
the valley saw the town defended
and the great battle that was raging:
four hundred picked men armed for waging
war and a thousand men on foot.
The castle's knights were staying put   2460
close to the gate they'd opened wide.
But when the warriors outside
saw their men lost, both dead and battered,
they rushed the gate: their ranks were scattered;
they were disordered and confused.

The knights from town held their ranks fused
before the gate in tight formation
and met them with determination.
Their men were weak, in short supply.
The warring knights were aided by   2470
their men on foot; a force so large,
their foes could not withstand their charge,
so they retreated to the town.
The archers on the gate shot down
into the troop's closebanded mass,
which struggled heatedly to pass
beyond the gate, until a small
group forced their way behind the wall.
So the invasion could be stopped,
the warriors in the castle dropped   2480
the great portcullis on those rushing*
inside the gate, which killed by crushing
the soldiers in its line of fall.
Then Clamadeu could not recall
a sight that caused him greater pain
than seeing that the door had slain
part of his army, shut him out,
and brought him to a halt; no doubt
another onslaught, in such haste,
would be but effort gone to waste.   2490
Once more his counsellor advised,
"My lord, nobody is surprised
when it turns out that worthy men
make blunders every now and then,
for at God's pleasure, at God's will,*
each man receives both good and ill.
You've lost the battle, at the least,
but what saint doesn't have his feast?*

v. 2481. The portcullis that kills Clamadeu's men by crushing them is similar to the
portcullis at Laudine's castle that nearly kills Yvain and cuts his horse in two, in *Yvain*,
vs. 907 ff (Roques edition).

    vs. 2495-2496 (2494-2495, Roach edition). Hilka notes (*Der Percevalroman*, p. 665)
that a similar thought about God's sending both good and ill is expressed in the *Disciplina
clericalis* 42, 37.

    v. 2498 (2497, Roach edition). Hilka notes (*Der Percevalroman*, p. 665) that this
proverb is listed in Morawski, *Proverbes français* no. 1376: "N'est saint qui n'ait sa feste."

Your men were crippled in the fray;
the castle's knights have won the day;   2500
the storm has come on you with fury,
but they will lose, you need not worry.
Pluck out my eyes and leave me blind
if in three days they've not resigned.
You'll win the castle and the tower
and have them wholly in your power
and at your mercy, if you stay
only tomorrow and today.
The castle will be in your hands;
the maid refusing your demands   2510
will beg you in the Lord God's name
to deign to take her." Soldiers came,
set up pavilions, pitched the tents,
and then the other regiments
camped out of doors as best they might.
The townspeople disarmed each knight,
although these prisoners were not chained
in dungeons, but the men ordained
they pledge, each as a loyal knight,
to do no harm nor take to flight.   2520
Once that these oaths had been exchanged,
in town the matter was arranged.
That day high winds blew violently
and drove a barge across the sea.*
Its cargo was a load of wheat
and many other things to eat,
and as God willed it, safe and sound,
it landed on the castle's ground.
When they beheld its passengers,
the townspeople sent messengers   2530
down to the moored barge to inquire
their names and what they might desire.
At once the messengers the town
was sending to the barge went down
to ask what kind of men they found,
where they were from, and whither bound.
"We're merchants," they began to tell,

---

vs. 2524 ff. Hilka notes (*Der Percevalroman*, p. 665) that there is a similar incident of
a ship rescuing a beleaguered city in the *Roman de Thèbes*.

"we are transporting food to sell.
We have salt bacon, bread, and wine,
and many oxen, pigs, and swine   2540
to slaughter, if you are in need."
They answered, "Blessed be God indeed
who gave the power to the gale
that blew you to us under sail.
Be welcome; come ashore; your freight
we'll purchase at as high a rate
as you dare ask our town to pay.
Come take your settlement away,
because you will be forced to count
and carry off the large amount   2550
of silver ingots and of gold
we give you when the wheat is sold,
and you may need a cart replete
with payment for the wine and meat,
or more at need!" So those who bought
and those who sold the cargo thought
the price was fair enough to charge.
The knights helped to unload the barge
and had the cargo sent ahead
so the townspeople would be fed.   2560
In town the people saw the food
arrive with joy and gratitude,
you may believe me, at the deal.
They hurried to prepare a meal
and worked as quickly as they knew.
Outside and idle, Clamadeu
would have an even longer wait,
because the knights within the gate
had oxen, swine, and salted meat
in plentiful supply, and wheat   2570
to last till harvest. Working fast,
the cooks were making the repast;
the kitchen boys were lighting fires.
The youth could follow his desires
and dally with his friend at leisure.
They gave each other joy and pleasure
as he kissed her and she hugged him.
The hall, no longer still and grim,
rang out with joy that filled the air.
The knights rejoiced about the fare,   2580

since they had yearned for it so long.
The cooks worked fast and made a throng
of men in greatest need of meat
sit down and dine; more come to eat
and took the seats of people leaving.
But Clamadeu and his men were grieving,
because the news had filtered down
of the good luck of those in town.
Some said to leave: there was no doubt
the castle could not be starved out,   2590
and many of his warriors thought
they had besieged the town for naught.
But Clamadeu, inflamed with rage,
sent word before he'd taken sage
advice and counsel, for he said
they should inform the knight in red
till noon next day, he could be found
upon the cleared and level ground
to battle with him, if he dared.
The maid heard of the fight prepared   2600
for her love and was vexed and sad
about the battle, but the lad
sent back this message to the knight:
since Clamadeu had asked to fight,
he would be glad to acquiesce,
which aggravated her distress.
No matter how the maid lamented,
the youth would never have consented
to let the challenge go unheeded.
The men and women begged and pleaded   2610
with him not to go out and fight
one who had never met a knight
who was a match for him before.
"Lords, you had better say no more.
Throughout the world there is no man
who could dissuade me from my plan;
I won't be stopped," the youth contended.
With these words all discussion ended.
They went to bed and took repose
till morning, when the sun arose,   2620
yet they were grieving for their lord
because, although they had implored,
the arguments they had employed

could not persuade him to avoid
the battlefield. All night his friend
beseeched the youth not to contend
with Clamadeu, to rest and feast,
since they no longer cared the least
for Clamadeu and for his train.
But all her pleading was in vain,   2630
which was most strange, for her cajoling
was very sweet and most consoling.
She kissed him softly, tenderly,
at every word, and put Love's key,
by using this persuasive art,
within its lock: the young man's heart.*
The maid discovered, nonetheless,
that she was having no success
in trying to dissuade the knight
from going out next day to fight.   2640
So, in the end, the youth demanded
his arms. The men he had commanded
brought them as fast as they could go
and armed him with the greatest woe,
for everybody there was grieving.
The youth commended them, on leaving,
to God the King of kings. With speed
he mounted a Norwegian steed
which they led up to him, and stayed
with them no longer nor delayed.   2650
When he had mounted, off he went
and left them making loud lament.
When Clamadeu beheld him nearing
to meet his challenge in the clearing,
he was so mad as to believe
he soon would make the young man leave
his saddle with an empty space.
The heath was a fine, level place,
and there were only to be two
to fight on it, for Clamadeu   2660
dismissed his men. When they were gone,
each warrior leaned his lance upon
the lance rest at the saddle's front,

---

vs. 2636 ff. Hilka notes (*Der Percevalroman*, p. 666) that the literary conceit of putting
Love's key in the lock of the heart appears in *Yvain*, vs. 4632 ff. (Roques edition).

and then they hastened to confront
each other, uttering no defiant
shouts, with ash lances, thick but pliant,
made with an iron cutting head.
Across the heath the horses sped.
The mighty knights, in mortal hate,
delivered blows so hard and great,   2670
their lances broke when they attacked,
the wood part of their bucklers cracked,
and both were knocked flat on the ground,
but, springing back up with a bound,
the two knights brought their swords in play,
continued fighting right away,
and battled fairly and at length.
Now, if I wished and had the strength,
I would describe it blow by blow
and tell you all you want to know.   2680
Why should I work so diligently?
One word is worth as much as twenty.*
But Clamadeu was forced at last
to beg for mercy, and, surpassed,
he promised all that he possessed,
just as his steward acquiesced,
lest he be sent to Belrepeire
a prisoner, nor would he dare,
for all the Empire ruled by Rome,
to go to Gornemant's fine home,   2690
the castle so well situated.
To be a prisoner, he stated,
at Arthur's court, he would consent.
He'd bring the message the youth sent
and tell the maiden that since Kay
had struck her in that brutal way,
he would avenge Kay's churlishness,
no matter whom it might distress,
if God would grant him power and aid.
The young man, in addition, made   2700
bold Clamadeu pledge more: he vowed
his prisoners would be allowed

---

v. 2682 (2681, Roach edition). Hilka notes (*Der Percevalroman*, p. 666) that the
proverb, "One word is worth as much as twenty," appears in the *Dolopathos* 2365 (Hilka
ed. Sammlung mittellateinischer Texte V, 1913).

to leave their cells and go upon
their way before next day at dawn.
As long as Clamadeu might live,
if foes besieged the town, he'd give
assistance till the siege was ended.
The maid would never be offended
or harmed by him or by his men.
So Clamadeu went home again   2710
to keep his pledges without fail.
He said the prisoners in his jail
should be released immediately,
and so the prisoners went free,
for his commands were executed
when they were given, undisputed.
They freed the captives, who collected
their things and left as he directed.
Their progress was not blocked or slowed.
But Clamadeu took to the road   2720
and started traveling on his own.
We find in writing there had grown
to be a custom that required
a knight to go to prison attired
as he had been when he competed
in battle and had been defeated;
the knight could not remove a stitch
or put on any new thing which,
when he had fought, he had not used.
In this guise, Clamadeu pursued   2730
Anguingueron's steps, traveling
to Dinasdaron, where the king*
would hold his court. At Belrepeire
they felt a joy beyond compare
the day the prisoners returned.
They'd suffered greatly and sojourned
in prisons vile, in desperate plight.

v. 2732. Loomis notes (*Arthurian Tradition*, p. 482) that Dinasdaron is composed of two elements: *dinas*, certainly the Welsh word for castle or fortress, and *daron*, which Loomis believed to be a corruption of Bran, since the ruinous castle of Dinas Bran in Northeastern Wales was the center of the Celtic traditions known to the Breton minstrels. Nitze and Williams believe that the fact that King Arthur is holding a plenary court suggests rather that Dinasdaron means Dinas d'Aron, castle of Aaron, who was the patron saint of Carlion, today Caerleon-on-Usk (*Arthurian Names*, p. 271).

The hall resounded with delight,
and the knight's rooms: in sanctuaries,
in chapels, and in monasteries,   2740
bells rang with joy, each monk and nun
gave thanks to God that they had won.
In streets and in the square's expanses
the men and women danced round dances.
Their spirits all began to soar;
the town no longer was at war.
While they rejoiced, Anguingueron
rode toward the court, and traveling on
his very heels was Clamadeu.
For three days and three nights he knew   2750
they stayed at the same lodging places
(Anguingueron had left clear traces),
till they arrived at Dinasdaron.
In Wales, with almost every baron
within his halls, a gathering great,
King Arthur held his court in state.
Then they saw Clamadeu come there
in armor, which he had to wear.
Anguingueron knew him on sight;
he came to court the previous night   2760
and told his story and relayed
the young knight's message to the maid.
The king had asked him to remain
within his council and his train.
He saw his master's clothes were red
with bloodstains, and at once he said,
"Lords, lords, wonder to behold!
I'm sure the youth of whom I've told
who bears red arms has sent this knight,
who is just coming into sight.   2770
The young man conquered him, it's clear:
he's smeared with blood I see from here
and recognize the man as well.
I am his vassal and can tell
my lord's name: Clamadeu of the Isles,
and he possessed such strength and wiles,
I thought there was no better man
within the Roman Empire's span.
Until now that was my belief,
but sometimes good men come to grief."   2780

Anguingueron had this to say
while Clamadeu came on his way.
The knights ran toward each other, meeting
within the courtyard for their greeting.
It was the feast of Whitsuntide;
the queen sat by King Arthur's side
upon the dais, with numberless
dukes, kings, counts, queens, and countesses.
The Masses had been celebrated:
the ladies and the knights who waited   2790
had just returned from church and heard
the services. The courtiers stirred
when they saw Kay the seneschal
come walking cloakless through the hall.
Now Kay held tight in his right hand
his little staff of office, and
he wore a cloth cap he had laid
on his blond hair, worn in a braid.
No knight more handsome walked the earth;
his looks and deeds were of less worth   2800
because his tongue was mean and snide.
His coat was of fine fabric, dyed
a crimson red, a deep, rich shade.
His belt was handsome, finely made
with golden buckle and bedecked
with gold trim, as I recollect
the book describes him in this way.
They made a path for steward Kay,
since everyone had learned to dread
the cruel and taunting things he said,   2810
and to avoid his cutting candor.
Those who are wise fear open slander,
whether in seriousness or jest.
The courtiers did so detest
both the malicious words he spoke
and the sarcastic way he'd joke,
that none spoke to the seneschal.
But Kay walked up in front of all
to Arthur's seat and told him, "Sire,
we dine whenever you desire."   2820
"Kay, leave me be," King Arthur said,
"for by the two eyes in my head,
I won't eat at a feast so great,

since I am holding court in state,
until I hear of something new."
While they were talking, Clamadeu
arrived at court and came on in
to give himself up and begin
his sentence of captivity,
in armor, as he ought to be.   2830
"God bless and save the best king living,
the highest born and the most giving
and generous of kings hereby,
as one and all will testify
who have been told or been informed
of the good deeds he has performed.
Sire, listen," he addressed the king,
"and hear the message I must bring.
Although it causes me distress,
I must acknowledge, nonetheless,   2840
that I was sent here by a knight
who overcame me in fair fight.
I must become your prisoner;
I have no choice. If someone were
to ask me if I know his name,
I would say no, but I can claim
to know this much of him," he said,
"his armor and his arms are red,
and he declares they came from you."
"Lord help you, tell me if it's true,   2850
if he is healthy; if you found
the knight at liberty and sound,"
the king said. Clamadeu was sure.
"You may feel utterly secure.
In combat, sire, the youth was shown
to be the finest knight I've known,
and he commanded me to tell
the maid who laughed, the demoiselle
whom Kay, disgracefully, in pique,
once slapped so hard upon the cheek,   2860
that soon he will avenge the maid,
if God will grant him power and aid."
The fool heard what the knight had vowed,
and leapt for joy, and cried aloud,
"Sir king, God bless me, for I know
she shall have vengeance for that blow,

and do not think I told a lie:
you will discover by and by
that Kay will have a broken arm
and can't avoid, for further harm,   2870
a dislocated collarbone."
Kay thought his foolishness full blown.
It was no trace of cowardice
that made the seneschal dismiss
the fool's words and not intervene:
he did not want to make a scene
before the king, who shook his head.
"I am so sorry, Kay," he said,
"the young man is not present too.
Thanks to your foolish tongue and you,   2880
he went away, to my regret."
Then, at these words, arose Giflet,*
who did the king's commands in haste,
and Sir Yvain, whose presence graced*
and bettered everyone he knew.
King Arthur said of Clamadeu
they should escort his prisoner
to where the queen's handmaidens were.
The rooms were gay and filled with laughter.
The knight bowed to the king, and after   2890
the knights King Arthur had appointed
escorted Clamadeu and pointed
the maiden out so she was clear.
His message she had longed to hear,
because she had been mortified,
and deeply grieved, and sorely tried,
since struck upon the cheek so lowly.
Although she had recovered wholly
from the hard buffeting she took,
she'd not forget nor overlook   2900
her deep embarrassment as yet.
To overlook and to forget

v. 2882 (2883, Roach edition). Hilka notes (*Der Percevalroman*, p. 669) that among other references, Giflet, son of Do, is mentioned in *Erec and Enide*, v. 1697 (Roques edition).

v. 2884. Sir Yvain, son of Urien, was a distinguished knight of King Arthur's court and the hero of Chrétien's previous romance, *Yvain; or, the Knight with the Lion*. See note v. 8149.

disgrace and injury is wrong.
Pain passes for the firm and strong:
embarrassment and sorrow last.
In knaves they cool and are soon past.
Once that this message was explained,
thereafter Clamadeu remained
a lifetime member, they report,
of Arthur's household and his court.   2910
The youthful knight who fought him for
the land and lovely maid Blancheflor,
found joy with her and great delight.
The land would have been his outright,
if he had wished, and if his mind
had not turned elsewhere and inclined
the youth toward thinking more and more
about his mother than before.
He saw her fallen in a swoon
and longed to go and see her soon,   2920
because her memory filled his heart.
He dared not ask leave to depart
of his dear lady, for she spoke
against it, telling all her folk
to beg him stay and to beseech him,
but nothing that they said could reach him,
save for the promise he would give:
that were his mother still to live,
to bring her to their castle, and
take full possession of their land   2930
to hold henceforth in feudal claim,
and, were she dead, to do the same.
The youth, on taking to the road,
vowed to return to their abode,
but left his gracious friend behind
in an unhappy frame of mind;
the others were as much cast down.
So the young man rode out of town
with such procession on his way,
it might have been Ascension Day,   2940
or at the least a Sunday morn.
The monks had all come out and worn
their silken copes, and nuns, all veiled,
had joined the monks. The youth they hailed,
"Sir, you who were the one to save us

from exile, who restored, and gave us
our houses, naturally we grieve
to learn how soon you mean to leave!
Our mourning is so very deep,
it can't be deeper!" "Do not weep,   2950
you must not mourn for me and cry,"
the young man told them in reply,
"I'll come back, with God's sanctioning,
and mourning is a useless thing.*
Don't you believe it would be good
for me to travel to the wood
called the Wild Forest, where I left
my mother lonely and bereft?
I'll come back whether or not I find
she's willing; I won't change my mind.   2960
If Mother lives, then I will take her
to join your order and will make her
a nun in veils; if she is dead,
each year I'll have a service said
for her upon the day she died,
so God will let her soul abide
in the bosom of holy Abraham*
with other pious souls. I am
sure, ladies fair, good monks, my leaving
should not be any cause for grieving;   2970
I shall provide well for her soul,
if Heaven brings me back here whole."
The monks and nuns and crowd departed.
With lance in rest, the young man started,
completely armed, as he had come.

v. 2954 (2955, Roach edition). Among other references, Hilka cites (*Der Percevalro-
man*, p. 670) *Cligès*, v. 2589 (Micha edition): "Mauvés est diax a maintenir," and Mo-
rawski, *Proverbes français* no. 1403: "Nul duel sordolier."

v. 2967 (2966, Roach edition). Hilka notes (*Der Percevalroman*, p. 670) that the ref-
erence to being carried into Abraham's bosom is from Luke 16:22.

THE GRAIL

The youth began his journey from
the castle, and the daytime whole
he did not meet one living soul:
no creature from the wide earth's span,
no Christian woman, Christian man   2980
who could direct him on his way.
The young man did not cease to pray
the sovereign father, God, Our Lord,
if He were willing, to accord
that he would find his mother still
alive and well. He reached a hill
and saw a river at its base.
So rapid was the current's pace,
so deep the water, that he dared
not enter it, and he declared,   2990
"Oh God Almighty! It would seem,
if I could get across this stream,
I'd find my mother, if she's living."
He rode the bank with some misgiving
and reached a cliff, but at that place
the water met the cliff's sheer face
and kept the youth from going through.
A little boat came into view;
it headed down the river, floating
and carrying two men out boating.   3000
The young knight halted there and waited.
He watched the way they navigated
and thought that they would pass the place
he waited by the cliff's sheer face.
They stayed in mid-stream, where they stopped
and took the anchor, which they dropped.
The man afore, a fisher, took
a fish to bait his line and hook;
in size the little fish he chose
was larger than a minnow grows.   3010
The knight, completely at a loss,
not knowing how to get across,
first greeted them, then asked the pair,

"Please, gentlemen, nearby is there
a bridge to reach the other side?"
To which the fisherman replied,
"No, brother, for besides this boat,
the one in which we are afloat,
which can't bear five men's weight as charge,
there is no other boat as large   3020
for twenty miles each way and more,
and you can't cross on horseback, for
there is no ferry, bridge, nor ford."
"Tell me," he answered, "by Our Lord,
where I may find a place to stay."
The fisherman said, "I should say
you'll need a roof tonight and more,
so I will lodge you at my door.
First find the place this rock is breached
and ride uphill, until you've reached   3030
the summit of the cliff," he said.
"Between the wood and river bed
you'll see, down in the valley wide,
the manor house where I reside."
The knight rode up the cliff until
he reached the summit of the hill.
He looked around him from that stand
but saw no more than sky and land.*
He cried, "What have I come to see?
Stupidity and trickery!   3040
May God dishonor and disgrace
the man who sent me to this place!
He had the long way round in mind,
when he told me that I would find
a manor when I reached the peak.
Oh, fisherman, why did you speak?
For if you said it out of spite,

v. 3038. There has been much debate about whether the Fisher King's castle is situ-
ated outside of conventional time and space and whether it disappears and reappears. In
the text, the Fisher King, Perceval, and Perceval's cousin cannot agree about its distance
from other lodging places (see vs. 3124–3129 and 3469–3495). Haidu discusses Mario
Roques's theory that the castle was a vision, and other theories that it was a physically
material dwelling, in a footnote in *Aesthetic Distance*, p. 168. Frappier notes, in *Chré-
tien de Troyes et le Mythe du Graal*, p. 109, that Perceval lost no time in getting to the
castle, and yet the Fisher King got there ahead of him.

you tricked me badly!" He caught sight
of a tower starting to appear
down in a valley he was near,   3050
and as the tower came into view,
if people were to search, he knew,
as far as Beirut, they would not
find any finer tower or spot.
The tower was dark gray stone, and square,
and flanked by lesser towers, a pair.
Before the tower the hall was laid;
before the hall was the arcade.
On toward the tower the young man rode
in haste and called the man who showed   3060
the way to him a worthy guide.
No longer saying he had lied,
he praised the fisherman, elated
to find his lodgings as he stated.
The youth went toward the gate and found
the drawbridge lowered to the ground.
He rode across the drawbridge span.
Four squires awaited the young man.
Two squires came up to help him doff
his arms and took his armor off.   3070
The third squire led his horse away
to give him fodder, oats, and hay.
The fourth brought a silk cloak, new-made,
and led him to the hall's arcade,
which was so fine, you may be sure
you'd not find, even if you were
to search as far as Limoges, one
as splendid in comparison.
The young man paused in the arcade,
until the castle's master made   3080
two squires escort him to the hall.
The young man entered with them all
and found the hall was square inside:
it was as long as it was wide;*

v. 3084. Loomis noted that the structure of the Fisher King's hall, with its central fire-
place and couches, is unlike anything that Chrétien would have seen in 12th-century
France (*Arthurian Tradition*, p. 375). As Nitze observed, it is similar to the Irish royal
banqueting halls at Cruachan and Tara ("Le 'Bruden' Celtique et le Château du Graal,"
Romania 75 [1954]: 231–232).

and in the center of its span
he saw a handsome nobleman
with grayed hair, sitting on a bed.
The nobleman wore on his head
a mulberry-black sable cap
and wore a dark silk robe and wrap.   3090
He leaned back in his weakened state
and let his elbow take his weight.
Between four columns, burning bright,
a fire of dry logs cast its light.
In order to enjoy its heat,
four hundred men could find a seat
around the outsized fire, and not
one man would take a chilly spot.
The solid fireplace columns could
support the massive chimney hood,   3100
which was of bronze, built high and wide.
The squires, one squire on either side,
appeared before their lord foremost
and brought the youth before his host.
He saw the young man, whom he greeted.
"My friend," the nobleman entreated,
"don't think me rude not to arise;
I hope that you will realize
that I cannot do so with ease."
"Don't even mention it, sir, please,   3110
I do not mind," replied the boy,
"may Heaven give me health and joy."
The lord rose higher on the bed,
as best he could, with pain, and said,
"My friend, come nearer, do not be
embarrassed or disturbed by me,
for I command you to come near.
Come to my side and sit down here."
The nobleman began to say,
"From where, sir, did you come today?"   3120
He said, "This morning, sir, I came
from Belrepeire, for that's its name."
"So help me God," the lord replied,
"you must have had a long day's ride:
to start before the light of morn
before the watchman blew his horn."
"Sir, I assure you, by that time

the morning bells had rung for prime,"
the young man made the observation.
While they were still in conversation,   3130
a squire entered through the door
and carried in a sword he wore
hung from his neck and which thereto
he gave the rich man, who withdrew
the sword halfway and checked the blade
to see where it was forged and made,
which had been written on the sword.
The blade was wrought, observed the lord,
of such fine steel, it would not break
save with its bearer's life at stake   3140
on one occasion, one alone,
a peril that was only known
to him who forged and tempered it.*
The squire said, "Sir, if you permit,
your lovely blonde niece sent this gift,
and you will never see or lift
a sword that's lighter for its strength,
considering its breadth and length.
Please give the sword to whom you choose,
but if it goes to one who'll use   3150
the sword that he is given well,
you'll greatly please the demoiselle.
The forger of the sword you see
has never made more swords than three,
and he is going to die before
he ever forges any more.
No sword will be quite like this sword."
Immediately the noble lord
bestowed it on the newcomer,
who realized that its hangings were   3160
a treasure and of worth untold.

v. 3143. Frappier says, in *Chrétien de Troyes et le Mythe du Graal*, pp. 111–112, that
"the sword forged by a wondrous smith in a distant land that is very difficult to reach does
not have its origins in Greek or Roman antiquity, in Biblical tradition, or in Christian
symbolism; it is an arm and a talisman of the Celtic Otherworld, comparable to the
magic swords of Irish and Welsh legend, especially King Arthur's Escalibor." According
to Celtic tradition, the sword forged in the Otherworld knows its owner in advance, and
it confers upon him a title and a power that are his by right. Frappier says that, "by the
sword, Chrétien suggests the exceptional nature of Perceval's destiny."

The pommel of the sword was gold,
the best Arabian or Grecian;
the sheath's embroidery gold Venetian.
Upon the youth the castle's lord
bestowed the richly mounted sword
and said to him, "This sword, dear brother,
was destined for you and none other.
I wish it to be yours henceforth.
Gird on the sword and draw it forth."   3170
He thanked the lord, and then the knight
made sure the belt was not too tight,
and girded on the sword, and took
the bare blade out for a brief look.
Then in the sheath it was replaced:
it looked well hanging at his waist
and even better in his fist.
It seemed as if it would assist
the youth in any time of need
to do a brave and knightly deed.   3180
Beside the brightly burning fire
the youth turned round and saw a squire,
who had his armor in his care,
among the squires standing there.
He told this squire to hold the sword
and took his seat beside the lord,
who honored him as best he might.
The candles cast as bright a light
as could be found in any manor.
They chatted in a casual manner.   3190
Out of a room a squire came, clasping
a lance of purest white: while grasping*
the center of the lance, the squire

---

v. 3192. The most widely accepted prototype of the bleeding lance is the Celtic lance
with which Balaain wounded King Pellehan through the thighs and brought devastation
upon his kingdom. Bruce, *The Evolution of Arthurian Romance*, pp. 271-273, and
Holmes, *Chrétien de Troyes*. p. 145, noted that the famous Celtic lance, the Luin of
Celtchar, was described as dripping blood on one occasion, and in another text bursts in-
to flame, kills nine at every cast, and cools off in a cauldron of blood. In addition to these
Celtic lances and the Holy Lance of Longinus, Helen Laurie noted that Chrétien was
probably familiar with Cephalus's javelin in Ovid's *Metamorphoses* (vii, 683-684),
which, when thrown, returned to its owner covered with blood ("Towards an Interpreta-
tion of the *Conte de Graal*," *Modern Language Review 66* [1971]: 781-782).

walked through the hall between the fire
and two men sitting on the bed.
All saw him bear, with measured tread,
the pure white lance. From its white tip
a drop of crimson blood would drip
and run along the white shaft and
drip down upon the squire's hand,   3200
and then another drop would flow.
The knight who came not long ago*
beheld this marvel, but preferred
not to inquire why it occurred,
for he recalled the admonition
the lord made part of his tuition,
since he had taken pains to stress
the dangers of loquaciousness.
The young man thought his questions might
make people think him impolite,   3210
and that's why he did not inquire.
Two more squires entered, and each squire
held candelabra, wrought of fine
pure gold with niello work design.
The squires with candelabra fair
were an extremely handsome pair.
At least ten lighted candles blazed
in every holder that they raised.
The squires were followed by a maiden
who bore a grail, with both hands laden.*   3220
The bearer was of noble mien,
well dressed, and lovely, and serene,

v. 3202 ff. Note the care with which Chrétien repeats three times that Perceval's failure to ask about the lance is due to Gornemant's warning about talking too much, and his naiveté in not realizing that the circumstances were exceptional. See vs. 3246 and 3293 for repetitions of Gornemant's warning.

v. 3220. Frappier discusses the word "graal" in *Chrétien de Troyes et le Mythe du Graal*, pp. 5–12, noting that the subject form is "li graaus," and the object form is "le graal." Loomis noted, in *The Grail: From Celtic Myth to Christian Symbol*, p. 29, that Helinand, Abbot of Froidmont in Beauvais, writing around 1215, defined "graal" as "a wide and slightly deep dish in which costly viands are customarily placed for rich people." Frappier notes that the word "graal," while not common, was not new; it appears in the *Alexandre*. The word "graal" became the medieval Latin "gradalis" and had slightly different forms in different regions of France. Chrétien's "graal" is closer to the Provençal "grazal" than to the very rare langue d'oil form, "greel."

and when she entered with the grail,
the candles suddenly grew pale,
the grail cast such a brilliant light,
as stars grow dimmer in the night
when sun or moonrise makes them fade.
A maiden after her conveyed
a silver platter past the bed.
The grail, which had been borne ahead,   3230
was made of purest, finest gold
and set with gems; a manifold
display of jewels of every kind,
the costliest that one could find
in any place on land or sea,
the rarest jewels there could be,
let not the slightest doubt be cast.
The jewels in the grail surpassed
all other gems in radiance.
They went the same way as the lance: 3240
they passed before the lord's bedside
to another room and went inside.
The young man saw the maids' procession
and did not dare to ask a question
about the grail or whom they served;*
the wise lord's warning he observed,
for he had taken it to heart.
I fear he was not very smart;
I have heard warnings people give:
that one can be too talkative,*   3250
but also one can be too still.
But whether it was good or ill,
I do not know, he did not ask.
The squires who were assigned the task
of bringing in the water and
the cloths obeyed the lord's command.

v. 3245. Frappier notes, in *Chrétien de Troyes et le Mythe du Graal*, p. 114, that Chrétien indicates the right question about the grail by repeating it three times: "Who is being served with the grail?" See vs. 3292 and 3302, and for the two correct questions about the lance and grail, vs. 3399-3401.

v. 3250. Among other references for this saying, Hilka cites (*Der Percevalroman*, p. 684) Ecclesiastes 3:7: "a time to keep silence and a time to speak," and Morawski, *Proverbes français* no. 1542: "On se peut bien trop teire"; no. 2276: "Sorparler nuit et trop se repuet l'en tere"; and no. 866: "Il est tens de parler et si est tens de teire."

The men who usually were assigned
performed these tasks before they dined.
They washed their hands in water, warmed,
and then two squires, so I'm informed,   3260
brought in the ivory tabletop,
made of one piece: they had to stop
and hold it for a while before
the lord and youth, until two more
squires entered, each one with a trestle.
The trestles had two very special,
rare properties, which they contained
since they were built, and which remained
in them forever: they were wrought
of ebony, a wood that's thought   3270
to have two virtues: it will not*
ignite and burn and will not rot;
these dangers cause no harm nor loss.
They laid the tabletop across
the trestles, and the cloth above.
What shall I say? To tell you of
the cloth is far beyond my scope.
No legate, cardinal, or pope
has eaten from a whiter one.
The first course was of venison,   3280
a peppered haunch, cooked in its fat,
accompanied by a clear wine that
was served in golden cups, a pleasant,
delicious drink. While they were present
a squire carved up the venison.
He set the peppered haunch upon
a silver platter, carved the meat,
and served the slices they would eat
by placing them on hunks of bread.
Again the grail passed by the bed,   3290
and still the youth remained reserved
about the grail and whom they served.
He did not ask, because he had
been told so kindly it was bad
to talk too much, and he had taken
these words to heart. He was mistaken;
though he remembered, he was still

v. 3271. Hilka cites other references to these properties of ebony, among them Pliny's
Natural History (*Der Percevalroman*, p. 685).

much longer than was suitable.
At every course, and in plain sight,*
the grail was carried past the knight,   3300
who did not ask whom they were serving,
although he wished to know, observing
in silence that he ought to learn
about it prior to his return.
So he would ask: before he spoke
he'd wait until the morning broke,
and he would ask a squire to tell,
once he had told the lord farewell
and all the others in his train.
He put the matter off again   3310
and turned his thoughts toward drink and food.
They brought, and in no stingy mood,
the foods and different types of wine,
which were delicious, rich and fine.
The squires were able to provide
the lord and young knight at his side
with every course a count, king, queen,
and emperor eat by routine.
At dinner's end, the two men stayed
awake and talked, while squires made   3320
the beds and brought them fruit: they ate
the rarest fruits: the nutmeg, date,
fig, clove, and pomegranate red.
With Alexandrian gingerbread,
electuaries at the end,*
restoratives, a tonic blend,
and pliris archonticum

v. 3299 (3301, Roach edition). "in plain sight." The phrase, "le graal trestot descovert," has been the subject of considerable discussion, and arguments based upon the premise that the phrase means "all uncovered, without a lid" have been proffered to show that Chrétien intended the grail to be a ciborium or other covered or veiled communion vessel. (It is important to note that women were forbidden to touch communion vessels in the Roman Catholic Church, and it is unlikely that Chrétien would have violated the edicts of the church.) Frappier states that the correct interpretation of the phrase is "completely visible, very apparent" (*Chrétien de Troyes et le Mythe du Graal*, pp. 176-177), an opinion which Loomis notes was shared by the First Continuator, in "The Grail Story of Chrétien de Troyes as Ritual and Symbolism," *PMLA 71* (1956): 847.

v. 3325 (3327, Roach edition). Electuaries are digestive medicines that are powdered and made into a paste with honey or syrup. In *Der Percevalroman*, pp. 689-691, Hilka includes detailed references to the properties of Alexandrian gingerbread, Pliris archonticum, and other electuaries.

for settling his stomach᳄.
Then various liqueurs were poured
for them to sample afterward: 3330
straight piment, which did not contain
sweet honey or a single grain
of pepper, wine of mulberries,
clear syrups, other delicacies.
The youth's astonishment persisted;
he did not know such things existed.
"Now, my dear friend," the great lord said,
"the time has come to go to bed.
I'll seek my room—don't thing it queer—
and you will have your bed out here   3340
and may lie down at any hour.
I do not have the slightest power
over my body anymore
and must be carried to my door."
Four nimble servants, strongly set,
came in and seized the coverlet
by its four corners (it was spread
beneath the lord, who lay in bed)
and carried him away to rest.
The others helped the youthful guest.   3350
As he required, and when he chose,
they took his clothing off, and hose,
and put him in a bed with white,
smooth linen sheets; he slept all night
at peace until the morning broke.
But when the youthful knight awoke,
he was the last to rise and found
that there was no one else around.
Exasperated and alone,
he had to get up on his own.   3360
He made the best of it, arose,
and awkwardly drew on his hose
without a bit of help or aid.
He saw his armor had been laid
at night against the dais' head
a little distance from his bed.
When he had armed himself at last,
he walked around the great hall past
the rooms and knocked at every door
which opened wide the night before,   3370

but it was useless: juxtaposed,
the doors were tightly locked and closed.
He shouted, called, and knocked outside,
but no one opened or replied.
At last the young man ceased to call,
walked to the doorway of the hall,
which opened up, and passed through there,
and went on down the castle stair.
His horse was saddled in advance.
The young man saw his shield and lance   3380
were leaned against the castle wall
upon the side that faced the hall.
He mounted, searched the castle whole,
but did not find one living soul,
one servant, or one squire around.
He hurried toward the gate and found
the men had let the drawbridge down,
so that the knight could leave the town
at any hour he wished to go.
His hosts had dropped the drawbridge so   3390
the youth could cross it undeterred.
The squires were sent, the youth inferred,
out to the wood, where they were set
to checking every trap and net.
The drawbridge lay across the stream.
He would not wait and formed a scheme
of searching through the woods as well
to see if anyone could tell
about the lance, why it was bleeding,
about the grail, whom they were feeding,   3400
and where they carried it in state.
The youth rode through the castle gate
and out upon the drawbridge plank.
Before he reached the other bank,
the young man started realizing
the forefeet of his horse were rising.
His horse made one great leap indeed.
Had he not jumped well, man and steed
would have been hurt. His rider swerved
to see what happened and observed   3410
the drawbridge had been lifted high.
He shouted, hearing no reply,
"Whoever raised the bridge," said he,

"where are you? Come and talk to me!
Say something to me; come in view.
There's something I would ask of you,
some things I wanted to inquire,
some information I desire."
His words were wasted, vain and fond;
no one was willing to respond.   3420

PERCEVAL'S COUSIN

He galloped toward the forest's bound
and rode in on a path he found,
where there were hoofprints, freshly made
by horses passing through the glade.
"This is the way the people took,
the ones for whom I came to look."
He galloped through the forest fast,
not stopping while the trail did last,
until by chance the young man spied
a maid beneath an oak, who cried,*   3430
bemoaned her fortune, and lamented
like some poor wretch, lost and tormented.
"Oh, evil hour that came to pass
when I was born! Unlucky lass!
Cursed be the hour of my conception
and of my birth! Without exception,
no act in my whole life," she stated,
"has left me so infuriated!
I wish that God had never willed
that I would hold my sweetheart killed,   3440
for what He should have willed instead
is that he live and I be dead.
Death, with the agony I've known,
why take his soul and not my own?
He's dead whom I loved most on earth,
and now what is my own life worth?
Without him I care nothing for
my life and self. Death, I implore,
come back and take my soul away
out of my body, so it may   3450
become the handmaid who attends
my love's soul, if he condescends."

v. 3430. Loomis notes that Perceval's coming upon a maiden mourning her newly slain lover is similar to an episode in the Finn saga, in which Finn, on the way to visit his uncle, comes upon a woman mourning her newly slain son and pursues and kills the slayer. Finn learns afterward that the slayer had wounded his father (*The Grail: From Celtic Myth to Christian Symbol*, pp. 84–85).

The maid's lament arose unquelled
over the headless knight she held.
The youth maintained a steady pace,
not stopping till he reached the place
where she was making such reproach.
He hailed her, and at his approach
she greeted him, but with head bowed,
and did not cease to mourn aloud.   3460
The young man asked the weeping maid,
"Who killed the knight whom you have laid
across your knees and hold so tight?"
"Dear sir, it was another knight,"
replied the maiden who was mourning,
"he killed my love this very morning.
God save me, what is it I see?
It very much amazes me,
since folks have ridden, so they say,
for forty leagues along the way   3470
from where you came and have not seen
a place, respectable and clean,
in which a traveller could abide.
Your horse has sleek, smooth flanks and hide;
if somebody had washed, brushed, fed
your steed on oats with hay for bed,
he'd not look any glossier.
You look yourself as if you were
well at your ease, in sweet repose
last evening, or I would suppose!"   3480
"My word, fair lady," said the knight,
"I was as comfortable last night
as I could possibly expect,
and if I look it, that's correct.
I do not have the slightest doubt,
if anybody were to shout
from where we're talking, they would hear
the sound where I stayed, loud and clear.
I think you must not have explored
the countryside: the bed and board   3490
I had last evening was the best
I've ever had, I can attest."
She said, "Then, sir, the dwelling which
is the possession of the rich,
Fisher King is where you stayed."
"I don't know, by the Saviour, maid,

if he's a king or fisherman,
but a most wise and courteous man.
All I can say is, late last night
I found two men who came in sight.   3500
I met the pair, who were out boating.
The boat was small and slowly floating.
One of the men was rowing, and
the other, hook and line in hand,
was fishing, and he told me where
he lived and gave me lodging there."
The maiden answered him, "Good sir,
he is a king, you may be sure,
but in a battle he was lamed,
so badly wounded, he was maimed.   3510
He cannot move and must have aid.
Hurt by a wound a javelin made
between his thighs, the king is still
in such pain, it's impossible
for him to ride, but when he wishes
to spend some pleasant hours, he fishes.
Placed in a small boat at his sign,
he fishes with a hook and line.
So he is called the Fisher King,
since fishing is the only thing   3520
to which the hurt king can resort
for recreation and for sport.
He suffers from the javelin's brunt,
and he can neither hawk nor hunt.
He has his fowlers, all the same,
and archers who can shoot the game
within his woods, and huntsmen near,
so he is happy staying here.
The Fisher King could not have found
another place the world around   3530
to suit him any more than it did.
He's built a manor house, well fitted
to be a rich king's residence."
"My word, I can give evidence
that you have spoken accurately.
I met the king and marvelled greatly
when in his presence yesterday.
I stood a little way away
from where he sat, and so he said
to sit beside him on the bed   3540

and told me if he did not rise
he hoped that I would not surmise
that he was haughty, for instead
he was too weak to rise from bed,
so I was seated at his side."
"Oh, what an honor," she replied,
"to seat you there within his manse.
Now tell me, did you see the lance
with bleeding tip, though it contains
no living flesh and has no veins?"   3550
"Indeed I did," the young man said.
"Then did you ask him why it bled?"
"So help me Heaven, I was still."
"Let me assure you, you did ill.
You saw the grail?" "Yes, I beheld it."
"In that case, can you say who held it?"
"A maid." "You saw her come from where?"
"A room." "Where did she go from there?"
"Another room, whence she proceeded."
"Tell me if anyone preceded   3560
the grail: did someone walk before?"
"They did, yes." "Who?" "Two squires, no more."
"The squires held . . ?" "Candelabra, maiden,
one in each hand with candles laden."
"After the grail passed, you beheld . . ?"
"Another maiden." "And she held . . ?"
"A little silver carving dish."
"Did you not ask, did you not wish
to learn where they went in procession?"
"Out of my mouth came not one question."   3570
"God help me, you're the more to blame.
Tell me, my friend, what is your name?"
Not knowing his real name at all,
he guessed his name was Perceval*

v. 3575. Perceval's guessing his name is a crucial point in the story. Frappier notes
(*Chrétien de Troyes et le Mythe du Graal*, pp. 120 ff) that for Perceval the intuition of his
name coincides with the intuition of his personality; until this point he existed only in re-
lation to others, but now he is aware of himself and his responsibility. Hilka notes (*Der
Percevalroman*, p. 695) that the name "Perceval li Galois" appears in *Erec and Enide*, v.
1506 (Roques edition) and in *Cligès*, vs. 4774, 4777, 4793, and 4797 (Micha edition).
Bruce, in *The Evolution of Arthurian Romance*, pp. 251-253, quotes W. Hertz, *Parzival
von Wolfram von Eschenbach, neu bearbeitet*, pp. 490 ff, that the name Perceval is
French and means "Pierce the valley, press on through the valley."

of Wales and said so, but the youth
did not know if it were the truth.
He spoke the truth, not realizing.
But when the maiden heard, arising,
she faced him, angry and estranged,
and said, "My friend, your name is changed!"　　　　　3580
"To what?" "To Perceval the wretch!
Unlucky Perceval, it's such
a dreadful pity you did not
ask all these questions on the spot!
To ask one question would procure
the king's recovery and his cure.
When the good king had once regained
use of his limbs, he would have reigned
in his land, to your benefit,
for much good would have come from it.　　　　　3590
Now learn disasters will ensue,
for other people and for you;
misfortunes caused by nothing other
than your great sin against your mother:
because of you, she died of grief.
I know you, it is my belief,
more than you know my name and line.
I'm your first cousin, you are mine,
Some years past you were reared with me
within your mother's nursery,*　　　　　3600
and now I feel as much distress
that you've had the unluckiness
not to have asked about the grail,
where it is borne, to what avail,
as I do that your mother died,
and that this knight lies by my side
whom I had loved so very dearly.
He called me dearest friend, and clearly
returned my love the way a true
and loyal knight would wish to do."　　　　　3610
"Oh, cousin," Perceval appealed,
"if all is as you have revealed,

v. 3600. In "The Fisher King and the Grail in Retrospect," *Romance Philology 6*
(1952-1953): 19-20, Nitze notes that the matriarchal relationship between Perceval, his
mother, the Fisher King, the Grail King, the hermit uncle, and the mourning cousin, is
one that appears frequently in Celtic legends. Gawain also encounters members of his
mother's family (see footnote v. 8728).

so I will not begin to doubt it,
please tell me how you know about it."
"I know she's dead," replied the maid,
"as one would know who saw her laid
beneath the ground." Said Perceval,
"May God be kind and merciful,
in His great goodness, to her soul.
You've told a tale of sorrow whole.   3620
When she is buried, as you speak,
what else is there for me to seek?
I traveled only to attain
my hope of seeing her again.
Now I must go another way,
and if you wish to come, you may;
I am most willing; this dead knight
can help no longer in your plight.
So come with me without misgiving:
the living should be with the living,*   3630
the dead be likewise with the dead.
I think it foolishness," he said,
"for you to keep the death watch there
all by yourself. Let's seek his slayer,
and if I ever overtake him,
I swear to you that I will make him
surrender, or he'll make me yield."
From her heart's depths, the maid revealed
the overpowering distress
she was unable to suppress.   3640
"My friend, it is impossible
for me to leave his side until
I've buried him, or go with you.
Take that stone roadway to pursue
the knight, so haughty and cold-hearted,
who took that road when he departed,
on slaughtering my dear, sweet friend.
So help me God, I don't intend
to tell you anything so grim
to make you want to follow him,   3650
although I wish him so much ill,

v. 3630. Hilka notes (*Der Percevalroman*, p. 697) that this proverb is listed in Morawski, *Proverbes français* no. 1098: "Li mort aus morz li vif aus vis," and is included in the *Eneas*, in Wace's *Roman de Rou* III 232 as "Li vif al vif, le mort al mort," and in other references.

it might be me he came to kill.
But answer me now, who supplied
the sword that hangs at your left side?
Because that sword is one that never
drew blood before, nor has it ever
been drawn in any time of need.
I know where it was forged; indeed
I know who forged it. Have a care,
and do not trust that sword you wear.   3660
It will betray you without fail,
for in a battle of great scale
it suddenly will fly to pieces."
"Last night, one of my good host's nieces
sent it, dear cousin, and the lord
pleased me by giving me the sword.
The things that you have told me here,
if they are true, fill me with fear.
Dear cousin, will you tell me now,
if the sword breaks, do you know how*   3670
and whether it can be repaired?"
"Yes, with much effort," she declared.
"But if you knew the road to take
near Firth of Forth to reach the lake,
in that place you could have the blade
rehammered, tempered, and remade.
So if by any chance you get
to Firth of Forth, find Trebuchet,
the smith who made that sword and who
will either forge the sword anew,   3680
or else no other hands, I swear it,
will ever manage to repair it.
There is no other living soul
who has the power to make it whole."
"And I shall be, make no mistake,
extremely angry, should it break,"
said Perceval. He went ahead;
she stayed beside the corpse instead,
because she did not wish to part
from him whose death so pained her heart.   3690

---

v. 3670. Loomis notes that Chrétien has worked into the romance the Celtic theme of
sword-mending, "a test of the hero's fitness to carry out his obligation to revenge the
murder of a kinsman" (*The Grail: From Celtic Myth to Christian Symbol*, p. 87).

THE PROUD KNIGHT OF THE MOOR

So Perceval went down the road
and followed all the tracks that showed.
He found a palfrey, thin and frail,
proceeding slowly down the trail.
The palfrey, to the young man's mind,
had fallen into hands unkind,
because the horse was so forlorn,
so miserable and travelworn,
so starved and lean, so gaunt and tired,
it looked much like a horse that's hired: 3700
by day it's ridden everywhere,
by night it's given little care,
that's what the wretched horse resembled.
The palfrey was so thin, it trembled
as if it were half frozen, stooping
with hairless neck and both ears drooping.
The hounds and mastiffs well might feel
the horse was destined for their meal.
Its frame was draped with hide alone.
The palfrey was but skin and bone.   3710
It had a bridle on its nose,
a saddle on its back, and those
were such as you would have expected
upon a creature so neglected.
A maiden rode this palfrey mean.
No maid more miserable was seen,
although, with any kinder fate,
her loveliness would have been great.
So dreadful was her wretchedness
that not a handful of her dress   3720
was of whole cloth. Her nipples showed
through her torn bodice which she sewed
with clumsy stitches here and there,
or tied a knot to close a tear
and try to keep the cloth attached.
The maiden's skin was badly scratched,
like scratches of a lancet blade,
with cracks and burns that had been made
by heat and cold and hail and frost.*

Her hair was loose, her cloak was lost,   3730
and there were many ugly streaks
of tears which showed upon her cheeks.
Unendingly, her tears were flowing
and left these many paths, still showing.
The tears ran down onto her breast,
the robe in which the maid was dressed,
and trickled down upon her knees.
The heart which suffers ills like these
might well feel wretched and abased.
But Perceval rode up in haste   3740
the very moment that he found her.
The maiden pulled her dress around her,
so her skin would not be exposed,
but tore new holes, for when she closed
one bad tear in the dress she wore,
she opened up a hundred more.
As Perceval drew near the maid,
who was so pale and disarrayed,
he heard her bitterly complain
about her suffering and pain.   3750
"Please, God," the maid began to say,
"don't let me live too long this way.
I have been miserable so long,
and yet I have done nothing wrong.
I beg of you not to observe
the suffering I don't deserve,
much longer, God, because you know
I never merited such woe.
Oh, God, send someone, if you please,
to save me from these miseries,   3760
or else deliver me from him
who shames me, for he is so grim,
so absolutely unforgiving,
that I cannot escape him living,

v. 3729. Frost and later snow after Pentecost, like the two feasts of Pentecost within the same year in Gawain's adventures (v. 9192) are among the most striking discrepancies in the romance. It is significant in view of the Celtic sources that both discrepancies occur after the hero's visit to an Otherworld castle. While it may not be the case for Chrétien's romance, there are tales in which the hero stayed in the Otherworld much longer than he realized, so that many months, sometimes years, seemed like one night.

and yet he will not murder me.
I do not know why it would be
he wants my company, unless
it makes him feel great happiness
to see my misery and shame.
Yet if he knew I were to blame   3770
and I deserved to be maltreated,
if he loved me, he would have meted
some mercy to me by and by;
once I had paid a price so high.
But he holds me in no regard
to make my life so very hard
by following him as I do."
"Fair lady, God deliver you,"
said Perceval, who'd reached her side.
The maiden heard him and replied   3780
in quiet tones and with a bow,
"My lord, who greeted me just now,
may your heart's wishes be fulfilled,
which I've no reason to have willed."
Then Perceval's face flushed with shame.
He said, "Why maid, in Heaven's name?
I can't recall a single case
in which I've ever seen your face
or ever done you any wrong."
"Indeed you have," she said, "so long   3790
have I lived on in misery,
that no one ought to speak to me.
I've broken into a cold sweat
when I was stopped by those I've met."
Said Perceval, "I can declare
that truly I was not aware
of any harm that I had caused.
I came along this road and paused,
but I did not seek out this place
to bring you trouble or disgrace.   3800
But now I see you look so bad,
so poor and wretched and ill clad,
that joy will never fill my heart,
if you do not at once impart
by what misfortune you sustain
such sorrow, suffering, and pain."
"Oh, sir, have pity; go away,

flee from this place and do not stay;
leave me in peace and go along.
To linger here with me is wrong;   3810
be wise and flee!" "You have not yet
told me what danger or what threat
should frighten me enough to flee,
when nobody is chasing me?"
"Please do not take offense, sir knight;
while you are able, take to flight
before the Proud Knight of the Moor,
for whom no things have more allure
than strife and violent endeavor,
returns and catches us together.   3820
He'll kill you on the spot, I fear,
if he comes back and finds you here.
He's so mad if I'm stopped," she said,
"no one's departed with his head
who made me stop to talk hereto,
if he arrived in time: he slew
a man a little while ago.
But first the Proud Knight lets them know
the cruel punishments he dreamt,
and why he treats me with contempt."   3830
But as the couple talked and stood,
the Proud Knight came out of the wood,
rode like a bolt of thunder, and
emerged from clouds of dust and sand.
He cried, "The hour was evil-laden
in which you stopped to join the maiden.
Learn that your end has come, because
you held her back, and made her pause
and fall a single step behind.
I'll let you live till I've defined   3840
the maiden's crime, the great misdeed
that is the reason I proceed
to make her live in such disgrace.
Now listen and you'll hear the case.
On one occasion, when I went
into the forest, in my tent
I left this maiden tarrying.
I loved her more than anything.
By chance a youth from Wales came there.
I don't know who he was or where   3850

he went when following his course,
except he kissed the maid by force,
as she confessed without denying.
What was the harm if she was lying?
If she was kissed against her will,
why didn't he next have his fill?
Whoever would believe they kissed;
then he decided to desist?
One thing leads to another, for
he who would kiss and do no more,*   3860
when there is nobody to spy,
is wrong to let the chance slip by.
Who yields her mouth without protest*
is all too quick to yield the rest;
that's just what she intends herself!
No doubt, though she defends herself,*
as everyone has always known,
she wants to lose this fight alone
and wants to win all other matches.
Although she grabs his throat, and scratches,   3870
and bites, and struggles, and delays,
she hopes to lose, for all she says.
However ardent a defender,
however timid to surrender,
she wishes to be roughly wooed,*
and then she feels no gratitude.
So I am certain that he lay
with her and took my ring away,
the one she wore upon her hand;
and that I simply cannot stand.   3880

---

v. 3860. Frappier notes, in *Chrétien de Troyes et le Mythe du Graal*, p. 128, that the proud Knight's tirade is a very original reworking of a passage from Ovid's *Art of Love*, I, v. 661–678: "To take a kiss and not the rest is to deserve to lose even those favors which were granted. What were you waiting for, after a kiss, to fulfill all your wishes?"

v. 3863–3864. Hilka notes that this comment is included in Morawski, *Proverbes français* no. 736: "Femme qui donne elle s'abandonne" (*Der Percevalroman*, p. 701).

v. 3866 ff. Hilka notes that these verses about the lady's protests are taken from Ovid's *Art of Love* I, v. 665.

v. 3875 (3874, Roach edition). Hilka notes (*Der Percevalroman*, p. 701) that a similar instance of women refusing what they want is mentioned in *Yvain*, vs. 1647–1648 (Roques edition).

Before he did, he drank strong wine
and ate good pasties, which were mine
and I had wanted saved for me.
But now my sweetheart, as you see,
continues doing, and has done
a splendid penance: let the one*
who yields to folly pay the price,
so she'll beware of yielding twice.
When I returned and learned about it,
I was incensed, you must not doubt it,　　　　3890
and what I did was right: I vowed
her palfrey would not be allowed
to feed on oats, would not be bled,
nor have new shoes when these were shed;
the maid would have no tunic nor
new cloak besides the ones she wore,
till I made sure the lad was dead
who'd forced her, and cut off his head!"
When Perceval this speech had heard,
he made this answer, word for word,　　　　3900
"Friend, do not doubt that she has done
her penance, for I am the one
who kissed her, to her deep distress,
against her will, and I confess
I took her ring, but I forbore
from taking or from doing more.
Let me assure you, though I ate
your pasty, one and half its mate,
and though I drank my fill of wine,
it was mere stupidness of mine."　　　　3910
The Proud Knight answered, "By my head,
what you admitted, what you said,
completely takes away my breath.
You've richly merited your death
if your confession is sincere."
"You'll find my death is not so near,"
said Perceval. Their speech was done;
the two knights let their horses run
toward one another. In their hurry
they came together with such fury,　　　　3920

v. 3886. Hilka notes (*Der Percevalroman*, p. 701) that this proverb is listed in Morawski, *Proverbes français* no. 1939: "Qui fait la folie si la boive."

they splintered lances, and were thrown
out of their saddles, and lay prone,
for each of them had lost his seat.
Then both the knights sprang to their feet,
and bared their swords as they arose,
and gave each other heavy blows.   3926
First Perceval drew out the sword*   a
he'd gotten at the lame king's board   b
to try it out upon his foe.   c
He struck the knight so hard a blow   d
upon his helmet, made of steel,   e
he snapped the blade off in his zeal   f
and left the Proud Knight unconcerned.   g
The blow was instantly returned: h
on Perceval's striped helm he hit   i
and knocked the flowers and jewels from it.   j
Then Perceval felt sad indeed   k
the sword had failed in time of need.   l
Unhesitatingly the lad   m
drew out the sword the Red Knight had;   n
they faced each other once again.   o
The broken sword, which once had been   p
the Fisher King's, the youth collected   q
within the scabbard, well protected.   r
A vicious battle was begun;   s
no man has seen a fiercer one.   t
The battle was both hard and stern,   3927
but I don't think I care to turn
more of their battle into rhyme:
I think it is a waste of time.   3930
The Proud Knight of the Moor, who lost,
sought clemency at any cost,
and Perceval, who had not ever
forgotten the great lord's endeavor

vs. 3926 a–t. Frappier notes that this passage is interpolated in only three manu-
scripts, H, P, and T, and expresses his opinion that it is ungenuine (*Chrétien de Troyes et
le Mythe du Graal*, pp. 110–111). There are parallels between this broken sword passage
and the final combat scene in Virgil's *Aeneid*. Turnus always carried his father Daunus's
fated sword, which had been forged by Vulcan and plunged into the waters of Hades,
but by mistake he carried a breakable sword into single combat with Aeneas. Turnus's
sword treacherously broke into pieces, and the victorious Aeneas slew Turnus. The flow-
ers decorating Perceval's helm were enamel.

to teach him warriors should be spared
who begged for mercy, soon declared,
"Knight, on my word, I never will
show any mercy to you till
you show some toward your lady-love.
She never has been worthy of   3940
the cruelties you've made her bear,
I can assure you and will swear."
The knight loved her more than his eye.
"As you say, sir," was his reply.
"I'll make amends to her in full.
There is no order that I will
be unprepared to execute.
Her misery was so acute,
my heart is dark with grief and woe."
The young knight ordered, "You must go   3950
and find the nearest place you dwell,
so that until she's healed and well
the maid can bathe herself and rest.
Then take your maiden, finely dressed,
before King Arthur: you must greet him
on my behalf, and then entreat him
to show you mercy and his grace,
armed the same way you leave this place.
Now if he wants to know my name,
tell him the person is the same   3960
whom he created a red knight
thanks to the counsel and foresight
of my lord Kay the seneschal.
Her penance and her suffering, all
that you have forced your maid to bear,
when every courtier is there,
you must repeat, so everyone
will learn about the things you've done,
including both King Arthur's queen
and her handmaids of fairest mien.   3970
One I esteem above them all;
she laughed at me. The seneschal
hit her so hard, it is no wonder
the blow he struck completely stunned her.
I order you to give that maid
this message from me you've conveyed:
I won't be moved by any plea

to join King Arthur's court, till she
is joyful once again to know
I've finally avenged that blow."   3980
The knight was glad to make his way
to Arthur's court and there convey
the message he was told to carry.
He promised that they would not tarry
except as long as she would need
to rest before they could proceed
and to prepare to make the trip.
He'd welcome the companionship
of Perceval along the road
and have him stay at their abode   3990
until his cuts and wounds were cured.
"Go on now," Perceval demurred,
"good luck to you; but I shall find
some lodgings of another kind."
Their conversation had abated,
and neither of the warriors waited
a longer time in that location:
they left without more conversation.
That very night the Proud Knight had
his sweetheart bathed and richly clad.   4000
She had good care where she sojourned,
and soon her loveliness returned.
The couple took the shortest road
to Carlion from their abode.*
King Arthur's court had gathered there:
a small and intimate affair,
a mere three thousand knights of fame.
To Arthur's court the couple came:
the Proud Knight entered court with her
to be King Arthur's prisoner,   4010
and stood, and said the following:
"I am your prisoner, lord King.
You may do with me what you will,
and that is right and reasonable;

---

v. 4004 ff (4003, Roach edition). Nitze and Williams note (*Arthurian Names*, p. 269) that Carlion, the most prominent seat of King Arthur's court, is the modern Caerleon-on-Usk. Hilka notes (*Der Percevalroman*, p. 703) that King Arthur's holding court in Carlion at Pentecost is mentioned in Geoffrey of Monmouth (Faral edition p. 242), and in Wace's *Roman de Brut* 10457.

those were my orders, so ordained
by a young knight who once obtained
red arms from you, as he requested."
The king heard what the knight attested
and grasped his meaning instantly.
"Remove your armor, sir," said he.   4020
"May he who sent you as my present
have greatest joy and fortunes pleasant,
and you yourself are welcome here.
For his sake you will be held dear
and honored in my house and train."
"There's something else I must explain
before the squires disarm me, sire.
Before I do so, I desire
to have the queen and maidens fair
come forth to hear the news I bear.   4030
His message cannot be conveyed
until the time a certain maid
appears at court to hear me speak:
the maiden slapped upon the cheek
because she laughed a single time.
Her laughter was her only crime."
He fell still. Since the king had seen
he meant to send word to the queen
to join the courtiers, sent for her.
The queen came in, and with her were   4040
her maids of honor, in a band.
The maidens entered hand in hand.
The Proud Knight of the Moor, defeated,
said these things when the queen was seated
before her lord the king, "My lady,
a knight I honor, for he made me
surrender to him in fair fight,
sends you his greetings. Of this knight
there's nothing more that I can tell.
He's sending you this demoiselle,   4050
my sweetheart, who is at my side."
"I thank him, friend," the queen replied.
And then the knight began to name
the acts of cruelty and shame
which, for so long, he had imposed,
the pain to which she was exposed,
the reason for her punishment,

and made a full acknowledgment.
They pointed out the maid whom Kay
the seneschal had struck that day.   4060
The knight said, "He, at whose behest
I came to court, made this request:
that you, on his behalf, I greet,
nor take my shoes off of my feet,
until you heard what word he sent:
there was no way he would consent
to join King Arthur's royal court,
for arguments of any sort,
so help him God, till he repaid
the blow upon the cheek that, maid,   4070
you once received on his account."
The fool had heard the knight recount
the message, and he cried, "Kay, Kay,
it won't be long before you pay,
God bless me!" leaping to his feet.
King Arthur said, "Kay, I repeat
that you were very rude, in truth,
upon that day you mocked the youth.
Yes, Kay, it was your mockery
that stole the youth away from me,   4080
so I've no hope of seeing him."
The king commanded, freeing him,
that his knight captive take a seat
before him, pardoned his defeat,
had him disarmed, as was required,
and then the lord Gawain inquired
from his seat at King Arthur's right,
"In God's name, sire, who is this knight
who vanquished, by his arms alone,
so fine a knight? I've never known   4090
or seen or ever heard the name
of any warrior who came
from all the islands of the sea,
whose feats of arms and chivalry
could rank with any he can claim."
"Dear nephew, I don't know his name.
I saw him but did not see fit
to question him or ask him it.
At court he asked me, at first sight,
to make him instantly a knight,   4100

and yet, because it was my feeling
that he was handsome and appealing,
I answered, 'Brother, with good will.
Dismount, though, while you wait, until
we send for arms with gilt overlaid.'
He answered he would not be made
to take them, nor dismount, nor walk
until he had red arms. His talk
astounded us: he would accept
no armor and no arms except   4110
the ones worn by that warrior bold
who carried off my cup of gold.
Then Kay, who was unmannerly,
and is still, and will always be,
who never says a civil word
to anyone, said, 'Lad, you heard,
the king decided to bestow
the arms upon you; you must go
at once and take them.' So Kay spoke.
The youth, who did not see the joke,   4120
believed that Kay meant what he said,
left to pursue the knight in red,
and killed him with a javelin blow.
How the fight started, I don't know,"
the king continued. "Of the fight
I know no more than the Red Knight
who's from the wood of Quinqueroi,
for his own reasons, struck the boy
a lance blow in a haughty fit.
He took his javelin up and hit   4130
the knight directly in the eye,
killed him, and took his arms, whereby
he has served me so well since then
that, by Saint David, to whom men
of Wales still pray, I now proclaim
I won't lie down within the same
abode or bedroom two nights, till
I know if he is living still
on land or sea, because I plan
to go and search for that young man."   4140
At the king's oath, all men at court
felt certain that the time was short;
the king was ready to depart.

BLOOD ON THE SNOW

You would have seen the packing start,
and people fill the chests with sets
of pillows, sheets, and coverlets,
and truss the pack horses, and load
the carts and wagons, where they stowed
the folded canopies and tents;
a sum of some significance.   4150
A clerk, well lettered, erudite,
could toil all day and never write
a baggage list of everything
they packed so quickly. Then the king
left Carlion and rode before,
as if he were to go to war,
with all his barons in his train.
No handmaids needed to remain;
they joined the queen, a company
of equal pomp and majesty.   4160
That night the court camped in a field
beside a wood. The sun revealed
much snow had fallen to enfold
the country, which was very cold.
On that same morning, Perceval
rose early, as was usual,
to seek adventure, knightly fame.
Directly to the field he came.
Upon its cloak of snow and frost
he saw the tents. Before he crossed   4170
to reach the royal camp, he heard
a flock of wild geese; every bird
had been bedazzled by the snow.
The flock of geese was flying low,
and they were honking loudly, keeping
far from a falcon, which was sweeping
upon them at tremendous speed.
He swooped upon the flock till he'd
found one goose who'd been separated.
He struck the wild goose, isolated   4180
from all the rest, and with a bound
he pounced and knocked her to the ground.

It was too early in the day,
he left and did not seize his prey.
The young knight saw the goose was stranded
and galloped toward the place she landed.
Hurt in the neck, the goose had shed
three drops of crimson blood, which spread
like blushes on the clear white snow.
The goose was not hurt by the blow   4190
and could still rise above the ground.
When Perceval arrived, he found
the goose had flown away again.
He saw the place the goose had lain;
the snow was pressed down when he found it,
with drops of crimson blood around it,
and started leaning on his lance
to contemplate them from this stance.
The blood and snow, both in one place,*
made him recall his lady's face,   4200
the colors of her bright complexion.
So Perceval fell in reflection
till he forgot himself outright.
The red contrasted with the white
complexion of his lady-love
in the same way the three drops of
red blood contrasted with the snow.
The combination pleased him so,
he thought he saw the colors clear
upon the face of one so dear.   4210

v. 4199. Nitze notes (*Perceval and the Holy Grail*, p. 311) a precedent for the blood-on-the-snow episode in the Irish Book of Leinster, dated before 1164, in which the Ulster cycle records the awakening of Deirdre's love for Naisi. Deirdre, seeing a raven drinking the blood of a newly slain calf which had flowed onto the snow, said: "Beloved would be the one man upon whom should be those three colors yonder: hair like the raven, and cheek like the blood, and body like the snow." Because of the 12th-century literary convention that all heroines were blonde, the reference to raven hair was eliminated. Frappier notes, in *Chrétien de Troyes et le Mythe du Graal*, p. 136, that Martin de Riquer, in "Perceval y las gotas de sangre en la nieve" (*Revista de Filologia Espanola 39* [1955]: 186–216), dissenting from the accepted view that Chrétien borrowed the motif of the wounded bird, blood, snow, and beloved woman from a Celtic tradition which is also reflected in the Welsh *Peredur*, pointed out that there are Flemish, Danish, English, Scottish, French, Italian, Catalan, Portuguese, Basque, Greek, Albanian, Bulgarian, Russian, and Finnish versions of the same story.

He thought about the drops and passed
the morning at it, till, at last,
the squires came out of the tent.
They saw him musing, all intent,
and they believed that he was sleeping.
Because King Arthur was still keeping
inside his tent and had not risen,
the squires met for a decision
by his pavilion, and they came
on Sagremore, with the nickname*   4220
of "Hothead" for his temperament.
"Tell me the reason why you went
in such a rush; don't hide a thing!"
"Sir," said the squires, answering,
"not far from our encampment site
we looked around and saw a knight
who's gone to sleep upon his horse."
"Well, is he armed?" "Oh, yes, of course."
"Then we shall have a parley short,
and I shall bring him back to court."   4230
He ran inside and woke the king
with, "Sire, a knight is slumbering
out in the field." The king agreed
that Sagremore might so proceed,
and he requested that they bring
the sleeping knight back to the king,
if he consented. Sagremore
ordered his war horse to his door,
and said to fetch his armor, and
squires rushed to follow his command.   4240
Armed fully, Sagremore rode out,
and he approached the knight to shout
"You must come to the king now, sir,"
to Perceval, who did not stir
and seemed not to hear Sagremore.
So Sagremore said it once more,
but Perceval stayed silent. Hostile,
he cried, "Saint Peter the Apostle,

v. 4220. Hilka notes (*Der Percevalroman*, p. 707) that Sagremore is mentioned in
Erec and Enide, vs. 1701, 2175, 2182, 2194 (Roques edition), and *Cligès*, vs. 4612, 4640,
and 4641 (Micha edition).

you'll come with me, will you or no!
Why was I asking you to go? 4250
It was an utter waste of breath!"
Then he unfurled to its full breadth
the pennant that was on his lance
wrapped round the shaft, and took his stance
in one part of the field, and spurred
his war horse, and again preferred
his challenge: let the knight beware;
he'd strike him if he did not care
to fight back for his own protection.
Perceval looked in his direction 4260
and saw the warrior's onslaught.
Emerging from his train of thought,
Perceval turned and spurred his horse,
and when they met in headlong course,
Sagremore's lance broke, end to end.
Perceval's did not break or bend;
he struck his foe, hurled him with force
onto the ground. The great war horse
head up, immediately went fleeing
back to the camp, where people, seeing 4270
the empty saddle's evidence
arose dismayed within their tents.
Kay could not keep from uttering
sarcastic words, came to the king,
and he began to jeer and joke.
"Sire, look at Sagremore," Kay spoke,
"he has returned and not been idle,
he holds the knight by rein and bridle
and leads him here against his will!"
"Kay," said King Arthur, "you do ill 4280
to jeer at such a worthy man.
Go in his place, see if you can
accomplish more than he could do."
"I'm happy that it pleases you
to let me go. I'll surely bring
the knight by force back to the king,
whether or not that is his aim,
and I will make him tell his name."
Kay armed himself and, mounted, went
to one on three drops so intent 4290
that they absorbed all his attention.

He did not heed Kay's intervention.
Kay, from afar, was bellowing,
"Come, vassal, come before the king!
You are to come to him, I say,
or otherwise I'll make you pay!"
But when he heard the threats Kay said,
Perceval turned his horse's head.
With spurs of steel he pricked his steed
toward the knight coming at top speed.   4300
Since each knight wished to do his best,
they met each other, not in jest.
Kay's lance broke as it hit the mark
and shattered as if it were bark,
for Kay put all his strength in it.
And Perceval, no slacker, hit
Kay on his shield above the boss
and overthrew him, with a toss,
onto a rock. Kay dislocated
his collarbone; the bone located   4310
in his right arm was snapped between
his elbow and his armpit, clean,
like a dry stick. The break inflicted
was one the king's fool had predicted
so often — a true prophecy.
As Kay passed out in agony,
his steed fled at a rapid trot
to reach the king's encampment spot.
The Britons saw the horse return
without the seneschal. To learn   4320
the reason for what had occurred,
the ladies, knights, and squires stirred.
When they had ridden out, they found
Kay sprawled unconscious on the ground.
They thought him dead, and one and all
lamented for the seneschal:
the women mourned him and the men.
But Perceval turned back again
to the three drops, braced on his lance.
The king, upset by the mischance   4330
that struck the injured seneschal,
was grieved and angered by his fall.
They told him not to be dismayed:
Kay would recover, with the aid

of a good doctor for his case
to put the collarbone in place
and set the fracture properly.
King Arthur loved Kay tenderly
and had his welfare much at heart.
He sent a doctor, wise in art,*   4340
and two maids schooled by him alone,
and they replaced the collarbone,
and set Kay's arm, and bandaged it,
so that the broken bone would knit.
They brought Kay to King Arthur's tent
and comforted him. Confident,
they told him that he must not feel
too worried, for the bones would heal.
The lord Gawain said to the king,
"Sire, sire, it's not the proper thing,   4350
so help me Heaven, as you know,
for you yourself have judged it so,
have always said, and said aright
it's always wrong for any knight
to jar another's train of thought.
On the occasion when they fought
I don't know if the two knights were
at fault or not, but it is sure
they've come to grief. Perhaps the knight
was thinking of some loss or plight   4360
that he had undergone, or maybe
somebody stole away his lady,
and he was downcast, ill at ease.
I'll go and see, sire, if you please,
and if the knight has ceased to brood,
and now is in a different mood,
I shall request him to appear
before you and ride over here."
Kay heard and grew enraged again.
He snorted, "Hah! My lord Gawain,   4370
you'll seize his bridle and escort

v. 4340-4341. Hilka notes (*Der Percevalroman*, p. 709) that there is a similar situation of a doctor being assisted by several women in *Erec and Enide*, vs. 5071-5072, and in *Yvain*, vs. 4691-4692 (Roques editions), in Marie de France's *Guigemar*, and in other references.

the knight unwilling back to the court!
Yes, what a feat if that rapt knight
allows it and concedes the fight!
We'll say 'well done' when it occurs;
that's how you take your prisoners.
When some tired knight has fought enough,
this warrior, so bold and tough,
asks leave to conquer him. Gawain,
upon my neck may curses rain,   4380
for you indeed are no one's fool,
we should take lessons at your school,
for obviously you know the way
to make your polished language pay.
And would you ever say a grim,
insulting, haughty thing to him?
A curse on anyone we know
who thought it or would think it so.
Why, you could wear a gown of silk
to run an errand of this ilk,   4390
and never be obliged to take
your sword in hand or lances break,
of which you should be very proud.
Count on your tongue to say aloud,
'God save you, sir, may God confer
good health and joy upon you, sir';
he will obey you willingly.
No lessons do you need from me;
when men are ruffled by some spat,
you stroke them as one strokes a cat.   4400
Then everybody starts to prattle,
'The lord Gawain fought a fierce battle!'"
The lord Gawain said, "Oh, Sir Kay,
you could speak in a kinder way.
Do you suppose to find redress
by venting your maliciousness
and rage upon me? If I can,
dear friend, I shall bring back the man
without a fracture of my own
or dislocated collarbone,   4410
for I dislike that sort of pay."
The king said, "Nephew, on your way.
The words you've spoken are polite,
and if you can, bring back the knight,

but carry all your arms; it's senseless
for you to go out there defenseless."
The lord Gawain, who'd won great fame
for all the virtues he could claim,
commanded he be armed with speed,
got on a strong and willing steed,   4420
and went straight to the knight, whose stance
was still of leaning on his lance.
He was not tired, and he still sought
to follow his pleasant train of thought.
The sun had melted down, by then,
two of the red drops which had been
shed on the snow within the clearing,
and now the third was disappearing,
so he was not so lost in thought.
When he approached the man he sought,   4430
the lord Gawain came at an amble
across the field, so his preamble
would not seem hostile. Then he stood
and told the knight, "My lord, I would
have hailed you, if I could have known
your heart the way I know my own,
but I will tell you this much, sir:
I am King Arthur's messenger,
and he has sent me to request
that you speak with him as his guest."   4440
"Two others," Perceval replied,
"have come already, and they tried
to lead me off as if I were
a captive or a prisoner,
or kill me, if I had not fought,
although I was so deep in thought
about a thing that touched my heart.
He who would force me to depart
would do so at his peril, sir.
Before me, in this place, there were   4450
three drops of fresh blood on the white.
They brightened it, and at the sight
I thought I saw, here in this place,
the colors of my lady's face,
and her fresh beauty did perceive.
I wished that I could never leave."
The lord Gawain replied, "Of course,

your thought was neither crude nor coarse,
but rather, courteous and refined,
and anyone who took your mind   4460
from it must be a brutish man.
I'd like to know, sir, what you plan
to do next, for if you agreed,
I would be very glad to lead
the way back to the court and king."
"But first, you must tell me one thing,
my dear friend," answered Perceval.
"Is Kay at court, the seneschal?"
"Yes, Kay is at the court, that's true.
He was just jousting here with you,   4470
and if you have not heard it, Kay
has broken his right arm to pay,
and dislocated his collarbone."
"Then I believe his fall has shown
that I have well avenged the maid.
The blow he struck has been repaid."
When Sir Gawain grasped what he meant,
he started with astonishment.
"God save me, sir, I must declare
our king has sought you everywhere.   4480
I must ask, sir: what is your name?"
"Sir, Perceval. I ask the same,
what is your name?" "Sir, be apprised
that I was given, when baptized,
the name Gawain." "Gawain?" "Yes, sir."
The youth could not be happier.
"I've heard so much of you from men
in many places I have been.
I greatly wish, sir, that we two
become friends, if you wish it too."   4490
The lord Gawain replied, "Why, yes,
our friendship would not please me less
than it would you, but rather, more."
So Perceval replied, "Therefore
I shall be glad to go with you;
it would be right for me to do.
My word, I'll go wherever you deem
that I should go, for I esteem
myself more highly, I contend,
now that I have become your friend."   4500

The knights went forward to embrace,
and then they started to unlace
helms, ventails, coifs, their heads to bare,
and pulled the mail down from their hair,
and left rejoicing. At the sight,
the squires who witnessed their delight
ran from the outpost where they stood,
and went as quickly as they could,
and came before the king again.
"Sire, sire, it's true, the lord Gawain   4510
has brought the knight, and they express
the greatest joy and happiness."
Then everybody left his tent
who heard the squire's news, and went
to meet them without tarrying.
Then Kay said to his lord the king,
"Sire, now the honors appertain
to your own nephew, Sir Gawain.
I think the fight in which he starred
must have been dangerous and hard;   4520
and I would never tell a lie,
for he's returned as hale and spry
and sound of limb as when he went.
So it is more than evident
that he did not receive one blow,
nor did he give one to his foe.
He uttered no defiant word;
let praise and glory be conferred;
let men proclaim that he has won
what other knights could not have done,   4530
despite our efforts and our might."
So Kay spoke, whether wrong or right,
the way it was his wont to speak.
The lord Gawain, who did not seek
to bring his comrade armed to court,
where weaponless he should report,
had him disarmed within his tent.
His private chamberlain was sent
to draw a garment from a coffer,
so that the lord Gawain could offer   4540
the robe to Perceval to wear.
When he was well dressed in a fair
surcoat and cloak and looking grand,

the pair proceeded hand in hand
to meet the king, before his tent.
The lord Gawain said, "I present
the very person, sire, whom you,
and I believe this statement true,
would have been very glad to know
not more than fourteen days ago,   4550
the man you said was on your mind,
the very man you went to find,
is this same man, whom I now bring."
"Thank you, dear nephew," said the king,
who showed his thankfulness to meet
the pair by rising to his feet.
He said, "Be welcome here, dear sir.
Please say what name you would prefer."
"My lord the king, I will not hide
my name, sire," Perceval replied,   4560
"my name is Perceval of Wales."
"Oh, Perceval, whatever prevails,
my dear friend, now that you have come,
I would not have you journey from
my court again, now you've returned.
Since first you came, I've been concerned
about you, for I did not know
the recompense God would bestow
on you and your high destiny.
The fool and maiden could foresee   4570
your fate and told my courtiers all,
when struck by Kay the seneschal
with the hard blows that he inflicted.
You have done all that they predicted,
and in a way no one could doubt
who recently had heard about
the knightly exploits you performed."
The queen appeared at that, informed
of news about the newcomer,
and after Perceval saw her   4580
and found out who she was, and after
the maid who broke out into laughter
when he had looked upon her face
came in as well and found her place,
then Perceval stepped forth meet them
and said these words to them, to greet them,

"Of all the ladies, God confer
great honor and great joy on her
who is most beautiful and best,
as all who see her will attest,   4590
and all who've seen her can aver."
"And you are more than welcome, sir,"
the queen said, "as a knight high-rated
whose prowess has been demonstrated."
By this time Perceval had seen
the maid of honor of the queen,
who laughed when first she saw his face.
He greeted her, with an embrace.
"And should you be in need, fair maid,
I shall become the knight whose aid   4600
will never fail you in distress."
The maid expressed her gratefulness.

THE UGLY MAIDEN AND GUINGANBRESIL

The king and queen and barons all
    rejoiced at meeting Perceval
of Wales, who went back on the way
to Carlion with them that day.
They celebrated all night long
and all the next day, and the throng
rejoiced the third day through as well.
That day they saw a demoiselle*   4610
upon a tawny mule's back, and
she held a scourge in her right hand
and rode toward court. They saw the maid's
black hair was twisted in two braids,
and if we can believe the book's
description of this maiden's looks,
then you would never find so fell
a creature in or out of Hell.
No one has seen, in any lands,*
black iron like her face and hands,   4620
and nonetheless these features were

v. 4610 (4612, Roach edition). Loomis notes the resemblance between Chrétien's grailbearer and the Sovranty of Ireland, who appeared traditionally in both beautiful and ugly forms. Although Chrétien established no link between the lovely grailbearer and the ugly maiden except their mutual knowledge of Perceval's silence, two continuations, *Peredur* and *Perlesvaus*, present them as the same person, based upon a common, remote source (*The Grail: From Celtic Myth to Christian Symbol*, pp. 49 ff). Frappier notes (*Chrétien de Troyes et le Mythe du Graal*, p. 144) that Chrétien's romance differs from its Celtic source in that the ugly maiden is an exteriorized image of Perceval's guilty conscience. She accuses him, she stresses his responsibility for the disasters to come, and she tells him that his failure cannot be corrected; the lost opportunity will never come again. Frappier notes that the mule's tawny color "fauve" was considered to be a symbol of deceit and ill omen and postulates that the ugly maiden may be trying to deceive or test Perceval by saying that the quest is hopeless (p. 142). Hilka notes (*Der Percevalroman*, p. 712) that a maid in disarray riding a tawny mule and whipping it appears in *Lancelot*, vs. 2781 ff. (Roques edition), among other references.

vs. 4619 ff (4618, Roach edition). Hilka notes (*Der Percevalroman*, p. 713) that there are parallels between the description of the Ugly Maiden and the Giant Herdsman in *Yvain*, vs. 292 ff., particularly since both are hunchbacks and have catlike noses. The messenger's exclusion of the hero from her greeting also occurs in *Yvain*, v. 2720 (Roques edition).

less ugly than the rest of her.
Her eyes were tiny holes; those eyes
were small as any rat's in size.
Cat-like or ape-like was her nose,
whereas her lips were more like those
of ox or ass, and when she spoke,
the maiden's teeth looked like egg yolk,
they were so deep a yellow shade,
and like a billy-goat, the maid   4630
was bearded, and a hump had grown
up from her chest, a bent backbone,
her shoulders and her hips were fine
to open balls! With hunchbacked spine,
the maiden's haunches seemed to be
like twisted wands of willow tree.
A perfect choice to lead the dance!
The maiden made her mule advance,
and no such maiden of this sort
was ever seen in royal court!   4640
She hailed the king and barons all,
with one exception, Perceval,
and him alone she left ungreeted.
Upon her tawny mule's back, seated,
she said, "Oh, Perceval, you'll find
that Fortune's head is bald behind,*
although a forelock hangs before.
A curse on him who greets you or
who hopes you're well or any better;
you'd not seize Fortune when you met her.   4650
You went inside the dwelling place
of the Fisher King; before your face
the bleeding lance came passing by.
You found it was too hard to try
to open up your mouth and speak.
You could not ask why, from the peak
of the white lance's point, that drop
of blood came springing from its top,
and when you saw the grail, in turn,

---

vs. 4646–4647. Hilka notes (*Der Percevalroman*, p. 715) several references for this description of the personified Goddess Fortune, among them *Disticha Catonis* I, 22, 2 (in *Phaedrus*, 5, 8): "fronte capillata, post est Occasio calva."

you did not ask or try to learn   4660
what nobleman was being served.
Unlucky he who has observed
exceptionally clement weather
and waits for better, altogether
unlucky, and that is your plight.
You saw the time and place were right
for asking, yet were taciturn.
You had a perfect chance to learn
but kept still in an evil hour.
If only you had had the power,   4670
the rich king, who is so afflicted,
would have been healed and, unrestricted,
would hold his land in peace and reign;
land he will never hold again.
Do you know what we must withstand,
if the king cannot hold his land
and for his wounds obtains no cure?
The married women will endure
their husband's deaths, lands will be wrecked,
and orphaned maids will live abject,   4680
with many deaths among the knights,
calamities and other plights,
and you will be the one to blame."
The maid turned to the king to claim,
"Don't be displeased, king, I must leave,
because tonight I must receive
my food and lodgings far from here.
I don't know if you've chanced to hear
of Castle Orgulous before:
by nightfall I must reach its door.   4690
There are within the castle wall
five hundred sixty-six knights, all
famed warriors of proven worth,
each with his lady, of high birth,
polite and fair, of noble station.
I'm giving you this information,
since nobody can reach that castle
without a jousting match or battle.
The knight who'd do bold deeds and fair
won't lack them if he seeks them there.   4700
The knight who seeks the greatest fame
the world around, for him I'll name

the place, the strip of land within it,
where such a warrior could win it,
if there is anyone who'd dare.
Upon the hill at Montesclaire
is a besieged, beleaguered maid,
and were a knight to bring her aid
and save her, when the siege was raised,
he would be honored, highly praised, 4710
and could, in safety, gird the Sword
with the Strange Hangings, if the Lord
allowed and showed him such compliance."
At that, the maid resumed her silence,
for she had said all that she pleased.
She left court, when her words had ceased,
and did not tell them any more.
The lord Gawain leapt up and swore
that he would go to Montesclaire
and strive to save the maiden there. 4720
Then Giflet said, the son of Do,
so help him God, that he would go
to find the Castle Orgulous.
"I'll travel to Mount Dolorous,"
Kahedin said, "which I will climb.
I will not rest a single time."
But Perceval, unlike the knights;*
said that he would not lodge two nights
in one place, nor would he arrange
to bypass any passage strange 4730
of which he heard, nor fail to fight
in combat when he met a knight
who claimed that he was best, and dare
even to fight against a pair,
until he learned about the grail
and whom they served with it, nor fail
for any suffering or mischance,

---

v. 4727. Frappier notes (*Chrétien de Troyes et le Mythe du Graal*, p. 145) that Perceval's choice of the quest of the grail is the sublime moment of the romance. The choice proves the freedom of the hero by allowing him to reject the consequences of his failure. Summing up Perceval's development at this point, Frappier comments that: "No uneasiness of a spiritual nature troubles his soul; he shows no sign of repentance; the Ugly Maiden has made no allusion to his sin against his mother, and he himself does not think of God" (p. 148).

until he found the bleeding lance,
until at last the truth was said,
and he discovered why it bled.   4740
When they had promised what they chose,
then up to fifty knights arose
to give the other knights their word,
for any adventure of which they heard,
that they would seek it out first hand,
though it lay in a cruel land.
While they made ready, one and all,
and armed themselves throughout the hall,
Guinganbresil came through the door*
and entered the great hall; he bore   4750
a shield of gold, and on its field
a band of azure crossed the shield.
The blue band occupied a space
that filled one third of the shield's face.
The knight Guinganbresil, who knew
the king, hailed him as was his due,
but did not greet Gawain, whom he
accused instead of treachery.
He said, "Gawain, you brought about
my lord's death, killing him without   4760
a word of challenge, to your shame.
You are dishonored and to blame;
now all these barons know the reason.
I am accusing you of treason;
I've uttered not one lying word."

v. 4749 (4747, Roach edition). Gawain's adventures are enlivened by an alliteration
of names beginning with "G": after being challenged by Guinganbresil, Gawain, riding
Gringalet, stays at Garin's house and eventually encounters Greoreas and the Guirome-
lant. Nitze and Williams (*Arthurian Names*, p. 281) cite Roland Smith's theory that the
etymon of the name Guinganbresil is the Irish *Find Bán Bresal* ("white, fair, contention"),
equating the Welsh *Gwyn Can Bresal* and the Breton *Guigan (Guegan) Bresal (Bresil)*.
Loomis's less accepted theory is that the name is a compound of the names Gui(n)gamor
and Bercilak (*Arthurian Tradition*, p. 485 ff). Loomis notes (p. 418) that there are par-
allels between the Guinganbresil-Escavalon episodes and the story of *Gawain and the
Green Knight*, in which "A strange knight, Bercilak, came bursting into Arthur's hall, is-
sued a challenge, and arranged a rendezvous with Gawain for a different place and a
later date; Gawain set out amid the lamentations of the courtiers, was welcomed at the
castle of his challenger, and was tempted by his beautiful hostess during her husband's
absence on the chase."

The lord Gawain, when he had heard
the warrior's words of accusation,
rose to his feet in indignation.
His brother, Agravain the Proud,
leaped up, and pulled him back, and vowed,   4770
"Sir, don't disgrace your line and name!
I will defend you from the shame
with which this knight is covering you.
I promise you I shall so do."
"I must defend my own name, brother,
not be defended by another,"
said Sir Gawain, "so it must be,
since he accuses none but me.
If only I could bring to mind
a single deed of any kind   4780
that I had done to wrong this knight,
then I would sue for peace outright,
and I would make the knight amends
determined by our sets of friends.
His words are wholly out of hand.
I will accept his challenge and
defend my honor anywhere
he chooses, whether here or there."
In forty days, not one day later,
the knight would prove him a foul traitor   4790
before the King of Escavalon,
far handsomer than Absalom;*
so, said the knight, was his opinion.
"I'll follow you to his dominion,"
the lord Gawain assured the knight,
"there we shall see which one is right."
At once Guinganbresil went back.
The lord Gawain began to pack
so he could follow in due course.
Each knight, who had a good, sound horse,   4800
good lance, or helmet, or a sword,

v. 4792. The expression "handsomer than Absalom" refers to King David's son Absalom, who rose up in rebellion against his father and was slain. He is described in 2 Samuel 14:25: "But in all Israel there was none to be so much praised as Absalom for his beauty: from the sole of his foot even to the crown of his head there was no blemish in him." Hilka notes (*Der Percevalroman*, p. 720), that Erec is compared to Absalom (*Erec and Enide*, v. 2210, Roques edition).

offered to lend it to the lord,
but Sir Gawain declined each loan
and only took what was his own:
two shields, and seven mounts to ride,
and seven squires at his side.
Before the lord Gawain departed,
the lamentation for him started,
and many a beaten breast, pulled tress,
and clawed face showed profound distress.   4810
The most discreet and dignified
of ladies grieved for him and cried.
The courtiers raised loud lament
for Sir Gawain before he went.
You'll hear me tell at greater length
about the trials and tests of strength
and fine adventures that he found.

THE MAID WITH LITTLE SLEEVES

A t first he saw, on open ground,
a band of knights in armature
who made their way across the moor.   4820
One squire was following the band,
a Spanish steed led in right hand,
a shield hung round his neck. "Oh, squire,"
the lord Gawain stopped to inquire,
"who leads those knights who just went by?"
to which the squire made this reply,
"Sir, Meliant de Lis, the bold."*
"Are you of Meliant's household?"
"No, sir, I am with Droes d'Aves,
as good as Meliant, no less."   4830
"What, Droes d'Aves? I know him well.
Where is he going? You must tell."
"Sir, to a tournament commenced
by Meliant de Lis against
Sir Tiebaut of Tintagel and*
I think you ought to take a stand
beside the knights in that redoubt
against the knights who are without."
Said Sir Gawain, "I am amazed,
Was Meliant de Lis not raised   4840
in Tiebaut's household as his ward?"
"God save me, so he was, my lord.
His sire was Tiebaut's trusted friend,
and on his deathbed, at the end,
since he held Tiebaut very dear,
he gave his son to him to rear.
So Tiebaut brought up Meliant
with every care that he could want.
Then he sought Tiebaut's daughter's love.

v. 4827 (4825, Roach edition). Hilka notes (*Der Percevalroman*, p. 721) that Meliant de Lis is mentioned in *Erec and Enide*, v. 1678 (Roques edition).

v. 483.5. Hilka notes (*Der Percevalroman*, p. 721) that Tintagel is mentioned in *Erec and Enide*, vs. 1909, 6460, and 6470 (Roques edition). The castle in Cornwall no longer seems to be associated with King Arthur or King Mark.

She answered she would not dream of   4850
according love to a mere squire,
so Meliant, filled with desire,
became a knight immediately
and came back to resume his plea.
'No, you will never find a way
to win my love until the day
that you will joust in front of me
and do such feats of chivalry,'
the maid made her demands precise,
'so that my love comes high in price,   4860
for things that you can get for free*
can never taste as savorously
as things for which you have to pay.
If you would win my love one day,
then ask my father to consent
to fight you in a tournament.
I must be sure that my affection
is not misplaced.' In such subjection
does Love hold people in its sway,
they never dare to disobey   4870
whatever Love deigns to command.
He yielded to the maid's demand
and undertook the tournament.
My lord, you would be negligent,
should you not take the castle's side.
If you are willing to provide
help for Tintagel, Tiebaut's court
has every need of your support."
"You have a lord you should pursue!
Go, brother, that's enough from you!   4880
Tend to your duties toward your master."
The squire departed all the faster,
and Sir Gawain rode without pause
straight toward Tintagel town, because
the castle could not be bypassed.
Within it Tiebaut had amassed
his cousins, relatives, and kin,

vs. 4861 ff. Haidu notes (*Aesthetic Distance*, pp. 204-205) that Gawain expresses a
similar sentiment in *Yvain*, vs. 2518-2520 (Roques edition) about small pleasures tasting
sweeter with delay.

and he had called his neighbors in.
They had assembled, one and all,
the young and old and great and small.   4890
His closest counselors, forthright,
persuaded Tiebaut not to fight
against his lord; they feared he meant
their downfall by the tournament.
So Meliant could be forestalled,
Sir Tiebaut had closed up and walled
each entrance way into the town.
The doors were sealed and weighted down
so firmly with hard stones and mortar
that they required no other porter.   4900
A little postern gate concealed
the only entrance left unsealed.
The doorway was not made of glass:
this door, through which the knights could pass,
would stand forever, and was made
of copper, with a bar, overlaid
with all the iron a cart could bear.
The lord Gawain had to go there
or else turn back; no other way
was less than seven leagues away.   4910
He headed toward the door, and went
with all of his accoutrement,
but found it closed and turned to face
a meadow at the tower's base,
enclosed by pointed stakes, where he
dismounted underneath a tree
and hung his shields upon the oak.
When many of the castlefolk
had started making loud lament
about the coming tournament,   4920
because the hour was drawing near,
they saw the lord Gawain appear.
There was a gentleman in town,
through lands and birth of great renown,
old, powerful, and well respected,
and nothing that this man directed,
whatever might be his decision,
was treated with the least derision.
When first he sighted Gawain's group,
and long before the little troop   4930

went in the field by stakes surrounded,
he went to Tiebaut and expounded,
"God save me, sir, I can report
I saw two knights of Arthur's court.
I think that they are coming here;
that is the way it would appear.
Two brave men are significant,
for one could win a tournament.
So the decision I have made
is we can tourney unafraid,   4940
for you have knights of high repute,
good men, and archers who can shoot
the horses of our rival's troop,
for I am certain they will group
before this gate and fight outside.
If they are brought to it by pride,
the victory is ours to claim,
and theirs will be defeat and shame."
So Tiebaut, following this plan,
permitted every able man   4950
to arm himself and go and fight,
if he desired, and every knight
was filled with joy in heart and mind.
The squires went running off to find
the steeds and saddles and prepare
the arms that would be needed there.
The ladies and the maidens went
on high to watch the tournament.
The ladies saw across the plain
the gear and steeds of Sir Gawain,   4960
and at first sight the ladies thought
that there must be two knights who brought
the pair of shields they saw which swung
upon the oak where they were hung.
We're born beneath a lucky star,
they thought, since they had climbed so far
to see whatever might be there,
to have a chance to watch a pair
of warriors arm themselves instead.
So some supposed, but others said,   4970
"Sweet Heaven! This knight has large amounts
of weapons, provender, and mounts,
so much he has enough for two.
Whatever will this warrior do

with two shields, since he is alone?
No other knight that we have known
has borne two shields instead of one."
While they discussed what he had done
and wondered why a knight would carry
two shields if he were solitary,   4980
for their astonishment was great,
the knights went riding out the gate.
The maid who sought the tournament,
Sir Tiebaut's elder daughter, went
up in the tower and stood on high.
The elder girl was followed by*
the younger, fashionably dressed
with narrow sleeves. She was addressed
as "Maid with Little Sleeves," so tight
her sleeves seemed painted at first sight.*   4990
The maids and ladies in a band
with Tiebaut's daughters, went to stand
high in the tower, looking down.
Before the great wall round the town
the foes were gathering to fight.
There was no handsomer a knight
than Meliant de Lis outside,
and so his sweetheart testified
to everyone who was around,
"My ladies, I have never found,   5000
and I would never tell you lies,
a knight as pleasing to the eyes
as Meliant de Lis can be.
If he is dressed so splendidly
(do you not find it a delight
to look at such a handsome knight?)
he must ride beautifully and wield
with greatest skill both lance and shield."

vs. 4986 ff. Frappier notes (*Chrétien de Troyes et le Mythe du Graal*, p. 222) that the rivalry between the two daughters of Tiebaut of Tintagel is similar to the quarrel between the two daughters of the Lord of the Black Thorn in *Yvain*.

v. 4990. Haidu observes that: "The fashion was for sleeves worn very tight as far as the wrist. She exaggerates this by omitting the usual puffed cuffs and tightening the sleeves so much that they seem "written" or "painted" on her arms" (*Aesthetic Distance*, p. 207, fn: Baist's comment, quoted by Hilka, note to line 4990, *Der Percevalroman*, p. 723). Frappier notes that sleeves were removable and were sewn on each time a garment was worn. Knights often carried a sleeve in tournaments in honor of the maid or lady from whom they received it (*Chrétien de Troyes et le Mythe du Graal*, p. 220).

Her sister, sitting next to her,
said there was one knight handsomer.   5010
The elder rose, infuriated,
to strike the girl for what she stated,
but all the ladies of her train
stopped her and held her, to restrain
the elder maid from striking her,
which made her even angrier.
The tournament began thereto,
and many lances snapped in two,
and many sword blows fell, and many
brave knights collapsed. Believe me, any   5020
who fought with Meliant de Lis
paid dearly and came seeking peace.
All knights who faced his lance soon found
themselves upon the stony ground.
If his lance broke, he drew his sword
and dealt great blows with it; the lord
was a fine fighter who outvied
the warriors on either side.
His sweetheart was so overjoyed,
this outburst she could not avoid,   5030
"You ladies will not see or hear
of any youth who is his peer.
He's marvellous; he is the best.
He is not only handsomest,
but better, in a joust or fight,
than any other warring knight."
The little sister said, "I see
a better, finer man than he."
The elder sister of the maid
came up and started to upbraid   5040
the little maiden, and, inflamed,
"You brat, how dare you," she exclaimed,
"for your misfortune, be so bold
to fault a man whom I've extolled?
You little wench, you must be crazed
to criticize when I have praised.
Now take this slap from me and guard
your tongue next time!" She slapped so hard,*

v. 5048. The slap that the older sister gives the Maid with Little Sleeves is a double for
the slap that Kay gives the maid who laughed (v. 1050).

her fingers left their mark in streaks
which showed up clearly on her cheeks.   5050
The ladies who were there that day
reproachfully pulled her away,
and then began to speak again
among themselves of Sir Gawain.
"Good Lord!" one of the maidens spoke,
"What keeps that knight beneath the oak?
Do you suppose his armor's lost?"
Another, more sarcastic, tossed,
"He made a vow he would not fight."
A third, "Don't tell me he's a knight!   5060
He is a merchant, and he leads
these mounts because he's selling steeds.
He's never heard of jousts or danger."
A fourth said, "He's a money changer
who'll give those poor young men who fought
those bags of money he has brought.
Don't you suppose I've told a lie;
he's gold and silverplate laid by
within those trunks he's brought along."
The little one said, "You are wrong;   5070
you've wicked tongues to be so quick
to say a merchant bears as thick
a lance as he is carrying.
You devils, saying such a thing!
It nearly kills me when I hear it.
By all I owe the Holy Spirit,
it's obvious that he is more
a jouster than a merchant or
a money changer; he's a knight."
The ladies said, "Perhaps he might   5080
look like one, but he's not, dear friend.
He's only trying to pretend
he is a knight, because his goal
is to avoid the tax or toll.
He is a fool who thinks he's wise,
because he doesn't realize
he will be taken and arrested
for common thieving," they attested,
"and in the end a rope will check
his cheating, hung around his neck!"   5090
The lord Gawain distinctly heard

these taunts and did not miss a word
the ladies said of him in blame.
He listened with distress and shame,
but he considered, and with reason,*
that since he was accused of treason
he had a prior obligation
to go defend his reputation,
lest he be thought dishonorable
and all his family as well.   5100
This fight had no significance,
he did not want to take the chance
of being taken prisoner
or being hurt, and did not stir,
although he longed to join the fray.
The knight could see, throughout the day,
the fighting grow more violent,
like Meliant de Lis, who sent
for bigger lances to strike harder.
The fight went on with growing ardor   5110
before the gate throughout the day.
The victors took the spoils away
for safekeeping at evenfall.
The ladies saw a bald squire, tall,
who had part of a lance's wreck
and wore a headstall round his neck.
One lady, silly and naive,
called, "Squire, God help me, I believe
you are a perfect idiot,
in this crush, to collect a lot   5120
of lance irons and bridle bits
and headstalls. Why, it ill befits
a man who calls himself a squire
to curb so sharply his desire
for spoils and plunder, and you seem
to hold yourself in low esteem.
Who will not profit when he can
must be a very foolish man.
I see in this field down below
not far from you, some things I know   5130
are valuable and undefended,

---

v. 5095. Gawain's explanation of his refusal to fight is repeated three times; see vs.
5190 and vs. 5309 ff.

and next to them is the most splendid
knight ever born: I have no doubt
that you could pull his whiskers out,
and even then he would not budge.
Don't take these paltry spoils they grudge
when you've an opportunity
to take those steeds and things we see,
for no one will contest your claim."
Across the field the squire came   5140
and started saying, as he hit
one of the steeds with his lance bit,
"Knight, tell me, are you hale and sound
to do no more than stand around,
and break no lance upon the field,
and put no holes into your shield?"
"Go to, why is it your concern?"
said Sir Gawain, "Perhaps you'll learn
the reason why I act this way,
but I swear it won't be today   5150
that I will deign to make it clear.
Go on your way, get out of here,
go back and do as you were told!"
The squire fled. None was so bold
to dare say one thing that offended
the lord Gawain. The fighting ended,
and many knights were captives, led
to prison, many steeds were dead.
Though the attackers of the town
displayed more courage and renown,   5160
yet the defenders won more loot.
They left with both sides resolute
to gather next day, as before,
upon the field and fight some more.
They parted as the sun went down,
and all the men who came from town
went back within its walls again;
upon their heels was Sir Gawain.
Before the castle gate, he met
the man who told his lord to let   5170
the fight and tournament begin.
And so, as Sir Gawain went in,
the most distinguished gentleman
asked Sir Gawain if he would plan

to stay with him, most graciously.
"Within this castle, sir," said he,
"your lodging place is all prepared.
You could stay with us, if you cared.
If you continue on your way
you'll find no proper place to stay,   5180
so I beseech you to remain."
"I thank you, sir," said Sir Gawain,
"I shall remain, I'm not adverse.
I have had offers that were worse."
The gentleman went to his dwelling
with Sir Gawain, and asked, while telling
of this and that, why, on that day,
he had not borne arms in the fray?
The lord Gawain told him the reason
was that he was accused of treason   5190
and greatly feared captivity
and any wound or injury
until he was exonerated.
If his arrival was belated,
and he did not appear on time
where he had been accused of crime
to fight and clear himself of blame,
his friends and he would live in shame.
The gentleman, with admiration,
said if the only explanation   5200
of his avoidance of the tourney
was not to risk a longer journey,
then he was more than justified.
He led the lord Gawain inside,
when they had gotten off their mounts.
The townspeople strove to denounce
the lord Gawain with bitterness.
They gathered in a crowd to press
their lord to have the knight arrested.
The elder sister, who detested   5210
her sister, worked with might and main
to bring disgrace on Sir Gawain.
"I well know, father, that today
you have lost nothing in the fray,
but I believe that you have won
more plunder than you think you've done,
and I will gladly tell you how.

You've only to give orders now
for someone to arrest that knight.
The lord who brought him here tonight   5220
won't dare to come to his defense;
he lives by cheating and pretense.
He has brought shields, and lances, and
war horses led in the right hand,
and has these trappings in plain sight
so he will seem to be a knight
(and be exempt from tolls and fares
while he goes peddling his wares).
Now punish him for what he's done.
He is at Garin's, Bertain's son,   5230
who lodged him underneath his roof.
He just went in, and I have proof:
I saw his host lead him inside."
And so the elder sister tried
to see the lord Gawain disgraced.
The lord got on his horse in haste
to go in person to the dwelling
of which his daughter had been telling,
where Sir Gawain had been invited.
Now, when the younger daughter sighted   5240
her sire, who sought the visitor,
she slipped away through a back door,
not to be seen by anyone,
and sped to Garin, Bertain's son,
the man who wished to entertain
and lodge his guest the lord Gawain.
It happened Garin had a pair
of daughters who were very fair.
They saw their little lady come,
and they began rejoicing from   5250
deep in their hearts: one on each side,
they took her hands and went inside.
They were rejoicing to the skies
and kissing her on mouth and eyes.
Then Garin, far from indigent,
remounted, and away he went
with his son Herman at his side.
The two of them began to ride
to court in order to confer
as usual with their seigneur.   5260

Instead, they met him in the street.
The gentleman began to greet
the lord and asked him where he went.
The lord said, for some merriment,
that he had come to pay a call.
Said Garin, "Well, that's not at all
displeasing, quite the contrary!
Come to my house, and you can see
the finest knight the world has known."
"That is not why I came, I own;   5270
I came to order his arrest.
He is a merchant, they attest,
who's selling horses in knight's guise."
"Not so! That is a pack of lies!
You are my lord and I your man,"
retorted Garin, "but I plan
to leave your service. Better I
and all my family defy
your lordship than endure this slur
you've brought against my dwelling, sir!"   5280
The lord said, "That's not what I meant,
so help me God! I am intent
on honoring your house and guest;
I promise I will do my best,
and I can tell you, I am scorning
the counsel I received in warning."
"I thank you," said the gentleman,
"I'm deeply honored that you plan
to come with me and see my guest."
They turned their mounts around and pressed   5290
along the street, so they could ride
back to his dwelling side by side.
The lord and gentleman once more
rode on until they reached the door.
Within the house, the lord Gawain
had taken lodgings with his train.
When Sir Gawain, who was well bred,
caught sight of them, he rose and said,
"Be welcome." The two men replied
and sat themselves down at his side.   5300
The worthy liege lord of the land
turned to the newcome warrior and
at once he asked the lord Gawain

why he had chosen to refrain
from fighting that day, as he ought.
Why had he come and then not fought?
The lord Gawain could see his case
but added it was no disgrace,
and then he told the lord the reason:
a knight was charging him with treason,   5310
so he was going to appear
at a king's court, where he would clear
his name in combat at his trial.
The lord replied, "Without denial,
it's an excuse and no disgrace.
Where is the battle to take place?"
"My duty, sir, is to go on
and find the king of Escavalon."
"I'll have some of my men escort
your party to that ruler's court,"   5320
the lord said, "Since you will be sure
to pass through wretched lands and poor,
I'll give you provender in packs
and steeds to bear them on their backs."
However Sir Gawain declined,
and told the lord, if he could find
supplies for sale, wherever he went,
he would have ample nourishment,
good lodgings, all that he required,
so there was nothing he desired.   5330
The lord rose with the matter cleared,
and then his little girl appeared,
seized Sir Gawain around the leg,
and started to beseech and beg,
"Dear sir, please listen to me, do.
I've come here to appeal to you
about my sister, for she hit
and slapped me, as she will admit.
Win justice for me, sir, please try."
The lord Gawain did not reply;   5340
he put his hand upon her head,
not sure to whom these words were said.
The maid tugged at his leg again.
"I'm talking to you, I complain
to you about my sister, sir.
I have no further love for her.

She shamed me on account of you."
"My lovely girl, what can I do?
Say what redress I can obtain,"
was the reply of Sir Gawain.   5350
Though at the door, the worthy lord
heard what his younger girl implored;
he had already said good-bye.
"Daughter, who said to come and cry
before this knight?" he questioned her.
The lord Gawain said, "My dear sir,
is she your daughter?" "Yes, indeed,
but you must pay her words no heed;
she's nothing but a silly child."
The lord Gawain said, "I'd be styled   5360
discourteous, did I not learn
what she is seeking in return.
Sweet, noble child, what can I do?
What justice can I win for you?
How can I take revenge on her?"
"For love of me, if you please, sir,
tomorrow only, do consent
to bear arms in the tournament."
The lord Gawain said, "Tell me, dear,
have you once asked a chevalier   5370
to do a deed of your invention?"
"Not once, sir." "Please pay no attention
to what she tells you is the matter;
don't listen to her silly chatter,"
the lord advised. "God grant me aid,
I think, for such a little maid,
she's spoken with such dignity,
I never could refuse her plea.
So, as she wishes, I will fight
tomorrow and will be her knight   5380
a short while," Sir Gawain avowed.
The maid said, with such joy, she bowed
down to her feet, "Dear sir, thank you."
They parted without more ado.
Sir Tiebaut placed his little daughter
upon his palfrey's neck and brought her
homewards, and asked what she had done,
and why the quarrel had begun.
The little maiden did not fail

to tell her father the whole tale   5390
from its beginning to its ending.
"My lord, my sister was contending
that Meliant de Lis could best
all knights and was the handsomest.
I didn't like her saying so.
This knight was in the field below;
I could not keep from telling her
I'd seen a knight far handsomer
than Meliant could claim to be.
My sister started calling me   5400
a stupid brat and slapped me hard,
and cursed be he who can regard
what she has done to me as fair.
I'd have my braids cut off, I swear,
right at my neck, close to my head,
to make me hideous," she said,
"if it would mean that, in the fray,
my champion would find a way
to strike down Meliant de Lis.
My lady sister's boasts would cease;   5410
she would be forced to change her tune;
she sang his praises night and noon,
and all the ladies are so bored!
Soft rain stills high wind!" Said the lord,*
"Dear daughter, now I shall decree,
since it would be a courtesy,
that you send him some token of
your admiration and your love:
send him a sleeve or else a wimple."
The maid, whose ways were very simple,   5420
responded, "Since you tell me so,
I'll gladly send him one, although
my sleeves are cut so small and tight,
if I dare send one to the knight,
he might not value it one bit."
"Dear daughter, let me see to it.
I'll give it thought, and with good will,"

---

v. 5414. The proverb, "Soft rain stills high wind," is often interpreted to mean that it
does not take much to calm violent rage. Hilka notes (*Der Percevalroman*, p. 725) that the
proverb is listed in Morawski, *Proverbes français* no. 100: "A petite pluie chiet granz
venz"; no. 506: "De grant venz petite pluie"; and no. 1624: "Petite pluie abat grant vent."

the lord responded, "now be still."
Conversing with her as he went,
he held her and was well content   5430
to hug and hold his daughter more,
until he reached his palace door.
But when the older girl beheld
her father and the maid he held,
with bitterness her heart was laden.
"Where has my sister been, the Maiden
with Little Sleeves? Sir, I believe
she has a few tricks up her sleeve;
she's learning young. Where have you sought her?"
"What business is it of yours, daughter?   5440
You'd best be silent; she is far
more of a lady than you are.
You pulled her braids and slapped her face,
which I believe was a disgrace;
it's put me in an angry mood.
I think you were extremely rude."
The elder daughter was ashamed
about the way her father blamed
her actions and was badly shaken.
The lord had crimson samite taken   5450
out of a trunk, and on his own
he had the fabric cut and sewn
to make a sleeve, both long and wide.
He called his daughter to his side.
"Now, daughter, do as I advise.
Tomorrow morning you must rise
and find the knight ere he can leave,
and you must give him this new sleeve
as a love token: he'll consent
to bear it in the tournament."   5460
The maid replied before daybreak
she would be sure to be awake,
and to be washed and well attired.
Her father, at these words, retired.
To do the bidding of the lord,
the joyful little maid implored
all her companions to keep
close watch lest she should oversleep,
for they must wake her right away
when first they saw the light of day,   5470

if they loved her, and once they heard,
the maid's companions gave their word.
As soon as they could see a ray
of sunlight, early in the day,
the moment that the bright dawn broke,
they dressed the maiden, whom they woke.
All by herself, the little maid
went to where Sir Gawain had stayed,
but though she was so early come,
he had arisen and gone from   5480
his lodgings to the church to hear
the mass, which they were chanting clear.
For a long time the maiden stayed
at Garin's dwelling, while they prayed
and heard all that there was to hear.
She jumped up when the men drew near
and finally came back again.
The maiden met the lord Gawain
and hurried to his side to say,
"God grant you honor, sir, this day   5490
and keep you in security.
Please carry, out of love for me,
this sleeve that I am holding here."
"Most willingly, thank you, my dear,"
said Sir Gawain. At once each knight
put on his armor for the fight
and went outside the castle wall.
Another time the maidens all
climbed with the ladies of the town
up to the high walls; looking down,   5500
they saw the strong, bold knights, in groups,
outside assembling their troops.
Before the rest, far in the lead,
was Meliant de Lis: with speed
he hurtled toward his foes combined
and left his comrades far behind,
two arpents and one half away.
His sweetheart could not help but say —
she found she simply could not hold
her tongue, to see her love so bold —   5510
"Oh, ladies, you must come and see:
he is the flower of chivalry,
the lord of knights!" the maiden cried.

The lord Gawain began to ride
as fast as war horse could convey him
at Meliant, which did not dismay him;
he broke his lance on Sir Gawain.
Then Meliant crashed to the plain,
as Sir Gawain dealt him a blow
that caused severest pain and woe   5520
and seized his war horse by the rein.
A squire came up, and Sir Gawain
told him the war horse should be brought
back to the maid for whom he fought.
He sent her the first thing he won,
now that the jousting was begun.
The squire led the saddled steed
up to the maiden, who, indeed
watched Meliant de Lis's fall
from a window in the tower wall.   5530
She said, "Look, sister, at the sight!
See Meliant de Lis, the knight
whom you were praising to the skies!
Upon the battlefield he lies.
Give credit only where it's due.
I've proven what I said was true;
God save me, everyone can see
there is a better knight than he."
The maid deliberately teased
her sister, who grew so displeased,   5540
she was beside herself and swore,
"Shut up, you brat! Not one word more!
I'll slap you so hard with my hand,
you'll have no leg on which to stand!"
The maid said, "Sister, now you ought
to keep in mind what God has taught.
If I have spoken truthfully,
you should not dream of slapping me.
I saw the way your warrior fell,
and you have seen it just as well.   5550
By looking at him, I surmise
that he is still too stunned to rise!
You may be mad enough to burst,
but sister, I will tell you first
we all can see him lying there
and waving both feet in the air."

The elder sister, as she vowed,
provided that she was allowed,
might well have slapped the younger hard,
a blow the ladies present barred.   5560
The squire came riding over, and
he held the horse by his right hand.
He gave the maiden, who was still
seated beside the window sill,
the charger Meliant had ridden.
Before the little maid had bidden
her men to take the horse of war,
she'd thanked him sixty times and more,
which he conveyed to Sir Gawain.
He seemed most likely to attain   5570
the tourney's championship: in fact
each knight whom Sir Gawain attacked
with the lance blows that he employed
though skillful, left his stirrups void.
He never had been so intent
on winning steeds in tournament.
He gave four steeds as gifts that day,
won by his own hand in the fray.
He sent the first war horse he won
to the small maid; another one   5580
delighted his host's wife; the third
and fourth war horses he conferred
on his host's girls. The tournament
came to an end, and then he went
back with the prize for which he vied,
the finest knight on either side.
When Sir Gawain went from the fray,
it was not even yet midday,
but he went riding through the gate
with such a troop of knights, they state   5590
the town was filled up with the band,
who wished to know his native land
and asked him what might be his name.
The knights went with him as he came
directly back to Garin's door.
The Maid with Little Sleeves, before
he could dismount, came out to meet him.
She seized his stirrup and, to greet him,
the words the maiden uttered were,

"Five hundred thousand thanks, dear sir."   5600
And, knowing what she meant to say,
"Until I have grown old and gray,"
the lord Gawain said gallantly,
"dear maid, wherever I may be,
and it may be some distant land,
I'll ever be yours to command,
and never too far, if I learn
you need assistance, to return.
All my commitments I will leave
at the first message I receive."   5610
"My deepest thanks," replied the maid.
Her father came in next and prayed
the lord Gawain with all his might
to stay with them another night,
but first he asked him, when he came,
if he would care to tell his name.
The lord Gawain chose to excuse
himself from staying; "I refuse
no man who asks me to reveal
my name, which I do not conceal:*   5620
Gawain, my dear sir, is my name.
If I've not said it since I came,
the reason is that nobody
till now has asked my name of me."
The lord's heart filled with great delight
to learn what guest had spent the night:
none other than the lord Gawain.
The lord said, "Sir, please do remain
one more night as my guest and stay,
he urged the knight, "for yesterday   5630
I did not do enough for you.
I swear to you, I never knew
in my whole life, a warrior
whom I have wished to honor more."
So Garin urged him to remain
beneath his roof, but Sir Gawain
made all excuses he could find.

v. 5620 (5622, Roach edition). Hilka notes (*Der Percevalroman*, p. 727) that there is a
similar comment in *Yvain*, v. 6260 (Roques edition). In Chrétien de Troyes' romances Sir
Gawain never hides his identity, although he tends not to volunteer the information.

The maid, not silly or unkind,
seized the knight's foot, gave it a kiss,
and when she finished doing this,   5640
the child commended him to God.
The lord Gawain, who thought it odd,
asked her to tell him what she meant,
and so she told him her intent:
that she had kissed the knight's foot so,
in every place that he might go,
he always would recall her face.
He said, "When I have left this place,
I won't forget you, my dear friend,
so put your doubting to an end,   5650
if God will grant me help and aid."
When he had spoken with the maid,
he left his host and all folk there,
commending them to Heaven's care,
whereby they might be safely kept.

ESCAVALON

The lord Gawain, that evening, slept
in a grange close to a monastery*
and had all that was necessary.
Next morning, early in the day,
he started riding on his way,   5660
until he found that he was gazing
upon a herd of wild deer, grazing
outside a forest on the border.
Then Yvonet stopped at his order
(he led one of the steeds, the best,
and held a huge, stiff lance at rest.)
The lord Gawain told Yvonet
to give the lance to him to set,
and make the saddle girth more tight.
He'd mount the steed held at his right   5670
and have the palfrey led away.
So Yvonet, without delay,
turned over to the lord Gawain
the huge lance and the horse's rein.
He chased the does, and dodged, and spun,*
until he caught a pure white one
beside a thornbush, so in check,
he laid his lance across her neck.
The doe fled, leaping like a stag.
The lord Gawain, who did not lag,   5680
pursued the deer with might and main
and nearly caught her once again,
when his horse cast a shoe complete
right off of one of his forefeet.
His master noticed, as he went
in search of his accoutrement,

v. 5657. Hilka notes (*Der Percevalroman*, p. 727) that an *obediance* was an estate or grange belonging to or dependent upon a monastery.

v. 5675. The hunting of white or fairy animals is often associated with a love adventure in Chrétien's romances (see Bezzola, *Le Sens de l'Aventure*, pp. 94 ff). Chrétien's first romance, *Erec and Enide*, begins with the hunt of the white stag (Haidu, *Aesthetic Distance*, pp. 212-213).

his charger's gait was growing crimped
and worried, wondering why he limped.
He thought perhaps the cause could be
he'd struck his foot against a tree.   5690
The lord Gawain called Yvonet
and told him to dismount and set
to caring for the hobbling steed;
his limp had grown severe indeed.
The squire did as he was bidden,
went to the horse his lord had ridden,
raised his lame leg, and looked, and knew
he limped because he'd lost a shoe.
"Your horse must be reshod," he said,
"we'll simply have to go ahead,   5700
and slowly, lest we overdo him,
until some farrier can reshoe him."
They went on, very much slowed down,
and saw men coming from a town,
a party ready for the hunt.
The men in short clothes were in front;
young men on foot with hounds to lead,
and then the hunters did proceed   5708
and brought the arrows and the bows;   5711
and then the knights went past in rows;   5712
the party ended with a pair
of knights upon two chargers fair.
One was a young man, handsomest,
of higher rank than all the rest.
He was the one man in that band
to greet the lord and take his hand.
He said, "Stop, sir, let me detain you.
Dismount and let us entertain you!   5720
Today is both the time and season,
if you agree, to find a reason
to break your journey on the way
and find a place to lodge today.
I have a sister, most polite,
who'd make you welcome with delight.
This knight you see here at my side
will lead you back where I reside."
He told the knight, "Go, my dear friend,
and lead this lord whom I shall send   5730
to meet my sister. Say I greet her,

and that I order and entreat her,
for love and for the loyalty
I feel for her and she for me,
that if she's ever loved a knight,
to cherish him, and to make quite
as much of him as she, on other
occasions, would for me, her brother.
Tell her she must amuse the lord
and keep him from becoming bored,   5740
until we have come back again.
When she begins to entertain
the knight and seats him at her side,
join us as fast as you can ride,
because, as early as I can,
I will return to see the man
and I will keep him company."
The knight left to accompany
the lord Gawain back to a place
where none had ever seen his face,   5750
but he was hated mortally.
He did not know that this could be,
so in this case his guard was down.
The lord Gawain looked at the town
placed high above the ocean's arm.
The town feared no assault nor harm;
the walls and tower were so strong.
The knight saw, as he rode along,*
the whole town filled with men well clad,
draped tables money changers had,   5760
who dealt with silver, coins, and gold,
and crafts diverse and manifold
were exercised by workmen skilled
in streets and squares completely filled.
They made so many things for sale:
one helms, another coats of mail,
plus saddle makers, blazoners,
makers of bridles, bits, and spurs.
Some polished swords, and others fulled,
or wove, or combed, or sheared, or pulled   5770

v. 5758. This description of Gawain's entry into the prosperous seaport of Escavalon is
the opposite of the description of Perceval's entry into the besieged town of Belrepeire.

fine fabrics. Other men in town
were melting gold and silver down.
Some men made lovely, costly things,
enameled jewelry, buckles, rings,
cups, goblets, every kind of plate,
and so you can appreciate
it seemed each day that there were fairs,
with stalls displaying different wares
throughout its many streets: there were
both gray and spotted types of fur, 5780
wax, pepper, every kind of spice
and merchandise to buy or price.
The knights, though they did not acquire them,
at intervals stopped to admire them,
and went on till they reached the keep.
The squires met them with a leap
and took charge of the steeds and train.
The knight alone with Sir Gawain
went on into the tower, and
he led the knight in by the hand 5790
to the maid's room. "My lovely friend,
your brother orders me to send
his greetings to you and to say
he is directing you to pay
this knight all honor due his state.
He tells you not to hesitate,
but greet him with as much good cheer
as if you were his sister dear
or he your brother. Do your best
to please and entertain our guest; 5800
be generous and openhearted.
Plan what to do when I've departed
to join the hunters in the wood."
The maiden, promising she would,
replied with great joy, "Blessed be he
who's lent such handsome company!
Clearly he was not being hateful,
and so I am extremely grateful.
Dear sir, come sit beside me here,"
the maiden said, "Since you appear 5810
to be a handsome, noble guest,
and since my brother did request,
you shall enjoy, as was his plea,

the pleasure of my company."
At that the first knight turned away
and stayed with them no more that day.
He left behind the lord Gawain,
who certainly did not complain
of being left alone with her.
The lovely girl made no demur;   5820
sophisticated, full of charm,
she did not think there any harm
in being left to entertain
her guest alone. The lord Gawain
and she began to talk of love.
They'd waste their time by talking of
another topic! Sir Gawain
requested that the maiden deign
to grant her love. This pledge he'd give:
he'd be her knight while he should live.   5830
She did not say no; from the start
she granted him her mind and heart.
Meanwhile a gentleman surprised
the couple, and he recognized
the lord Gawain, unfortunately.
The maiden and the knight were greatly
enjoying themselves with a kiss.
The gentleman, who saw their bliss,
found that he could not hold his tongue.
"Shame on you, woman, shame!" he flung.*   5840
"May God confound you; you're disgraced
to let yourself be held, embraced,
and kissed, and cuddled, and caressed,
by him whom you should most detest!
Poor, foolish woman, good-for-naught,
you've done exactly as you ought,
but you should use your hands to wrest
and tear his heart out of his chest,

vs. 5840 ff. Haidu observes that: "Gawain and the sister of the King of Escavalon represent the conventions of a literary ethic and a mode of life codified by that ethic. The situation in which they were discovered was typical of that mode: the knight and lady, sitting by each other's side, exchanging vows of love and social compliments — this is half the *raison d'être* of the characters, the mode, the ethic. It is not only a couple which is under fire, but the conventional ethic according to which they were acting" (*Aesthetic Distance*, p. 218).

and not your mouth! Now, if your kisses
could reach down to the knight's heart, this is 5850
one way to pull it from his breast,
although I think you would do best
to use your hands to tear it out;
and so you should have done, no doubt.
Yet, if a woman did not sin,
you could not call her feminine.
Who hates the bad and loves the good
can't be called 'woman', for she would
be forfeiting her right to own
the name by loving good alone. 5860
I see you're a real woman too.
The man you're kissing, next to you,
has killed your father; he's at ease.
When women can do as they please,
they go too far and do not care."
He jumped back and rushed out of there
before the lord could say a word.
The maiden fainted, when she heard,
and lay some time on the paved floor.
The lord Gawain raised her once more; 5870
he was both furious and sad
about the fright that she had had.
When she revived at last, she said
to Sir Gawain, "Now we are dead!
I'll perish undeservedly
because of you and you for me,
for I am wholly positive
the vulgar, common folk who live
in town will storm the tower door.
There'll be ten thousand men and more 5880
outside this tower, that is clear.
Still, there are many weapons here;
I'll arm you now before the strife.
One brave man could defend his life
against an army from this tower."
Though far from calm at such an hour,
the maiden fetched the arms in haste.
When all the armor had been placed
on Sir Gawain, they felt secure,
but to his great discomfiture, 5890
he could not find a shield: instead

he picked a chessboard up and said,
"Dear, this is all I want to wield,
don't search for any other shield."
He spilled the chessman on the floor.
They were of ivory, ten times more
huge than most chessmen and more hard.
The lord Gawain thought he could guard
the entrance to the tower from
whoever might intend to come.   5900
He belted on Escalibor,
and it was far superior
to other swords, because it could
cut iron as if it were wood.*
Meanwhile the gentleman went down
and found some people of the town:
the mayor, and the aldermen,
the ordinary citizen,
and side by side these neighbors sat.
The townfolk were so sleek and fat,   5910
no purgatives had they been trying.
The gentleman ran toward them, crying,
"To arms, let's get traitor Gawain,
for by his hand our lord has slain!"
"Where is he, where?" the people cried.
"I've found him out," the man replied.
"Gawain the traitor, a proven one,
is in this tower having fun,
hugging our maiden, kissing her,
and she complies without demur.   5920
No, she responds and means to let him.
Come on now, and we'll go and get him!
To hand him over to my lord
would be a service: your reward
will be his deepest gratitude.
The traitor ought to be subdued
and treated roughly, but contrive
to carry off the knight alive.
My master would prefer him living:

v. 5904. Traditionally, Escalibor is King Arthur's sword but Chrétien specifically says
that Gawain borrowed nothing (vs. 4803–4804). Loomis notes that there is another tradi-
tion, included in the *Vulgate Merlin,* according to which King Arthur gave Escalibor to
his nephew when Gawain was knighted (*Arthurian Tradition,* p. 421).

a dead man can have no misgiving, 5930
for he has nothing left to fear.
Arouse the town, assemble here,
then go and do your duty, men."
At once the mayor arose, and then
the aldermen rose in a flurry.
You could have seen the oafs, in fury,
snatch up a pole ax, or an ax,
or strapless shield. Like maniacs,
for shields, the rabble picked up doors
or baskets from the threshing floors. 5940
The cryer cried the news throughout
the town, men gathered, bells rang out,
so nobody would stay behind.
The poorest fighters rushed to find
clubs, pitchforks, picks, or flails to lug.
To slaughter a defenseless slug,
they caused such uproar, you'd not see
its equal down in Lombardy.
The worst men gathered in that band
with weapons of some sort in hand. 5950
The lord Gawain would have been killed
without the help that God had willed.
Courageously enough, the maid
shrieked at the crowd, to bring him aid,
"Back, rabble, back, mad dogs, vile peasants!
Who in the devil sought your presence?
Whom have you come here to annoy?
May Heaven never grant you joy!
God help me, you won't interfere
or hurt the knight who is in here! 5960
God willing, he will leave, instead,
some of your number crushed and dead.
He came here by no secret way;
he did not fly in here today!
My brother sent him as a guest,
and I was strongly urged and pressed
to show this knight as much affection
as my own brother. What objection
can you have, if I gave the knight
companionship, joy and delight? 5970
He who would hear it, let him hear it.
I kept him joyful, full of spirit,

as I was bidden by my brother.
That was the reason, nothing other.
I never had a thought immoral,
so I despise you and your quarrel!
You acted most insultingly
by drawing out your swords at me
at my own door. Were you to try,
you could not say the reason why,   5980
for it is certain, if you knew it,
you have not told me why you do it!
You make me angry and distraught!"
While she was saying what she thought,
the men were breaking down the door
with the long axes that they bore.
The mob's blows split the door in twain.
Within, the porter, Sir Gawain,
could well defend it: with the sword
that he was carrying, the lord   5990
repaid so well the first who tried,
the other men were terrified.
Nobody dared to come ahead,
because each man feared for his head
and lacked the courage to advance.
They kept their distance from that stance,
because they feared the porter so,
and dared not raise a hand or go
one step ahead in such duress.
The maiden belted in her dress,   6000
threw chessmen lying on the floor,
tucked up her skirt, and furiously swore,
as she was hurling chessmen down,
she'd see the people of the town
destroyed, if it would be allowed,
before she died. The rabble vowed,
as they retreated, they would tear
the tower down upon them there,
if their resistance were not ended.
The maid and Sir Gawain defended   6010
themselves with more and more success
with huge men from the set of chess.
They hurled down pieces; many backed
away when they were thus attacked.
Then with steel pickaxes, they all

began to undermine the wall
in order to destroy the tower,
because the porter made them cower.
That door was narrow, and so low,
believe me, two men could not go   6020
through it abreast without a squeeze.
One man could hold the door with ease,
if he were brave enough for it.
To strike a bare head, and to split
the skull in two through teeth and brain,
no better porter than Gawain
could have been summoned. Though the lord
who offered him both bed and board
knew naught, as early as he could,
he left off hunting in the wood.   6030
Meanwhile the townspeople combined,
with steel pickaxes undermined
the tower's foundations. Unexpected,
Guinganbresil, who'd not suspected
the mob would riot and attack,
came to the castle, speeding back,
and when he heard the way they pounded,
Guinganbresil was quite dumbfounded.
He had not realized at all
Gawain was in the castle wall,   6040
but when he learned of it, instead
Guinganbresil prohibited
each person there to be so bold,
for any reason, did he hold
his body dear, upon his own
to dare pry loose a single stone.
The people cried they did not care
about his threats, that they would tear
the tower down in the interim,
and they would even bury him,   6050
if he took sides with those inside.
Guinganbresil soon realized
his threat was useless, and he thought
he'd meet the king, who should be brought
to see the violent crowd's affront;
he was returning from the hunt.
He met the king and told him then,
"My liege, your mayor and aldermen

all treat you with contempt and scorn.
They started rioting this morn,   6060
and they besieged your tower all day.
Now, if you do not make them pay,
I'll hold a grudge, and for good reason.
I have accused Gawain of treason,
as you know with no need of proof.
You welcomed him beneath your roof,
and you gave lodgings to the knight,
so it is reasonable and right
that, as your house guest since he came,
he should not come to harm or shame."   6070
The king said to Guinganbresil,
"Advisor, he'll have no ill will,
nor fear of peril and disgrace,
as soon as we can reach that place.
If he is hated and despised
within the town, I'm not surprised,
but what's occurred enrages me.
I'll shield the knight from injury
and prison if at all I can,
since I gave shelter to the man."   6080
They went on to the tower and found
the people circling it around;
their rioting was growing worse.
He told the mayor to disperse
the rabble, and the mayor sent
the crowd home; they obeyed and went.
There was a gentleman of worth
who'd lived within the town from birth,
and since he was extremely wise,
they called upon him to advise   6090
the people in the country round.
He said, "My lord, you should have sound
and loyal counseling from me.
The man committed treachery
the day he took your father's life,
therefore, no wonder there was strife,
nor that he was attacked, because
they hate him to the death, with cause.
Still, you must do your very best
to shield him, since he is your guest,   6100
from death and from imprisonment.

To tell the truth, it's evident
Guinganbresil here should protect
the lord Gawain, which is correct,
because he traveled to report
his treachery to Arthur's court.
The lord Gawain, as we know, came
to your court to defend his name.
His trial by combat for his crime
should be postponed for one year's time.   6110
Instead, the lord should make a trip
to seek the lance whose iron tip
bleeds even when it is wiped clean.
A drop of blood is always seen
upon the tip or forming there.
So have the lord Gawain declare
himself your prisoner of war,
completely at your mercy, or
have him obtain this lance for you.
You'll have a better reason to   6120
detain him in your prison than
you have now, for you could not plan
a punishment, I understand,
too dreadful for him to withstand.
One should impose the harshest tests*
upon a man whom one detests.
If you seek vengeance on your foe,
there's no worse punishment I know."
The king thought his advice was sage.
He found his sister in a rage.   6130
His sister stood up when he came;
the lord Gawain did just the same;
he did not whiten or appear
to tremble or show any fear.
Guinganbresil went toward the knight.
He hailed the maid, who did turn white,
and said a word or two in vain.
"My lord Gawain, my lord Gawain,
I realize I had agreed
to shield you in an hour of need.   6140

v. 6125–6126. Hilka notes (*Der Percevalroman*, p. 733) that this proverb is included in Morawski, *Proverbes français* no. 688: "En totes les manieres que l'en puet doit on grever son enemi," among other references.

If you recall what you were told,
I asked you not to be so bold
as to come to the castle and
the towns within my liege lord's land,
unless you could not pass them by,
and so, as you cannot deny,
you have no right to raise objection
nor to complain you lacked protection."
The wise man, with these words exchanged,
said, "Sire, it all can be arranged.   6150
God help me, how can anyone
be blamed for what these oafs have done
when they attacked him? All involved
would think the matter unresolved
until the final Judgment Day.
It should be settled in the way
my lord the king would have it be.
I say, as he's commanded me,
provided that Guinganbresil
and Sir Gawain agree, they will   6160
do battle one year from this day,
and Sir Gawain can go away,
though he must take a solemn vow,
and tell my lord, one year from now,
he will turn over to his keeping
the lance whose tip is always weeping
a drop of crimson blood, for some
have written that the hour will come
when the entire realm of Logres,*
in olden days the land of ogres,   6170
will be demolished by that lance.
His majesty my liege lord wants
this affirmation and this oath."
Said Sir Gawain, "I would be loath
to pledge my word to that, for I
would rather stay with you to die
or languish seven years, than take
an oath I might be forced to break.

vs. 6169–6170. Nitze notes that Logres is the name of Arthur's land in Geoffrey of
Monmouth (Faral edition, p. 93) and that the ogres must be the giants that inhabited Al-
bion, according to Wace (*Brut*, v. 686), in "Le Bruiden et la Lance-qui-saigne," *Roma-
nia 75* (1954): 517.

I don't fear death; I would prefer
to suffer dying, if I were   6180
to die and leave an honored name,
than break an oath and live in shame."
"Dear sir," the man replied in haste,
"you won't be lessened or disgraced.
You need but promise in advance
that you will seek the bleeding lance,
that you will do all in your power,
that you will come back to the tower
if you can't fetch it: we'll allow
in such that case you kept your vow."   6190
"On those conditions," he declared,
"as you have said, I am prepared
to take the oath that's necessary."
A very precious reliquary
was brought forth, and the lord Gawain
avowed with all his might and main
that he would seek the bleeding lance,
and in this way the combatants
resolved the battlefield to leave
and gave themselves one year's reprieve.   6200
But when he and Guinganbresil
put off their test of knightly skill,
Gawain escaped from peril fell.
He told the noble maid farewell
before he left the tower, and
he told his squires to seek their land
and take the mounts he called his own,
all steeds but Gringalet alone.*
And so the squires went to find
their homes and left their lord behind.   6210
The squires went riding on their way.
There's nothing more I wish to say,
for they were mournful but compliant.
Now at this point the tale falls silent,
and tells no more of Sir Gawain,
but starts with Perceval again.

v. 6208 (6209, Roach edition). Hilka notes (*Der Percevalroman*, p. 736) that Gawain's horse, Gringalet, is mentioned in *Erec and Enide*, vs. 3935, 3945, and 4063 (Roques edition).

PERCEVAL'S HERMIT UNCLE

The story tells us Perceval
had lost his memory of all
events that had occurred before,
so he remembered God no more.   6220
The months of April and of May*
had come five times and gone away;
yes, five entire years had passed
since he had been to chapel last
or prayed to God or to His cross.
He spent five years thus, at no loss
for strange adventures to pursue,
and dangerous and hard ones too,
which he kept seeking, all the same,
while in pursuit of knightly fame,   6230
and he fought well and held his own.   6233
As captives, in five years alone,
some sixty famous knights he sent
to Arthur's court. The young knight spent
five years in combats of this kind;
no thought of God once crossed his mind.*
When five years ended, nonetheless,
while traveling through a wilderness,   6240
completely armed, as was his way,
he met three knights along the way
with ladies ten, and all on foot,
unshod, in woolen gowns, who'd put
their heads within the hoods they wore.
The mounted, armored warrior
who held his lance and shield upraised,
left all the ladies much amazed,
for, to ensure their souls' salvation,

v. 6221. Perceval's five years of wandering, repeated six times for emphasis, is one of the most glaring discrepancies in Chrétien's time sequence, because it occurs in the middle of Gawain's single year of adventure.

v.6238. Haidu notes that: "Like Yvain, Perceval in the Hermit Episode is at the nadir of his existence. For both, the Hermit Episode is the bottom of the abisme . . . , a place where their resurgence begins, thanks to the charity of the hermit" (*Aesthetic Distance*, p. 222).

the ladies felt an obligation   6250
to go on foot, a penance fitting
the sins that they had been committing,
in penitence for every fault.
One of the three knights made him halt.
"Don't you hold Jesus Christ in awe,
the One who wrote down the New Law
and gave this law to Christian men?
It is not good or righteous, then,
but very wrong," he testified,
"to bear arms on the day Christ died."   6260
Since Perceval had in no way
considered time or hour or day,
his heart was so dispirited,
"What day is it today?" he said.
"What day is it? You don't know then?*
It is Good Friday, when all men
should hold the cross in reverence,
weep for their sins in penitence.
Christ, sold for thirty shillings pay,
was hung upon the cross this day.   6270
Though He was free of any sin,
He saw mankind lay fettered in
foul sin throughout the whole world's span
and for our sins became a man.
He was both God and man in one,
because the Virgin bore a son,
one of the Holy Ghost conceived.
Both flesh and blood our God received;
the flesh of our humanity

v. 6265. Haidu makes the interesting observation that Perceval receives a more pro-
found religious instruction from the knight than he does from the hermit (*Aesthetic Dis-
tance*, pp. 222-223):

> From the knight, Perceval hears of the Passion of Christ; a reference to original
> sin; the paradox of the God-Man; the Virgin's conception by the Holy Ghost; the
> Harrowing of Hell, and the paradox that great good came from the Jews' crucifix-
> ion of Christ.
>   By comparison, the hermit's teaching is far less ambitious . . . [and] . . . is
> merely repeating the lessons Perceval failed to learn from his previous teachers.
> The hermit . . . undeceived by the knightly armor . . . offers simple spiritual
> food to one who is still a simpleton.

to cover His divinity.   6280
Whoever doubts this was the case
will not set eyes upon His face.
Born of a Virgin, He began
to take the form and soul of man,
and of sacred divinity.
Upon this day, in verity,
they crucified Him, and as well
He led His friends all out of Hell.
This death was holy, for Our Lord
both saved the living and restored   6290
the dead from death to life again.
The traitor Jews, who should be slain
like dogs, established in their hate
our great good and their wretched state,
for when they raised Him on a cross,
they saved us and ensured their loss.
All who hold Christ in reverence
should spend this day in penitence.
No man of faith in God should wield
or carry arms on road or field."   6300
"Then from what place have you just come?"
asked Perceval. "We're coming from
a holy hermit, wise and good,
whose dwelling place is in this wood.
So holy is this man, he's known
to live by Heaven's grace alone."
"In God's name, sirs, what was your task?
What did you seek? What did you ask?"
One of the ladies said, "What, sir?
We sought the hermit to confer   6310
about our sins and make confession,
a task that is the chief profession
of faith a Christian can accord,
who would draw nearer to Our Lord."
Then Perceval began to cry.
Their words had made him want to try
to go and talk with that good man.
So Perceval said, "If I can,
I wish to go to his abode,
if I could learn the path or road."   6320
"Whoever wants to go there, sir,
should take the path on which we were,

go straight on through this forest thick,
and watch for every branch and stick
which we have knotted, which we bent
with our own hands, because we meant
each knotted branch to show the way,
so nobody would go astray
who sought the holy hermit's dwelling."
They separated, after telling   6330
each other that they were commended
to God's care, and their questions ended.
He found the path, and made a start,
and sighed from deep within his heart,
for Perceval felt he had sinned
and was repentant and chagrined.
In tears beneath the foliage,
he rode up to the hermitage,
dismounted, laid his arms aside,
to a hornbeam his charger tied.   6340
The young knight found, when he went in,
the hermit, ready to begin
the service in a chapel small,
with him a priest, and they were all
assisted by an acolyte.*
It is the noblest, sweetest rite
that ever can be celebrated
in church or chapel consecrated.
As Perceval knelt down in awe,
the good man called him, for he saw   6350
the knight was humble and was weeping;
the water from his eyes was sweeping
in rivulets down on his chin.
The knight, in terror of the sin
he feared he had committed, grasped
the hermit by the foot, and clasped
his hands, and bent down low, and prayed
the hermit for advice and aid
of which he was in urgent need.
The good man told him to proceed,   6360

vs. 6345–6346. Hilka notes that this service is not the mass, but the midday Good Friday liturgy with its veneration of the Holy Cross and the Holy Sepulchre (*Der Percevalroman*, p. 739).

because the youth could not be blessed
and pardoned till he had confessed
and signs of his repentance shown.
"Sir, for five years, I have not known
where I was, and did not believe
in God or love God. I perceive
my deeds were evil, in the end."
The good man answered, "Ah, dear friend,
tell me why you have done so ill,
and pray God may have mercy still   6370
upon the soul of His poor sinner."
"Sir, at the Fisher King's, at dinner,
I saw the lance and that, indeed,
its white point did not cease to bleed.
I did not ask about the drop
of blood suspended from the top
against the steel of shining white.
I've done no better since that night.
I don't know who was being served
out of the grail that I observed.   6380
Since then I've been so sorely tried
that I would willingly have died,
and I forgot about Our Lord.
His mercy I've not once implored
nor done one deed that I can see
would make Him merciful to me."
"Oh! friend," the worthy man exclaimed,
"do tell me now how you are named."
"Sir, Perceval," the knight replied,
and at that name the good man sighed,   6390
for he had recognized the name.
"A sin for which you feel no shame
has brought misfortune on you, brother.
It was the grief you caused your mother
the day you left; a grief so great
she swooned and fell before her gate
next to the drawbridge, on her side,
in so much anguish that she died.
It was this sin that made you fail
to ask about the lance and grail.   6400
Then your misfortunes came along.
You could not have held out so long,
without your mother's parting prayer

that God would have you in His care.
Her commendation had such power
that God preserved you, since that hour,
from death and from imprisonment,
because she blessed you when you went.
You did not ask the reason why,
each time the lance's tip passed by,   6410
from which the blood, unstaunched, has sprung,
because your sin cut off your tongue.
You were a foolish man to fail
to learn whom they serve from the grail.
The man they serve is my own brother;
my sister, and his, was your mother;
and also the rich Fisherman
is that king's son, son of the man
who has himself served with the grail.
Now do not let the thought prevail   6420
that from the grail he takes food like
a salmon, lamprey, or a pike,
because from it the king obtains
one mass wafer, and it sustains*
his life, borne in the grail they bring;
the grail is such a holy thing.*
He is so very spiritual
that he's required no food at all
except the host the grail contained;
the last twelve years he has remained   6430
inside the little room wherein
you saw the grail borne. For your sin
I wish to give your penance now."
"I'll do it, uncle, that I vow,"

v. 6424. In *The Grail: From Celtic Myth to Christian Symbol*, pp. 60-61, Loomis cites other precedents for people being nourished solely by the host: "Caesarius of Heisterbach gives an instance of a woman who was sustained solely by the Body of Christ. Under the date 1180 the chronicler Guillaume de Nangis told of a paralytic young herdswoman of the diocese of Sens who, unable to take other food, was likewise kept alive by the host; the rumor of this could have easily reached Chrétien if he was living in or near Troyes."

v. 6426 (6425, Roach edition). Haidu notes (*Aesthetic Distance*, pp. 225-226) that Chrétien never uses the expression, "the Holy Grail"; "The grail is such a holy thing" is the closest that the noun and adjective come on the one occasion that they are linked in the *Story of the Grail*, and the expression "tant sainte chose" is unusual in Chrétien's works.

said Perceval, "with my whole heart.
Since Mother was your sister, start
to call me 'nephew'; I therefore
should call you 'uncle' and love you more."
"We should, but listen. I cajole,
if you have pity on your soul,   6440
dear nephew, and you do repent,
attend church, as a penitent,
each morning, the first thing you do.
It will be very good for you.
I say you must not fail to go
for any reason, if you know
there is a church or chapel near.
Go when the bell rings and you hear
or earlier if you have risen.
You won't repent of your decision;   6450
your soul will prosper. Should you pass
and find the priest has started mass,
so much the better, you must stay
until he's ceased to chant and pray.
If you are willing to remain,
you'll grow in merit and obtain
first honor and then paradise.
Love God, believe in God, arise*
and worship God time and again;
respect good women and good men;   6460
when priests are in your presence, stand.
It is a simple gesture, and
God greatly loves this courtesy,
because it shows humility.
If any woman seeks your aid,
a widow, orphan, or a maid,
assist her, and you will do well.
This service is commendable,
and you, as well, will benefit;
it's one that you must not omit.   6470
Perform this penance in all places,

---

vs. 6458 ff. Frappier notes (*Chrétien de Troyes et le Mythe du Graal*, p. 155) that the
hermit's advice resembles a passage from Ecclesiasticus 7:29-36, which begins "Fear the
Lord with all your heart and reverence his priests. Love your Maker with all your might
and do not leave his ministers without support."

so that you may regain the graces
that, years ago, you once possessed.
Now will you do as I request?"
"Yes, sir, and very willingly."
"I ask you now to stay with me*
for two entire days and dine
in penance on such food as mine,"
which Perceval agreed to share.
The hermit taught the knight a prayer   6480
by whispering it in his ear
time and again, till it was clear
that he could say it back the same.
Such potent forms of Our Lord's name*
were in this prayer, so great and many,
no one should utter it on any
pretext except in fear of death.
Once he had taught, under his breath,
the prayer to Perceval, he said
that for no reason save in dread   6490
that greatest danger would betide
should he say it. The knight replied,
"No, I will not, sir." So he stayed
with joy and heard the service, prayed
when it was over to the cross,
and wept and mourned his sins and loss.   6496
The holy hermit filled his plate   6499
that evening with the food he ate.   6500
No more did that good man possess
than beets and chervil, lettuce, cress,
and millet, oat and barley bread,
and spring water. The hermit fed
one pan of barley every day

v. 6476. Perceval vowed not to spend two nights under the same roof until he had learned where the grail was carried and whom they served with it, and until he had found the lance and had discovered why it bled. He has obtained the information he sought about the grail, and he stays two nights with the hermit, perhaps a sign that his quest is partly fulfilled.

v. 6484. Frappier notes (*Chrétien de Troyes et le Mythe du Graal*, p. 157) that perhaps this prayer reflects the belief in the 56, or 72, or 76 names of Jesus. Chrétien could also have taken it from traditions that came from the Orient and passed into Latin sequences and hymns (see also Hilka, *Der Percevalroman*, p. 743, and W. Kellerman, *Aufbaustil und Weltbild Chrestiens von Troyes im Percevalroman*, pp. 199–202).

to the knight's horse and gave him hay.   6506
That's what they ate at evenfall.   6509
And so it was that Perceval   6510
found out that God was crucified
upon a Friday, and He died.
At Easter, worthily, he took
communion. At this time the book
relates no more of Perceval,
but I've heard more material
about the lord Gawain, much more
than you have heard me tell before.

GREOREAS AND THE EVIL MAIDEN

The lord Gawain then rode along,
once he escaped the tower strong   6520
on which the angry mob had hewn.
Between the hours of nine and noon,
he came upon a little ridge
and a huge oak with foliage
shade-giving and profusely sprung.
Upon the oak a shield was hung;
a lance, beside it, stood upright.
He spurred toward it till he caught sight
of a black palfrey which was grazing
before the oak, which seemed amazing;   6530
he had seen nothing similar.
The palfrey and the arms for war,
he thought, did not belong together.
Now if the palfrey on its tether
had been a steed, he'd understand
some knight who'd ridden through the land
was up upon the ridge and came
in search of glory and of fame.
Beneath the great oak, in the shade,
the lord Gawain could see a maid.   6540
The maid was sitting there, and had
this maid looked joyful or been glad,
he thought that she would have been fair;
she ran her fingers through her hair,
which she tore out by strands and rent,
and she was raising loud lament
about a knight. She uttered cries
and kissed his forehead, mouth, and eyes,
and as the lord Gawain drew near,
he saw the knight's wounds were severe.   6550
His face was all cuts, and he had
a head wound which was very bad
and had been given by a sword.
From both his flanks two blood-streams poured.
The knight passed out time and again,
for he was suffering so much pain,

until he fell asleep at last.
The lord Gawain, when riding past,
could not tell whether he was dead.
"Fair maiden," Sir Gawain then said,   6560
"how goes it with that knight you hold?"
The seated maid, in answer, told
the lord Gawain, "Sir, you can see
that he is injured critically!
Look at the harm his wounds have done:
he could die from the smallest one."
The lord Gawain said, "Be so kind,
my dear friend, if you do not mind,
and wake him up to tell me what
is happening around this spot."   6570
"I'll never wake him, I'd prefer
to be cut up in pieces, sir.
I've never felt a love so strong,
nor will I ever, my life long,
for any man I've met before.
I'd be a foolish wretch and more,
when he is sleeping in repose,
to do one thing that I suppose
would make him speak a word of blame."
"I mean to wake him all the same."   6580
He turned his lance round as he spoke
and gave the knight a gentle poke
with the lance butt upon the spur.
The lord Gawain did not incur
his anger when he woke the knight.
His touch was gentle, very light;
he did not hurt him by the poke.
The knight thanked him when he awoke,
"Thank you five hundred times, dear sir.
When poking me awake, you were   6590
so gentle that you caused no pain.
But I implore you to remain
here in this place for your own sake.
You would be foolish not to take
my good advice and go ahead.
Trust me, stay here," the hurt knight said.
The lord Gawain, when he had heard,
asked, "Stay here? Why?" "Upon my word,
I'll tell you, since you want to learn.

No knight's been able to return   6600
who crossed those fields and roads in order
to get across the Galloway border.
No knight can come to that frontier,
cross over it, and come back here.
No knight has managed to escape
except for me, in such bad shape
I think I will not live till night.
Within that land I met a knight,
brave, daring, strong, and arrogant.
I've met no man as valiant,   6610
nor fought so strong a personage.
You'd best not go along the ridge;
turn back instead, be on your guard,
for coming back is much too hard."
"My word," the lord Gawain replied,
"I did not come to turn aside,
for people would consider me
to have been very cowardly
upon this trip, if I departed
or turned back from the way I started,   6620
so I'll go on until I learn
why no one ever can return."
"I see you're bent on doing so,"
the hurt knight answered, "you will go
with eagerness in expectation
of a more famous reputation.
Now if you'll do as I request,
I'd like to ask that, in this test,
if Heaven grants you victory,
one granted no knight previously,   6630
a victory I don't believe
that any warrior will achieve,
including you and other men,
for any reason, sir, but when
you travel back this way again,
I beg of you to ascertain
if I am still alive or dead
or better off or worse instead.
If I am dead, for charity,
and for the Holy Trinity,   6640
I beg you, keep this maid protected,
so that she will not be subjected

to pain and shame. You should accord
this boon with pleasure, for the Lord
will never make, nor has He made
a nobler or a finer maid."   6646
And so the lord Gawain consented: 6651
he vowed, if he were not prevented   6652
by prison or another plight,
he would return to see the knight,
and he would give the maid as good
advice and counsel as he could.
He left the pair, and rode along
through field and forest to a strong
walled town which had upon one side
a port where many boats were tied.   6660
As large as Pavia in size
was this walled town upon its rise.
Its castle was of noble mien;
nearby the vineyard could be seen,   6664
and the great river lower down   6667
flowed to the sea around the town   6668
and castle, cut off therewithal
by water all around the wall.   6670
The lord Gawain, who crossed the bridge,
went in a field high on a ridge,
the place that was best fortified,
and underneath an elm he spied
a gentle maiden in the place,*
and she was looking at her face
and mouth within a looking glass.
Her face snow's whiteness would surpass;
a slender band adorned her head
embroidered with fine golden thread.   6680
The lord Gawain spurred from his amble
and went for her without preamble.
She called to him, "Slow down, slow down!
Sir, don't come riding like a clown
across the meadow at top speed.

v. 6675. Frappier notes (*Chrétien de Troyes et le Mythe du Graal*, p. 236) that in the whole gallery of Chrétien's female characters, the only portrait missing was one of a vamp. Here she is, complete with the troubled childhood (see vs. 8640 ff) and the unhappy youthful love adventure that caused her to hate men (see vs. 8932 ff). Frappier calls this episode the meeting of Chrétien's vamp and his Don Juan.

You really shouldn't make your steed
break from his amble when he's spurred.
What work for nothing! How absurd!
Fool he whose labors are in vain!"
"God bless you, maid," said Sir Gawain.   6690
"Dear friend, if you will be so kind,
please tell me what you had in mind
when, for no reason that I know,
you said my pace should be more slow."
"I know my reasons and," she said,
"what thoughts are passing through your head."
Asked Sir Gawain, "What could they be?"
"To pick me up and carry me
back down this hill and make the trek
with me upon your horse's neck!"   6700
"I must admit that that is true."
"Of course it is, how well I knew,
but cursed be he who ever thought
of treating me so, and you ought
not dream that I would give you leave.
I'm no maid, silly and naive,
like those whom knights take pleasure bearing
upon their horses' necks when faring
in search of deeds of chivalry!
You won't go riding off with me!   6710
But all the same, sir, if you dared,
I would go with you, if you cared
to take the trouble to enharden
your nerve and go into that garden
to fetch my palfrey here for me.
Then I would keep you company,
and I would travel with you till
disgrace and pain and every ill
befall you while you're at my side."
"To go with you, fair friend," he sighed,   6720
"will I need more than bravery?"
"Not to my knowledge," answered she,
"there is no more that you will need."
"But, maid, where shall I leave my steed,
if I cross over, for the weight
of my war horse is far too great
to go across upon that board?"
"Then give your horse to me, my lord,

and you can cross that plank on foot.
I'll try to keep him, once he's put   6730
into my care, and hold his rein.
You'd better hurry back again,
for I could never keep him checked
unless he's still and circumspect,
and then somebody might use force
before you come and steal your horse."
The lord Gawain said, "That is true,
and I will cast no blame on you.
If he's led off, it's not your fault,
nor if he bolts and will not halt."   6740
He gave the maid the horse and thought
he'd take his weapons, all he'd brought,
to have them there in case he found
some knight within the garden ground
who wanted to prevent his taking
the palfrey back to her by making
an uproar or a battle grim
to keep the palfrey there with him.
The lord Gawain crossed on the board
and met some people, quite a horde,   6750
who looked at him and said, astounded,
"Maid, may you ever be confounded,
and may one hundred devils burn
your wicked body, you who spurn,
but never love, a gallant man!
We are so sorry that you can
have cost the heads of warriors brave.
Ah, knight, why come here? Though you crave
the palfrey, you could never know
what evils you will undergo   6760
if you but touch it with your hand.
If you could only understand
what great misfortunes and disgrace
will come upon you in this case,
if you dare lead her mount from here,
sir, truly, you would not come near."
The men and women standing there
spoke in this way in hopes to scare
the lord Gawain and turn his course
away from going near the horse.   6770
Although he heard how they insisted,

the knight would never have desisted.
He made his way along each street
and greeted all he chanced to meet.
The men and women all returned
his greetings but were much concerned
about the safety of the lord.
Yet Sir Gawain kept heading toward
the maiden's palfrey and extended
his hand toward it, for he intended   6780
to seize its bridle, nothing loath.
It had a saddle and bridle both.
A huge knight sitting quietly
beneath a leafy olive tree
said, "Knight, you have come here for naught
to fetch the palfrey, for you ought
not take it; you are arrogant.
Nevertheless I do not want
to fight to force you to forsake it,
if you so greatly wish to take it,   6790
but I think you should go away
and leave the palfrey here to stay.
You'll fight for it elsewhere, I've heard."
"No matter, I am undeterred,"
said Sir Gawain, "by your objection.
The maid admiring her reflection
beneath the elm has sent me here.
If I desist, it will be clear
I failed to get the thing I sought.
I would be shamed; I would be thought   6800
a worthless coward far and wide."
"Dear brother," the huge knight replied,
"you would be thought unlucky, rather,
because, by God the Sovereign Father,
to whom my soul I would account
no knight has ever touched that mount,
the way you wish that you could do,
without immediately going through
such perils that he lost his head,
and you will do the same, I dread.   6810
Though I'm opposed, no harm was meant.
I'm not the one who will prevent
your leading it off as you plan,
no more than any other man,

but you will be unfortunate
if you are so importunate
to take the palfrey out of here,
for you may lose your head, I fear."
The lord Gawain, quite undeterred
by the dire warnings that he heard,   6820
did not delay but promptly led
away the palfrey, and its head
was partly black and partly white.
It crossed the plank before the knight
and had no difficulty, for
it crossed so many times before,
it was well trained: the lord Gawain
controlled it by its silken rein.
He found the elm; in that direction
the maiden gazed at her reflection   6830
deep in the looking glass's pane.
Her cloak and wimple she had lain
upon the meadow to admire
her body to her heart's desire,
and see her face times without count.
The lord Gawain gave her her mount,
completely saddled and arrayed.
He said to her, "Come over, maid,
I'll help you on your palfrey now."
"God! that I never will allow!   6840
In no court will the tale be told
that I permitted you to hold
my body in your arms," she swore.
"Were you to touch one thing I wore
or lay bare hands upon my dress,
I would believe it shamefulness.
I would feel dreadful and abhorred
if it were known or told abroad
that you had ever touched my skin.
I'd rather skin and flesh had been   6850
cut to the bone in such a case;
and I shall say it to your face!
Give me my horse; leave me alone;
for I can mount it on my own.
I do not need your help or want it.
My prayer today, and may God grant it,
is to see you as I predict.

I pray that Heaven will inflict
disgrace upon you before night.
Go any place that you think right,   6860
but don't come nearer; don't suppose
that you could touch me or my clothes,
for I will follow you until
misfortune or some dreadful ill
has struck you down because of me.
I shall abuse you terribly,
so you cannot escape from dying."
The lord Gawain, without replying,
heard how the maiden reprimanded
his gesture scornfully, and handed   6870
her palfrey to her in due course.
The maiden gave him back his horse.
The lord Gawain then started bending
down to the ground by her, intending
to pick her cloak up off the ground
and help her wrap the cloak around
her shoulders, but at once the maid
took notice and was not afraid
to speak an insult to a knight.
She asked him, "Just what interest might   6880
you have, sir, in my cloak and wimple?
Good Lord, I am not half so simple
as you suppose that I must be!
I will not have you wait on me.
Your hands aren't clean enough to dare
to handle anything I wear
or which I put upon my head.
Should you be handling a thread
of any garment that I place
upon my frame, mouth, brow, or face?   6890
May Heaven honor me the less
if I accept your services."
On saying that, the maid arose;
when she had fastened on her clothes
and by herself got on her steed.
She said, "Now, knight, you may proceed
wherever you may wish to fare,
and I will follow everywhere,
till you are treated shamefully
before my eyes because of me,   6900

today, if it be Heaven's will."
To that the lord Gawain kept still,
nor by a single word replied;
he was completely mortified.
He mounted as the maiden spoke
and turned his bowed head toward the oak.
He'd left the wounded warrior there
in dire need of a doctor's care.
Bad wounds the lord Gawain could treat
better than anyone you'll meet.   6910
He had observed an herb which grew
within a hedgerow, one he knew
worked well for taking out the pain
of deep wounds, so the lord Gawain
picked it and rode until he found
the maid sitting on the ground
lamenting underneath the oak.
When she caught sight of him, she spoke,
"Oh, sir, this knight is dead, I fear,
because he can no longer hear."   6920
The lord Gawain dismounted, and
he felt the warrior with his hand.
He found the hurt knight's pulse was strong,
and he was not too cold along
the lips and armpit. Answering her,
the lord Gawain said, "I am sure
that this knight is not dead already.
His pulse is strong, his breathing's steady,
his wounds aren't mortal. I have brought
an herb with me which surely ought   6930
to help alleviate a part
of the deep, throbbing pain and smart
that he has suffered and long felt
from the sore wounds that he was dealt.
You'll find no herb, were you to look,
as good for deep wounds, says the book;
it leaves so powerful a mark
that even on a sick tree's bark
whose wood is not entirely dried,
when this strong herb has been applied,   6940
the ailing tree will put down roots,
will flower, and put out leaves and shoots.
Your sweetheart need not fear to die:

this potent herb we shall apply
to every open wound and bruise
and bind them up, but we must use
a fine-spun wimple, clean and white,
to make a bandage for the knight."
"I'll give you right away," she said,
"the one I'm wearing on my head, 6950
because I haven't brought a spare."
The maiden, with a joyful air,
removed her wimple; it was one
made of white fabric, finely spun,
and Sir Gawain cut up and tore
the cloth to the right shape, before
he took the strong herb, and applied it
to every wound, and tightly tied it.
The maiden helped as best she knew
and did whatever she could do. 6960
The lord Gawain stayed by the oak
and waited till the warrior spoke.
He took a deep breath. "May the Lord
bless the physician who restored
my voice and speech to me hereby.
I was in terror I would die
without a chance to make confession,
and all the devils, in procession,
were coming here to seek my soul.
Before I'm buried in a hole 6970
I wish to be confessed today.
A chaplain lives not far away,
and if I only had a mount
I'd find that chaplain and recount
my every failing and transgression,
and after I had made confession
I'd take communion in no fear,
but knowing, when my death was near,
that I had made acknowledgment
and had received the sacrament. 6980
If you will do as I desire,
give me the pack horse of that squire,
the one who's coming at a trot;
give me that wretched nag he's got."
When Sir Gawain heard what he said,
he noticed, as he turned his head,

an ugly squire who came their way.
What did he look like? Let me say:*
his hair was tangled, stiff, and red,
and stood on end upon his head   6990
like an indignant porcupine.
His eyebrows were so thick of line,
they covered all his face and nose
and twisted, long mustachios.
His mouth was nothing but a slit;
his beard was bushy, thick, and split
with forked ends, frizzling past the prong;
his neck was short; his chest was long.
The lord Gawain thought he would go
and meet the squire, so he would know   7000
if he could have the nag outright.
Before he went, he told the knight,
"I don't know him, so help me Heaven,
 but I would rather give you seven
war horses, if they were with me,
than his poor nag, whoever he be."
"Sir, you should realize that man
is going to harm you if he can.
He came with only that intent,"
the knight warned Sir Gawain, who went   7010
to meet the squire and to inquire
where he was bound. The surly squire,
asked, "Why are you intent on knowing
from where I've come or where I'm going?
Whatever road I take, I pray
misfortune strikes you on your way!"
The lord Gawain, quite rightly, served
the surly squire as he deserved:
he slapped him with his open palm,
with armored hand, without a qualm,   7020
because he meant to strike him hard.
He left the saddle void and jarred
the squire completely off his horse.
And when the squire rose in due course,
he staggered, falling as before.

v. 6988. Loomis notes that Chrétien's portrait of the ugly squire is in the tradition of
conventional portraits of malevolent dwarfs (*Arthurian Tradition*, p. 434).

He fell down seven times or more
in less space than a lance of pine
would occupy (no joke of mine).
When he was upright and collected,
"You struck me, sir," the squire objected.　　　　7030
Said Sir Gawain, "I struck you, true,
but did not do much harm to you.
As God's my witness, I regret
the way I struck you down, and yet
it was a stupid thing to say."
"I've more to say about the way
you'll pay for doing me such harm.
Were you to lose the hand and arm
with which you struck the blow you hit,
I'd never pardon you for it."　　　　7040
While this went on, the weakened heart
of the hurt knight began to start
to beat at a more normal pace.
He told Gawain, "Sir, in this case,
please pay no heed to what you heard.
He never says a civil word
to anyone, so let him be
and you will act most sensibly.
Bring me his wretched nag to ride.
Protect this maiden at my side.　　　　7050
Assist her, hold her palfrey still,
and help her mount it, if you will.
I will not stay here any longer;
if I have grown a little stronger,
I'll mount the squire's animal
and search for a confessional.
My search is one I will not leave
until the last rites I receive
and take communion, well confessed."
The lord Gawain, at his request,　　　　7060
gave the squire's pack horse to the knight.
Meanwhile the wounded warrior's sight
had much improved and grown more keen,
and once the wounded knight had seen
the lord Gawain, he placed his face.
Meanwhile, with courtesy and grace,
the lord Gawain raised up the maid
on her fine palfrey, and he made

sure she was settled for her ride.
While Sir Gawain was occupied,   7070
the hurt knight seized his great war horse,
and mounted, and began to force
the mighty steed to prance around.
The lord Gawain looked back and found
the hurt knight galloping and bounding
upon the hill, which seemed astounding.
The lord Gawain called out with laughter,
"Sir knight, upon my word, and after
your wounds, you are a fool indeed
to be out prancing on my steed!   7080
Dismount at once and end your ride,
or else your wounds will open wide;
give me my horse before you're hurt!"
The wounded knight's reply was curt.
"Gawain, be still! You'd best get on
the nag, because your horse is gone.
You've lost your charger; I shall make him
 prance, if I choose, and I shall take him."
"What! When I've helped you, now I learn
that you would harm me in return?   7090
Don't take my horse away from me;
to do so would be treachery."
"Gawain, I wish that I could wrest
your beating heart out of your chest
and hold it in my hands to see,
no matter what becomes of me."
The lord Gawain said, "I suppose
I've heard the proverb, one which goes
'Do good and break your neck to pay.'*
But I do wish that you would say   7100
why you desire to have my heart,
and steal my charger, and depart.
I have no wish to do you wrong
and did you none my whole life long.
I think my horse should be returned;
I don't believe this trick was earned,
for to my knowledge on that score,

---

v. 7099 (7100, Roach edition). Hilka notes (*Der Percevalroman*, p. 750) that this
proverb is listed in Morawski, *Proverbes français* no. 463: "De bien fait col frait."

I've never seen your face before."
"You have, Gawain, you saw my face
that time you brought me to disgrace. 7110
Think of that man you did mistreat;
for one whole month you made him eat
down with the hounds, the hunting pack,
with his hands tied behind his back!
You acted foolishly that day,
and now you'll be disgraced to pay."
"Are you Greoreas? Of course,
that man who took the maid by force
and finally had his will of her.
But you knew perfectly well, sir, 7120
about King Arthur's firm direction:
in his lands maidens have protection.
He's given them safe conduct, and
has them escorted through the land,
and keeps them in security.
Therefore it does not seem to me
that you should hate me or resent
my conduct and the punishment
which I imposed in justice loyal,
as is established in all royal 7130
decisions in the king's domain."
"I know you punished me, Gawain,
and now the time has come for you
to suffer from the things I do.
I shall lead off your Gringalet
in vengeance, and you'll have to get
the squire's pack horse to replace him,
the squire you knocked down to disgrace him.
This is the worst thing I could do;
there'll be no other mount for you!" 7140
Then Sir Gawain was left behind.
Greoreas sped off to find
his love, who'd ridden off with speed.
He rode on Sir Gawain's fine steed
at a fast trot and followed after.
The evil maiden said, with laughter,
"Sir, sir, what are you going to do?
We certainly can say of you:
'Fools never are in short supply.'
It is hilarious to try 7150

to follow you! I'll gladly ride
with you and never turn aside;
I will go with you everywhere.
I wish that you could ride a mare
and not a nag," the maiden stated,
"you would be more humiliated."
The lord Gawain, will he or not,
got on the nag and made it trot,
as one who could not mend his fate.
It was ridiculous in gait.   7160
The nag was ugly and ill fed,
with a lank neck and outsized head,
long dangling ears, and all the flaws
and blemishes old age can cause:
its lips agape a finger wide,
its vision murky, bleary-eyed,
its feet were scabbed; its sides were scarred
by spurs when it was ridden hard.
The nag was long and lank of line;
thin hindquarters, a twisted spine.   7170
The reins and bridle that it had
were mere cords, with no blanket pad
beneath the saddle, and it too
was very far from being new.
The stirrup straps were short and fragile;
the lord Gawain dared not be agile
enough to lean on them, they tell.
"Ha! Things are going very well,"
the disagreeable maid stated.
"I shall be joyful and elated   7180
to go wherever you decide,
for it is right for me to ride
with you, and follow willingly
a week, or two full weeks, or three,
or one whole month, as I think fitting.
You've a fine harness, and you're sitting
on a fine charger, well arrayed:
a fine knight to escort a maid!
Now I intend to watch, for fun,
all the misfortunes, one by one,   7190
that will befall you, I've no doubt.
You have a new horse; try him out,

prick with your spurs a little bit,
don't be afraid of doing it;
he is a swift and willing steed.
I'll follow you, for we've agreed
that I am never going to leave you,
until dishonor comes to grieve you;
it's bound to happen in the end."
The lord Gawain said, "My dear friend,   7200
you may address me any way,
and yet no maiden ought to say
such nasty things, and taunt, and scold,
once she is over ten years old.
She ought to be well bred by then,
polite to women and to men,   7206
if she has wit enough to learn."   a
"How dare you have the nerve to turn   b
and lecture me?" the maiden flung.   7207
"Go on your way and hold your tongue!
I've no concern for your tuition;
you're in exactly the condition   7210
I hoped to see you in today."
The couple rode along the way
in silence till the evening fell.
The knight went on, the demoiselle
came afterward, but he could not
induce his nag to run or trot
for anything, and did not know
what could be done. Will he or no,
he had to ride on at a walk.
When spurred, the squire's nag did not balk;   7220
it headed onto rough terrain
and shook and jostled Sir Gawain
so badly that he could not face,
at any price, a faster pace.
Therefore he rode the nag reviled
through forests lonely, deep, and wild,
until he came to open land
crossed by a deep, wide river, and
it was so wide, no mangonel,
crossbow, nor catapult as well   7230
could possibly have shot or thrown
across an arrow or a stone.

Across the water was a grand,*
strong castle, well designed and planned.
I won't allow myself to lie:
no living man has laid an eye
on any fortress so extensive,
so grandiose, and so expensive,
built on a cliff, on living rocks.
The palace wall was built of blocks   7240
of dark brown marble, and there ran
along the palace walls more than
five hundred windows, open wide,
and maids and ladies looked outside,
grouped at the windows of the rooms,
on fields and gardens filled with blooms.
Now, many maidens were arrayed
in robes of samite silk brocade
and tunics of all shades and hues,
and most wore silks on which they use   7250
bright patterns worked in beaten gold.
Outside the walls you could behold
the maidens at the windows there.
They showed their shining heads of hair
and their fine bodies could be traced
above the belts worn at the waist.
The wickedest of maidens found
in any place the world around
led Sir Gawain so she could ride
her palfrey to the river side.   7260
She stopped, and she dismounted from
her dappled palfrey, when she'd come

v. 7233. Frappier notes (*Chrétien de Troyes et le Mythe du Graal*, p. 244) that this
castle of ladies and maidens is in the Otherworld: the water is a mythical separation of
the two worlds; the glass windows recall the Isle of Glass which is mentioned in *Erec and
Enide* (vs. 1897–1901, Roques edition), and the castle is in the tradition of Celtic para-
dises, blessed isles, where beautiful women lure heroes to a life of delights, a fairyland,
without death, but instead a wondrous longevity.

  There are certain overtones of the Virgilian Underworld as well. Like the Celtic
Otherworld, the Underworld was accessible from the real world. Both Aeneas and Ga-
wain are ferried across the river by a ferryman and enter the land with a guide. Both he-
roes come to a sort of Elysian Field, filled with dancing and song, where Aeneas talks with
his father and Gawain with his grandmother, mother, and sister. Both worlds are ex-
ceedingly difficult for a mortal to leave.

upon a boat at a stone block
held tightly by a chain and lock.
Within the boat an oar was thrown.
The lock-key lay upon the stone.
The evil maiden, who possessed
a wicked heart within her breast,
got in the boat. Without demur
her little palfrey followed her   7270
into the boat moored at the shore,
as, often, it had done before.
"Sir knight, you must dismount," said she,
"and come into this boat with me,
and bring your nag that's so absurd;
it's thinner than a chickie-bird!
Undo this barge. You'll be disgraced
if you don't cross this stream in haste,
or if you don't know how to swim,"
the evil maid instructed him.   7280
"Why, maid?" "You don't see what I see,
sir knight, for you would quickly flee,
if you saw what is taking place."
The lord Gawain then turned his face,
and he looked back, and to be sure,
a knight was riding on the moor,
completely armed and coming near.
"My dear friend, I would like to hear,
and if you know the truth, please tell,"
he turned and asked the demoiselle,   7290
"who that man on my horse can be?
The horse that traitor stole from me
this morning, once his wounds were cured!"
"Yes, by Saint Martin, rest assured*
I'll tell you," said the maid, aglow.
"Although I want to have you know
I would not say a word of it,
if it were for your benefit.
Since I am positive he came
to harm you, I won't hide his name: 7300
he is Greoreas's kin,

v. 7294. Hilka notes (*Der Percevalroman*, p. 754) that there is a reference to Saint
Martin in *Lancelot*, v. 1476 (Roques edition), among other references.

his nephew, and the knight has been
sent by his uncle for a task
which I will tell you, since you ask.
His uncle told him to pursue
your trail until he slaughters you
and brings your head back as a present.
If you don't wish to die at present,
take my advice, dismount, and board
the barge, and flee!" Replied the lord,   7310
"Be certain I won't flee in fear;
I will await the rider here."
"A goal that I would not gainsay,
I'll just keep still. What a display
of spurring and of galloping
you'll give those maidens marvelling
and leaning out the window there!
They are so noble, and so fair,
so filled with joy and with delight,
and they have come to watch you fight.   7320
Spur on! They're glad on your account,
you're sitting on a splendid mount,
and you look like a gallant knight
who is just spoiling for a fight."
"Fair maid, whatever it may cost,
I shall go out there to accost
that rider and not dodge the fight.
I'm going to confront that knight,
and if I'm able to regain
my war horse," said the lord Gawain   7330
"I shall be glad, you may be sure."
He turned his nag's head toward the moor
and met the knight, who spurred his horse
across the sand in headlong course.
The lord Gawain stood still, and faced
the knight, and waited, and he braced
himself so hard, at last the lord
snapped the left stirrup's fragile cord.
He drew his foot out of the right
and waited that way for the knight,   7340
because his pack horse would not budge.
He spurred it hard, but could not nudge
the nag and make it move ahead.
"Alas," the lord Gawain then said,

"what wretched mounts pack horses are
for knights to do great deeds of war."
Toward Sir Gawain the rider came
upon his steed, which was not lame,
and gave the lord so hard a blow,
his lance bent back into a bow   7350
and broke in two. The iron stuck
in Sir Gawain's shield, and he struck
the knight right on his shield above
the buckler, hard enough to shove
the lance on through the shield: the blow
went through the coat of mail below
and knocked the knight onto the sand.
The lord Gawain held out his hand,
and seized his horse, and leapt astride.
The venture left him satisfied   7360
and filled with joy, as much and more
as he had ever felt before
at any dangerous affair.
He went to seek the maiden fair
within the boat, but at that place
the lord Gawain could find no trace
of her or of the boat as well.
So he had lost the demoiselle,
to his extreme discomfiture.
He wondered what had become of her.   7370

THE WONDROUS BED

W hile deep in thought about the maid,
     he saw a boatman, who conveyed
a dinghy, and the boatman rowed
across from the fine walled abode.
The boatman said, when at the port,
"Sir, I am coming to transport
those maidens' greetings. They have told
that you must not try to withhold
my rightful, lawful property,
so, if you please, give it to me."   7380
"May God bless each and every maid
and then yourself. You'll not be made
to forfeit anything you name
to which you have a rightful claim,"
said Sir Gawain. "I've no desire
to wrong you, but may I inquire
to what of mine your claim applies?"
"You overcame, before my eyes,
another knight, and so, of course,
I am entitled to the horse.   7390
If you don't wish to be unjust,
give me the horse, sir, as you must."
"Friend, it would cause me too much pain
to give him up," said Sir Gawain.
"I'd have to go on foot, you see."
"If I can't have my property,
those maidens watching in plain sight
will think you a disloyal knight
and call your conduct a disgrace.
I've never heard or seen a case   7400
in which a knight who chanced to meet
another knight and met defeat
down at this port beside the sea
did not give up his horse to me.
If I can't have the horse outright,
I think I ought to have the knight."
The lord Gawain told him, "My friend,
the knight is yours; I don't intend

198

to counter such a worthy plan."
"My word," replied the ferryman,   7410
"I don't want such a present, sir,
for I believe that if he were
to try resisting, you well might
have trouble capturing the knight
if he decided to attack.
But if you can, sir, bring him back,
and we'll be quits." "If I walk there
and put my charger in your care,
can I trust you to keep my horse?"
The ferryman said, "Yes, of course,   7420
I'll keep him in security
and give him back most willingly.
I will not harm you while I live,
this promise I shall freely give."
"I shall believe the things I've heard;
I trust you and shall take your word."
To this the lord Gawain agreed.
Dismounting from his new-found steed,
he placed him in the boatman's care.
The boatman promised to be fair   7430
while keeping him, and so the lord
Gawain proceeded with drawn sword.
He found the knight, who could abide
no further wounds: he'd hurt his side
so seriously, much blood was lost.
The lord Gawain went to accost
the warrior, who was terrified
and told him, "Sir, I cannot hide
my injury is deep, and clearly
I could not be hurt more severely.   7440
It seems to me that in a flood
I lost about eight pints of blood;
I'm at your mercy." Sir Gawain
said, "Get up now," and with much pain
the hurt knight struggled to his feet.
The lord Gawain led him to meet
the boatman, who was very grateful.
The lord Gawain asked for the hateful
maid he had chosen to escort.
He asked the boatman at the port   7450
if he could shed some light upon

that maid or where she might have gone?
The ferryman responded, "Sir,
you need not give a thought to her
or where she went; no maid is she,
but worse than Satan ever could be.
Down to this seaport she has led
many a knight who's lost his head.
If you'll take my advice today,
you'll come along with me and stay   7460
within a dwelling like my own.
It is unwise to stay alone
and linger on this river strand.
This is a wild, mysterious land,
with many mighty wonders filled."
"My friend, because you have so willed,
I'll take your counsel faithfully,
no matter what becomes of me."
The lord Gawain did so and let
the ferryman lead Gringalet   7470
into the skiff and go before.
The men came to the other shore
and very near the water's edge
they found his dwelling: they allege
a count could stay there, think it fit,
and be extremely pleased with it.
The ferryman led in his guest
and prisoner, and did his best
to honor them as they deserved.
That night the lord Gawain was served   7480
with a lord's supper, which was pleasant:
good venison and partridge, pheasant
and plovers, wine, clear red and white,
both old and new, all strong and bright.
The ferryman was much impressed
by both his prisoner and his guest.
The men kept eating till the table
was carried off by servants able,
and washed their hands. The lord Gawain
felt he had managed to obtain   7490
good lodgings and was gratified.
He was extremely satisfied
with the boatman's hospitality.
As soon as Sir Gawain could see

the daylight starting to appear
next morning, knowing dawn was near,
he rose, as he had always done;
he'd always risen with the sun.
The boatman also was awake
and rose with him for friendship's sake.   7500
They leaned to view the vast terrain
from turret windows. Sir Gawain
saw fields and woods and did not miss
the castle on the precipice.
"Host," said the lord, "If you don't mind,
I wish to ask of you and find
who rules this land, so wide and fair,
and that great castle over there."
"Sir, I don't know," his host replied.
"You do not know? I'm mystified   7510
by your reply, for I believe
you serve the castle and receive
an ample income, yours to claim,
yet you don't know your liege lord's name!"
The boatman answered, "That is so.
As I have said, I do not know
and never knew his name before."
"Dear host, in that case, tell me more:
who guards the town and citadel?"
"Sir, it is guarded very well: 7520
five hundred crossbows and great bows,
of which the castle can dispose,
are always poised for an attack,
and they would not stop shooting back
and never tire of it nor shirk;
that's how the bows were made to work.
Let me describe the situation.
There is a queen, of highest station,
a lady of outstanding worth,
rich, wise, of very noble birth.   7530
The queen came here with all her treasure
of gold and silver beyond measure
to live within this country long
and to construct this manor strong.
Also the queen brought with her here
a lady she holds very dear,
and ever since the great queen brought her,

she's called the lady 'queen' and 'daughter'.
That second queen is too a mother
and has a daughter fair, another   7540
who does not shame her noble birth.
I think you could not find on earth
a lady with more poise and grace
nor with more beautiful a face.
Both by enchantment and by art
their hall is guarded in each part,
as I will tell you presently.
A clerk, wise in astronomy,
a learned man whom the queen brought
to the great palace there, has wrought   7550
the many wondrous things there are;
I've heard of nothing similar.
No knight goes in that citadel
and stays an hour alive and well,
if he is full of cowardice,
or flattery, or avarice,
or guilty of some sin or vice.
By some enchantment or device
no traitor, coward can survive;
no perjurer can stay alive;   7560
inside that palace, cheats die fast;
within its walls they do not last.
Within there young men congregate
from many lands who serve, and wait,
and learn to use the arms they bear;
more than five hundred men are there,
some bearded, some not: in that place
one hundred have no beard nor trace
of mustache, but one hundred show
the beards they've just begun to grow.   7570
One hundred others shave and shear
their beards each week throughout the year.
One hundred's hair is white as wool;
one hundred's hair with gray is full,
and there are ladies, aged, bereft,
who have no lords and husbands left
to hold their lands and are deprived
unjustly of the wealth derived
from landholdings and revenues.
Young ladies who are orphans choose   7580

to keep the two queens company.
The queens treat them most graciously.
They come and go, and as they stir
they wait for what will not occur:
for the arrival of a knight
who will protect them by his might,
restore the ladies' revenues,
and after he has done so, choose
good husbands for the maids, and then
make knights out of the younger men.   7590
But no, the sea will turn to ice
before a knight without a vice
appears and stays alive in there.
The knight must be entirely fair,
intelligent, uncovetous,
bold, nobly born, brave, generous,
and loyal, free from vice and sin.
If that knight came and lived therein,
he'd rule the castle, and restore
the ladies's lands, and end the war,   7600
and marry off the maidens then,
and make knights of the younger men,
and banish every magic spell
from the enchanted citadel."
The lord Gawain was pleased by such
good news and liked it very much.
He said, "Host, let's be on our way;
give me my arms without delay,
and bring my charger to the door.
I will not wait here anymore;   7610
I'm leaving now." "Where to, sir? Stay,
may God protect your life today,
tomorrow, and in days ahead."
"Not at this moment, host," he said.
"Blessed be your house! With Heaven's aid,
I'll go and see the spells they've laid,
the maids, and wonders which they did!"
"Don't say that, sir, and God forbid
that you do something so absurd!
Stay here with me and take my word."   7620
"Be quiet, host! To hear you speak,
you think me cowardly and weak.
May Heaven never have my soul,

if I pursue another goal,
or do as someone else thinks wise."
"Sir, I'll be still, for I surmise
it's wasted effort, and I know
that if you wish to go, you'll go.
I must escort you, which is sad.
No company you could have had   7630
will win you there, as is well known,
as much respect as will my own.
So I shall take you, but I ask
a boon before I start the task."
"What is it, host? I want to know it."
"First promise me you will bestow it."
"I'll do your bidding, host, provided
it is not shameful," he decided.
Then he commanded them to lead,
out of the stable stall, his steed   7640
already harnessed, and he sought
his weapons, which the people brought.
He armed himself, and turned, and rode
off from the ferryman's abode.
The ferryman turned back and went
to mount his palfrey, for he meant
to take the knight most faithfully
to where he thought he should not be.
They went until they reached the flight
of stairs before the palace site,   7650
and at the foot, they noticed that*

---

v. 7651. This man with the silver leg may be a double for the Fisher King. Haidu notes
(*Aesthetic Distance*, p. 248) that both men are wounded in the leg, wealthy, engaged in
pastimes (presumably forced upon them by their disabilities); both arouse curiosity, but
neither succeeds in drawing a question from the hero. Frappier notes (*Chrétien de
Troyes et le Mythe du Graal*, p. 241) that there are other interpretations of this mysteri-
ous figure: Sheila Fynn saw him as an allegorical symbol of the pagan man, and he might
also be a devil or a pagan divinity from Hell, such as Pluto, was was often called "the
Rich." Loomis notes (*Arthurian Tradition*, pp. 445-447) that in the Welsh tale, "The
Dream of Maxen," this figure was seated on an ivory throne, carving chessmen from a
golden rod, and that perhaps because of confusion by Chrétien or his source between the
words "eschace" (wooden leg) and "eschacier" (man with a wooden leg), and the words
"eschac" (chessman), "eschec" (chess piece), and "eschequier" (chessboard), it was not
the rich man's *leg*, but his *chessboard* that was of silver, banded with gold, and set with
precious stones.

there was a one-legged man who sat
upon a bunch of gladioli.
His leg was made of silver wholly,
or else of silvered metal, banded
with gold and jewels. Not empty-handed,
the one-legged man sat all alone
and used a pocket knife to hone
a stick of ash wood. To detain them
the cripple spoke no words to rein them.   7660
They spoke no words to him nor tried.
The boatman pulled the lord aside.
"What's your opinion, sir, I beg,
about that man who has one leg?"
"His leg is not of aspen wood,"
said Sir Gawain, "My word, I could
see beautiful jewels set in it."
"This one legged man does benefit
from properties which he can claim,
great ones and beautiful. God's name,   7670
the income makes him very rich!
You would have heard a few things which
would have displeased you at that spot,"
the boatman said, "if it were not
that I accompanied you past there."
They went ahead until the pair
came to the palace by and by.
The entrance way was very high.
The doors were beautiful and rich;
the hinges and the catches which   7680
were in the bolt were of fine gold,
according to the story told.
One of the doors was ivory,
and carved and sculpted beautifully,
paired with another, ebony door,
as well carved as the one before.
Each door was trimmed with gold and shone
with many a magic, precious stone.
The paving was of many hues
of black, white, violets, reds, deep blues,   7690
placed skillfully in a design
and polished to a brilliant shine.
Within the palace was a bed,
and none of it was wood; instead

it was all made of gold, in hoards,
except the silver mattress cords.*
I tell no tales nor lies bare-faced:
where the cords met and interlaced,
small bells were hanging from the bed.
It had a great silk samite spread,   7700
and on each bedpost, held there fast,
there was a carbuncle, which cast
its light across the room as bright
as four well-lighted candles might.
The bed was resting on a pair
of statues of fierce dogs: teeth bare
and grimacing with silent squeals.
The dogs were set upon four wheels.
So freely did they roll and slip,
that if you used one fingertip   7710
to give the bed a little shove,
the bed would roll from one end of
the great room to the other end.
So was the bed, and I contend
it is the truth that I recount.
No bed owned by a king or count
was ever like this bed at all,
and centered in the palace hall.
The palace (trust me when I talk)
was not in any part of chalk.   7720
The walls were marble, and above
were rows of glassed-in windows of
such clearness that, if you took pains,
you could see through the window panes
all entering the walled estate
once they had passed beyond the gate.
The walls were painted costly hues;
the finest colors one could choose,
but I won't start describing all
the things within the palace wall.   7730

v. 7696. The Wondrous Bed is similar to the perilous bed upon which Lancelot lay
(*Lancelot*, vs. 503-534, Roques edition). Lancelot was nearly killed by a flaming lance
that descended at midnight, grazed his side, and set fire to the bed. Loomis (*Arthurian
Tradition*, pp. 443-444) notes that Gawain's adventure has parallels with the Irish saga
of *Bricriu's Feast*, in which the hero Cuchulainn undergoes similar trials in Curoi's re-
volving fortress (echoed in the wheels of the Wondrous Bed).

It had — and even more than those —
four hundred windows which would close,
one hundred others open wide.
The lord Gawain went on inside
and walked through, looking everywhere,
inspecting everything with care.
When done, he called the ferryman
and said to him, "Dear host, I can
find nothing in the palace here
to give a stranger cause to fear. 7740
What you say now, and what was meant
by your attempting to prevent
my coming here and seeing it?
For I would like to rest and sit
a little while upon the spread.
I've never seen a richer bed."
"What! My dear sir, may God forbid!
Do not go near it. If you did,
you'd die the worst death any knight
has ever died in any plight." 7750
"In that case, host, what shall I do?"
"What, sir? I will explain to you,
since you've decided to preserve
your life a while more, I observe.
At home, when you were so intent
on coming here, before we went
I asked you for an unknown boon,
and now the time seems opportune
for me to ask it. You will learn
the favor is that you return 7760
to your own land to tell each friend
and person there that you contend
the palace is superior
to any you have seen before
or anyone has ever known."
"I say God hates me, and I own
that I'm disgraced and brought to shame,
the two together! All the same
I think that you are saying it
since it is for my benefit, 7770
but I refuse to be gainsaid.
I plan to sit upon the bed
and see the maidens who were leaning

over the window sills last evening."
His host retorted, pulling back
to strike him harder or attack,
"I tell you, you will not behold
one of those maids of whom you've told.
Go back at once the way you came,
for, on no pretext you could name,   7780
could you behold them with your eyes.
God save me, you should realize
the ladies, queens, and maidens too
are watching you this instant through
those glassy windows. Be aware
that they are in their chambers there."
"My word," the lord Gawain then said,
"at least I'll sit upon the bed,
if I can't see a single maid.
I can't believe this bed was made   7790
for any other end or plan
except for a great nobleman
or lady to recline on it.
Upon my soul, there I shall sit,
be done to me whatever will."
At that the ferryman fell still.
He could not stop the lord Gawain,
but he did not wish to remain
within the palace wall and stay
to watch him sit. He went his way   7800
and said, "How bitterly I grieve
about your death, sir. I believe
upon that bed no knight has lain
or sat upon its counterpane,
because it is the Wondrous Bed,
on which no man may lay his head,
nor sleep, nor take repose, nor sit,
and rise alive and whole from it.
It's such a pity you must take
such risks and put your life at stake,   7810
and with no ransom or reprieve!
Since you will not agree to leave
for love or reasons I extoll,
may God have mercy on your soul.
I do not have the heart to stay
and watch you die." He went away.

At once the lord Gawain sat down,
armed as he'd come into the town,
his shield hung round his neck and head.
When he sat down upon the bed,   7820
the mattress cords let out a scream;
the bells rang out to the extreme
ends of the palace; they were rung
and echoed back. The windows flung
themselves wide open at the bells,
which set in motion magic spells.
The palace wonders were unveiled.
First great and lesser arrows sailed
out of the windows toward the floor,
and more than seven hundred tore   7830
through Sir Gawain's shield, where they stuck.
He did not know how he'd been struck.
The magic spells were of a kind
made so no one could see or find
from where the giant arrows came,
nor see the archers. All the same,
you could have heard great noises rending
the air, from bows and crossbows bending
and shooting arrows. Sir Gawain
would not have chosen to remain,   7840
not for one thousand marks as pay.
The windows, though, without delay,
shut by themselves; no human passed
to push the windows closed and fast.
The lord Gawain began to pluck
out the thick arrows which were stuck
fast in his shield, and often felt
blood flowing from the wounds they'd dealt.
Before he'd pulled them, he was put
through one more trial, for with his foot   7850
a peasant kicked another door.
It opened: with a ferocious roar
a proud and wondrous lion, kept
half starved, strong and gigantic, leapt
through the door with a single bound,
attacked the lord Gawain, and ground
his sharp claws in the shield, with tracks
as deep as if the shield were wax;
his claws went through the shield with ease.

The knight was brought down to his knees,   7860
but he leapt up. At once the lord
Gawain drew out his naked sword
and struck the beast a blow so dread,
he severed his front paws and head.
The lord was joyful, for the paws
stayed on his shield hung by the claws.
Part of the claws hung on its face,
and part of them were still in place
forced through the shield by the attack.
Well pleased, the lord Gawain went back,   7870
once he could see the lion dead,
and sat once more upon the bed.
His host, who had a happy face,
returned and found him still in place.
He said, "I promise, sir, from here
you will have nothing more to fear.
Remove your armature of war;
you've come and ended evermore
the marvels that the palace raised.
You will be honored, highly praised   7880
above all other men, extolled,
and waited on by young and old,
so praises be to God our Lord!"
To Sir Gawain there came a horde
of younger men who knelt and were
clothed in fine tunics. "My dear sir,
you are the one for whom we've waited
and long desired to see," they stated,
"we offer you our services."
"I think that your opinion is   7890
that I have stayed away too long."
One man began it, then the throng
removed his armor, shield, and sword,
and while the youths disarmed the lord
and helped him set his armor down,
some other young men of the town
went out for his horse, which they stabled.
And while the younger men enabled
the lord Gawain to doff his arms,
a maid came in, with many charms,   7900
and she was lovely to behold.
She wore a circlet of pure gold

upon her hair, with every strand
at least as golden as that band.
Her face was beautiful and white,
by Nature's hand with crimson bright
illuminated; she was straight,
well formed, and tall, of agile gait.
Behind her other maidens came;
as lovely and of noble name.   7910
One young man came with them, no more,
and up against his neck he bore
a surcoat, tunic, robe, and cloak.
The cloak, the one of which I spoke,
was lined with ermine interlaid
with sable, mulberry black in shade;
without it was of scarlet wool.
Their entrance seemed so wonderful
to Sir Gawain, and so surprising,
he could not keep himself from rising   7920
and springing to his feet to meet them.
He said, "Be welcome, maids," to greet them.
The first maid told him, with a bow,
"Dear sir, the queen, my lady, now
sends me on her behalf to greet you.
Her people she commands to treat you
as if you were their rightful lord.
Without deception I accord
my services before the rest,
and furthermore I can attest   7930
these maidens from the citadel
will treat you as their lord as well.
They've longed for you and feel delight
at seeing you at last, sir knight,
who are the bravest of the brave.
I have no more to tell you, save
that we are at your service now."
All of the maidens made a bow
and knelt to show that from that day
they honored him. Without delay   7940
he had the maidens of the town
arise at once and then sit down.
They were a joy to contemplate,
first since their loveliness was great,
and second, they were pleasing since

they had made him their lord and prince.
The lord Gawain was joyful, more
than he had ever been before;
such honors had the Lord endowed.
The maid stepped forward from the crowd   7950
and went to meet him and declare,
"My lady sends this robe to wear
before she sees you, from her sense
of courtesy and common sense.
She thinks that you were so maltreated
by your trials, you are overheated.
Put on the robe, try wearing it,
and let us see if it will fit.
It's prudent to endeavor not
to get chilled after being hot,   7960
you may become chilled to the bone,
which riles the blood. Upon her own
she sent this robe of ermine fur,
so nothing harmful will occur.
My lady queen, to be precise,
thinks just as water turns to ice,
so does the blood congeal and cake,
when people tremble hard and shake
after becoming overheated."
The courteous lord Gawain entreated,   7970
(the finest man the world has seen,)
"The Lord preserve my lady queen;
God is all goodness and your Saviour.
You are so gracious in behavior
and are so very eloquent.
The thoughtful messagers she sent
show me she must be very wise.
Indeed, she seems to realize
exactly what a knight requires.
Thanks be to her, since she desires   7980
to send this robe; thank her for me."
The maiden answered willingly,
"I promise you I shall do so,
and you can put it on and go
and look upon the countryside
out of those windows, or decide
to mount that tower, where you could
look out on river, field, and wood

until I have come back again."
She turned and left. The lord Gawain   7990
put on the ermine robe, one which
was very costly, very rich,
and fastened it beneath his chin
by clasping it with a brooch pin
hung from the collar of his gown.
He sought the tower to look down
upon the scenery from its height.
His host the boatman and the knight
went up around the spiral stair
beside the vaulted palace fair,   8000
until they reached the tower's summit
and viewed the lands surrounding from it.
The country round the citadel
was lovelier than one can tell.
So, from on high, the lord Gawain
admired the river and the plain
and forest filled with birds and deer.
"By God, host, I'll like living here,"
said Sir Gawain, "for I can go
and hunt with arrows and a bow   8010
within this forest that we see."
"Sir, say no more of that to me,"
the boatman told him, "Hush, instead,
because I've often heard it said
the man whom God would love so well,
he would be called by those who dwell
within 'defender, master, lord',
it would be certain, underscored,
that he could never leave the site,
no matter if it's wrong or right,   8020
so you must never speak to me
of hunting or of archery.
Within these walls you will remain
and never go outside again."
"Host, say no more to me; I find
that shortly I will lose my mind,
if you have more advice to give!
I'll have you know I cannot live
for seven days or seven years
times twenty, unless it appears   8030
that I can leave at any hour!"

The lord Gawain went from the tower
into the palace hall to brood,
for he was in an angry mood,
sat on the bed, and stayed in place,
and pulled a sad and mournful face,
until the maid returned, the same
who had been there when first he came.
When Sir Gawain saw she was present,
he was ill-tempered and unpleasant   8040
when he arose and greeted her.
She saw his words and face both were
much altered, heard the angry way
he spoke what words he had to say,
and realized from what she heard
that something that had just occurred
must have annoyed him, but she dared
not let him notice, and declared,
"My lady, when you send for her,
will come in here to see you, sir.   8050
Your meal is ready; you may go
and dine above or down below,
where and whenever you decide."
"Fair maiden," Sir Gawain replied,
"I am not interested in eating.
I hope my body will be meeting
misfortune if it once finds pleasure
in food before I hear some measure
of better news, so I refuse.
I need to hear some better news!"   8060
The maiden, in great consternation
at hearing his recrimination,
left the great hall without a word.
The queen asked her what had occurred.
"Please tell me in what frame of mind,
dear granddaughter, did you just find
the good lord God has given us?"
she asked the maiden to discuss.
"Oh, honored queen, in my belief
I am about to die of grief!   8070
My heart must be completely broken!
Our noble, kind lord has not spoken
a word that's not irate or cross;
I am completely at a loss,
because he gave no explanation.

I dared not ask for information,
but I can say this much," she said,
"first he was eloquent, well bred,
and filled with joy and with well being,
so that we did not tire of seeing   8080
his countenance, so bright and gay,
and hearing all he had to say.
His manner changed so by and by,
that I believe he wants to die,
for everything seems to displease him."
"Now, granddaughter, I will appease him;
do not be so distressed," said she.
"The moment he lays eyes on me,
though great his anger, have no doubt
that soon it will be driven out,   8090
and joyfulness will take its place."
The great queen, at a regal pace,
went in the palace with the other
queen, who accompanied her mother,
and was most glad to go with her.
Two hundred fifty maidens were
behind the queens, and in their train
as many youths or more again.
When Sir Gawain saw one queen and
the other holding to her hand,   8100
his heart, for often hearts can guess,
informed him with assuredness
the lady entering the room
must be the mighty queen of whom
he had been told so steadily.
He could have guessed it readily,
for she had white hair hanging down
below her hips and wore a gown
of white silk trimmed with flowers of gold
embroidered finely to behold.   8110
When Sir Gawain saw her, he sped
to greet her, and the great queen said,
"My lord, I am the lady who
rules in this palace after you.
Yours is the lordship: I have turned it
over to you since you have earned it.
Tell me, are you affiliated
with Arthur's household?" "Yes," he stated.
"Are you, I'd like to be informed,

a knight of the Watch, who have performed   8120
great deeds in such a valiant way?"
"I'm not, my lady." "As you say.
Please tell me if you can be found
among the knights of the Table Round;
that company whose strength and worth
makes them the most admired on earth?"
"I dare not claim, since you inquired,
to be among the most admired;
I would not rank me with the first
nor think myself among the worst."   8130
"My very dear sir," answered she,
"you've spoken with great courtesy
when you reject the best men's fame
and yet reject the worst men's shame.
How many sons, throughout his life,*
had King Lot by his lawful wife?"
"Four, lady." "Name the sons." "Gawain
was eldest, next was Agravain
the Proud, with hard hands, and the others
who followed their two older brothers   8140
are Gaheris and Gareth." "Yes,*
so help me God, they did possess
those names," she said, "as I recall.
Please Heaven that his four sons all
were with us now! Do tell me, then,
if you have met King Urien?"
"Yes, lady." "Has he sons at court?"
"Yes, lady, two of wide report
with famous records to maintain.*

v. 8135. Hilka notes (*Der Percevalroman*, pp. 762-763) that Lot, King of Orkney,
was married to Arthur's sister Morcadés, by whom he had four sons: Gawain, Agravain,
Gaheris, and Gareth. King Lot is mentioned in Geoffrey of Monmouth (Faral edition, p.
225), in Wace's *Brut* 9056, among other verses, and also in *Erec and Enide* v. 1705 and in
Yvain, v. 6261 (Roques editions), among other references.

v. 8141. Hilka notes (*Der Percevalroman*, p. 763) that Gaheris is mentioned in *Erec
and Enide*, v. 1695 (Roques edition).

v. 8149 ff. Loomis notes (*Arthurian Tradition*, p. 492) that the first Yvain (also men-
tioned in v. 2844) is Yvain, the legitimate son of King Urien, the historic Owain who was
a prince of the North Britons in the late 6th century. He is the hero of Chrétien's preced-
ing romance. Yvain the Bastard, according to a Welsh account, was the illegitimate son
of King Urien and Mordron. Hilka notes (*Der Percevalroman*, p. 763) that the two
Yvains are mentioned in *Erec and Enide*, vs. 2174, 1685, and 1686 (Roques edition).

The first son is the lord Yvain, 8150
the courteous and nobly born,
and when I see him in the morn,
it makes me happy all the day,
so wise and courteous is his way.
The second son's named like the other,
but he is only his half brother
and called "the Bastard": Urien's whelp
has beaten all knights to a pulp
who were paired with him, when they fought.
The two Yvains at court are thought 8160
to be extremely courteous knights,
intelligent and brave in fights."
"Dear sir, how is King Arthur, then?"
"Much better than he's ever been;
strong, healthy, full of vigor, more
than he has ever been before."
"But that is normal, sir, in truth,
because King Arthur's still a youth;
one hundred at the very most.*
Indeed, King Arthur could not boast 8170
of being older, I don't doubt.
Please tell me something more about
the queen's condition and well being."
"My lady, there's no disagreeing:*
she is so very beautiful,
so very courteous, so full
of wisdom, that God in His grace
has not created any place
of other law or language where
one could find anyone so fair. 8180
No lady's been so glorified
since the Lord God took Adam's side
and the first woman was thus raised,
and she deserves to be so praised.

v. 8169. Queen Ygerne, who considers King Arthur young at 100, may well be living outside of mortal time. There were biblical precedents, however, for people living to be several hundred years old, with which Chrétien was undoubtedly familiar.

v. 8174. Gawain's description of Queen Guinevere's graciousness, eloquence, wisdom, and beauty emphasizes those sides of her character that are included in the descriptions of the queen in *Erec and Enide* and *Yvain*. Her less attractive qualities are emphasized in the portrait of the queen as the capricious and adulterous heroine of *Lancelot*.

As the schoolmaster, wise and keen,
instructs small children, so the queen
instructs us, and is always giving
the world a model of good living.
From her all virtues radiate,
and spring forth, and originate,   8190
and everyone at court who grieves
is comforted before he leaves.
Our gracious queen has always guessed
each person's true worth and how best
to please him, and has done or said it.
The man with fine deeds to his credit
has learned them from the things she taught.
No man, however overwrought,
has left my lady angrily."
"Nor will you angrily leave me."   8200
"Once I would not have thought it true,
but I have seen you, and I do.
Before I did not even care,
I felt so much distress in there,
and now, though I was so annoyed,
I could not be more overjoyed."
"By God, who gave me birth, sir knight,"
replied the queen with hair of white,
"your joy will double and increase
each day, and it will never cease.   8210
Since you are joyful now, and feel
much happier, please eat your meal
when you are ready for it, sir,
in any place that you prefer;
perhaps upstairs, or you could go
and eat within those rooms below."
"My lady, I'd not trade this hall
for any palace room at all.
They said no knight sat here or ate."
"No knight, my lord, at any rate,   8220
who thereinafter had the power
to leave, or stay alive an hour
or half an hour in this place."
"Then I will dine here, in that case,
my lady, if I have your leave."
"Most willingly, and I believe
you are the first knight of them all

to dine within the palace hall."
The queen departed, leaving there
two hundred fifty maidens fair,   8230
the fairest in the palace fine,
who with the lord Gawain would dine
and serve him and perform each task
it might occur to him to ask.
The courtiers gladly served the knight.
Some men's hair was completely white;
some men had gray streaks in their hair,
some had no gray hairs anywhere.
Some had no mustache and no beard;
two of these younger men appeared.   8240
The young men knelt before the lord,
and while one youth brought wine and poured
the other young man served the meat
out of a platter. At the seat
by Sir Gawain his host was placed.
The two men did not dine in haste;
it was no quick meal: their repast
took longer than a day would last
around the feast of Trinity.
Before the last amenity,   8250
the heavy darkness had returned,
and many torches had been burned.
Their talk ranged widely while they ate.
The people strove to celebrate
for their lord in these circumstances,
with many dances and round dances
at dinner's end, to end the day.
And when he went to bed, he lay
again upon the Wondrous Bed,
a pillow placed beneath his head   8260
by a handmaiden, where the knight
slept comfortably till it was light.
By morning they'd prepared for him
a samite robe with ermine trim.
The ferryman of whom I spoke
assisted him when he awoke
to wash his hands and dress and rise.
Moreover Clarissant, the wise,
the eloquent, the true, the loyal,
the maiden beautiful and royal,   8270

was present at this rising scene.
She left and knelt before the queen,
who turned around to question her.
"Now, by the faith, dear granddaughter,
you owe me as a rightful debt,
had your dear lord arisen yet?"
"My lady, yes, some time ago."
"Sweet graddaughter, where did he go?"
"My lady, he went out to climb
the tower, but whether by this time   8280
he has descended, I don't know."
"Dear granddaughter, I want to go
and find him, for today, God please,
he shall have joyfulness, and ease,
and nothing but complete content."
The queen arose, because she meant
to join the lord, and walked until,
high at the tower window sill,
she saw him watching as a maid
and knight clad in full armor made   8290
their way across the meadow wide.
The two queens entered, side by side,
but from a different direction,
and found both men deep in reflection
by windows at the passing scenes.
"Good morning," said the pair of queens,
"Our glorious Father high above,
the one who made His mother of*
His daughter grant you joy and mirth."
"Our Lord, who sent His son to earth,   8300
exalting Christianity,
grant you great joy, so may it be.
Now ladies, if it be your will,
come over to this window sill.
Who is that maiden in that field?
A knight who bears a quartered shield
accompanies her, and both appear
to be intent on coming here."
The queen looked and began to say,

v. 8298. "The one who made His mother of His daughter" refers to the belief that the
Virgin Mary was both a daughter of God, born without sin to Saint Anne, and the moth-
er of God through the immaculate conception of her son, Jesus Christ.

"Sir, I can tell you right away.   8310
She is the maiden, evil-ridden,
who followed you when you had ridden
toward here last night to stay awhile.
She is too arrogant and vile
for you to pay her any heed.
That knight whom she appears to lead
is one I beg you not to fight,
because you ought to know the knight
is the world's bravest and the best.
His many battles are no jest;   8320
for many knights, I can report,
were put to death here at this port."
"My lady," said the lord Gawain,
"I want to speak with her again,
if you will give me leave to try."
"Sir, may it not please God that I
grant you my leave to hurt yourself.
Please leave the maiden to herself,
because she is so full of malice.
Please God you never leave this palace   8330
for goals so futile to achieve,
for you would wrong us if you leave."
"Ah, woe is me! My noble queen,
my anguish could not be more keen,
for I would never be content
within this palace, if it meant
I could not leave! May God prefer
I not be long a prisoner!"
"Oh, lady queen," the boatman said,
"allow the knight to go ahead   8340
and do as he thinks good or ill.
Don't keep him here against his will;
he'll die of grief, I do believe."
The queen said, "I will let him leave,
provided, if God spares the knight,
he vows he will return tonight
and sleep within the palace here."
"My lady, you need have no fear,
for if I can, I will return.
I'll ask a favor in my turn: 8350
I beg of you, please do not seek
to learn my name before one week,

if you don't mind," said Sir Gawain.
"Since you desire it, I'll refrain,"
the white-haired queen reciprocated.
"Although I don't wish to be hated,
but had you not forbidden me,
the first thing I'd have asked would be
to have you tell us all your name."
Back down the tower stair they came.   8360
Men ran to bring the arms he'd need
to arm himself and fetched his steed.
Completely armed, the lord Gawain
remounted, and rode down again,
and reached the port beside the sea.
The boatman kept him company.
The pair got in the boat once more
and headed for the other shore.
The rowers took the oars and rowed
across the river; when they slowed,   8370
the lord Gawain got off the skiff.

THE GUIROMELANT

The other knight said, "Dear friend, if
you know that knight in armor's name,
who's by the river bank and came
to meet us here, please tell me so."
The merciless maid answered, "No,
but he's that same knight, I can say,
who brought me here just yesterday."
"God keep me safe," the warrior swore,
"he is the one I'm looking for,   8380
and I was so afraid he might
escape my clutches, for no knight
of mortal mother born will say
he crossed the border of Galloway
and boast elsewhere that he traversed
this country if I find him first.
Now since I see that God has let
the knight come to me, I will set
upon him, for I mean to hold
a prisoner this warrior bold,   8390
who as my captive shall remain."
He hurled himself at Sir Gawain,
with no threat nor defiant word.
He lifted up his shield and spurred.
The lord Gawain went riding toward
the knight and struck him, and the lord
severely hurt his side and arm,
but did the knight no mortal harm.
So solid was his hauberk's chain,
the iron lance of Sir Gawain   8400
could not completely pierce its strength,
except the tip, a finger's length,
went in his body, and the knight
fell to the ground. When he caught sight
of his own blood, which flowed undried
through the bright mail at arm and side,
the knight was grieved, and fell upon
the lord Gawain with his sword drawn,
but soon he tired; he was not strong

enough to hold his ground for long,   8410
and asked that mercy be conferred.
The lord Gawain first took his word
and afterward bestowed the man
upon the waiting ferryman.
Meanwhile the maid demoniac
dismounted from her palfrey's back.
The lord Gawain next greeted her.
"Remount, friend," he entreated her,
"I must go back across the stream,
and you with me; I would not dream   8420
of leaving you alone back here."
"Ha, ha!" the maid began to sneer,
"you're so proud of yourself, sir knight.
You should have had a harder fight.
My friend's old wounds have worn him out,
or your boasts would not fly about.
Your silence would not be more great
had you been cornered in checkmate!
How can you feel superior,
in battle, to that warrior,   8430
because you've beaten him, although
you've seen so often, and you know
the weak can overcome the strong?
Now, if you dared to come along,
to leave this port beside the sea,
and ride beside me to that tree,
and at that place a task discharge,
done by my friend placed in the barge,
I would consider you as fine
a fighter as this friend of mine   8440
and cease to treat you with disdain."
"If, maiden," said the lord Gawain,
"I need go only to that tree,
I'll do as you have asked of me."
"Please God," the maiden said in turn,
"that I may not see you return."
They went the way the maiden led;
he followed, and she went ahead.
Within the palace, maidens fair
and ladies pulled and tore their hair.   8450
They tugged it as they cried, "Alas!
Why, when we see it come to pass

that he who should have been our lord
is going of his own accord
to his destruction and his death,
do we continue drawing breath?
The evil maiden leads the knight,
whom she has riding on her right,
to where no knight returns alive.
When we had just begun to thrive,   8460
alas! our hearts will break in two,
for God had sent a man who knew
all goodness, and there was in fact
no noble quality he lacked,
not courage nor another one."
The palace maidens had begun
lamenting for their lord, who went
off with the maid malevolent.
Eventually, when he and she
had ridden over to the tree,   8470
and had arrived and halted there,
the lord Gawain said, "Maiden fair,
tell me if we are quits now, or
if you would have me manage more.
If I am able, I will do
whatever deed might gladden you."
The evil maiden asked the lord,
"Now do you see that river ford,
where both the banks are very steep?
I think the river is more deep   8480
beneath that ford than anywhere.
My dear friend used to cross it there."   8486
"Oh, lovely one, no one would try!
Both river banks are steep and high,
and no one could get down that slope."
"You dare not cross; I had no hope   8490
that you possessed the nerve to dare
to go across the river there,"
the evil maiden told the lord,
"for this place is the Perilous Ford.
Unless he's magic powers extreme,
no man would dare to cross that stream."
The lord Gawain led his war horse
to the bank by the river's course.
Below him rushed the water deep,

and the embankment, sheer and steep,   8500
rose sharply on the other side,
and yet the river was not wide.
When Sir Gawain saw it, he told
himself his horse, in days of old,
much wider ditches often spanned;
and he had heard in many a land
that he who crossed the Perilous Ford
and its deep water, in reward
would have the greatest glory found
in any place the world around.   8510
He drew back from the stream a bit,
then galloped rapidly toward it
to jump across it, but he fell;
he did not take the jump too well.
His charger jumped and landed him
deep in the ford; the horse could swim
and touched the bottom, with a thump,
on all four feet and tried to jump.
He hurtled up, with one great leap,
the other bank, extremely steep.*   8520
When he had reached the other shore,
the great war horse could move no more;
he stood still and would not proceed.
The knight dismounted from his steed,
for after such a great event
he found his charger wholly spent.
The lord Gawain got down with speed,
and took the saddle off his steed,
and turned it upside down to try
to wipe it off and get it dry,   8530
then took the blanket off his mount,
so drenched with water an amount
ran down his legs from ribs and back.
The lord then put the saddle back
and rode with short steps at a walk.

v. 8520. Gringalet's leap echoes the leap Perceval's horse makes from the drawbridge
of the Fisher King's castle (v. 3407). Gawain's caring for the helpful steed recalls the
scene in which Yvain cares for the wounded lion. Frappier notes (*Chrétien de Troyes et le
Mythe du Graal*, p. 250) that Loomis (in *Arthurian Tradition*, pp. 448-454) traces the
first model of the episode of the Perilous Ford and the meeting with the Guiromelant to
the story of Pwyll, Prince of Dyved.

One knight who had a sparrow hawk
and who was hunting was revealed.
There were, in orchard and in field,
two bird dogs who had gone before.
The knight was very handsome, more   8540
than any man's lips could explain.
Approaching him, the lord Gawain
first greeted him, then said, "Dear sir,
may God, who made you handsomer
than any living creature, give
good luck and joy while you shall live."
The knight replied, "You are a good,
brave, handsome man, and yet you should
be willing to give me the reason
you left the maiden full of treason   8550
upon the other bank alone.
She had an escort of her own;
where is he now?" The lord said, "Sir,
the time that I encountered her,
a knight who bore a quartered shield
was leading her across the field."
"What did you do?" "I won the fight."
"And then what happened to the knight?"
"The ferryman led him away;
he said he wanted him as pay."   8560
"Dear brother, he spoke truth thereof.
The maiden was my ladylove
but not the sort to condescend
to love me or to call me friend.
Unless I forced her, to be sure,
I could not give a kiss to her.
She'd grant no favors willingly.
I loved her; she did not love me.
She always had her sweetheart there,
accompanying her everywhere.   8570
I killed him, took the maid away,
and strove to serve her, every way.
My services she would not claim;
when opportunities first came,
the maiden seized her chance, and fled,
and found another friend instead,
that man you sent away this morn.
That is no knight to treat with scorn,

for he is very brave, God save me.
Since then he's never acted bravely   8580
enough to dare to come around
a place he thought I might be found.
You've done a deed that hitherto
no knight has ever dared to do,
but since you dared, and since you've done
this knightly exploit, you have won
the whole world's glory in reward.
You leapt across the Perilous Ford
and showed your courage was extreme.
No knight has lived to cross that stream."   8590
"Why, sir," the lord Gawain replied,
"the evil maiden must have lied!
She made me think that truly, sir,
her sweetheart, out of love for her,
would cross the deep ford once a day."
"How treacherous! So did she say?
Would she would drown, she is so evil!
That maiden is full of the devil,
if she could tell you such a lie.
She hates you, I cannot deny,   8600
to seek to send you plunging down
that swirling water's depths to drown.
The fiend's damnation be assured!
But now you must pledge me your word,
and likewise I will pledge you mine:
I promise I will not decline
to tell you what you wish to know,
whether it brings me joy or woe;
and I am under obligation
to give you fullest information,   8610
and you will tell me in return
whatever I would like to learn,
and you will never lie to me
if you know what the truth may be."
They made this promise, man to man,
and first the lord Gawain began.
He told the knight, "Sir, first I care
to ask about that city there.
What is that city and its name?"
"My friend," the knight said, "I can claim   8620
to tell the truth: let it be known

the town is mine and mine alone
with no restriction to be borne;
I'm answerable to no man born;
I hold it from God, no one else.
The city's name is Orqueneseles."
"What is your name?" "Guiromelant."
"A noble man and valiant,
and I have heard of many lands
whose lordship lies within your hands.   8630
By what name goes the demoiselle
of whom, both near and far, they tell
no good, as you can testify?"
"No one knows it as well as I.
She should be held in greatest fear;
she's evil, and she loves to sneer.
'The Proud Woman of Nogres'," with scorn
he said, "the land where she was born
and taken out of as a child
is how that wicked maid is styled."   8640
"What is the name of her dear friend,
the reluctant knight I had to send
to be the boatman's prisoner?"
"He is a wondrous warrior,
friend, I would have you know outright,
and so his name is the Proud Knight
of the Passage with the Narrow Way
who guards the border of Galloway."
"Next tell that lofty castle's name,
mighty and fair, from whence I came   8650
and where, last night, I drank and ate?"
The Guiromelant, disconsolate
about what Sir Gawain had said,
turned sadly on his heel instead,
and he began to walk away.
The lord Gawain called him to say,
"Sir, answer me and come back now!
Remember that you made a vow."
The Guiromelant came to a halt
and turned his head for this assault.   8660
"The hour when I saw you first
and pledged my word to you be cursed!
Go on your way,for you are free
from any pledge you made to me;

free me of any obligation!
Although I wanted information
about the castle as my boon,
you know as much about the moon
as you could know about the town."
"Sir, I was there, and I lay down   8670
last evening on the Wondrous Bed.
It's like no other bed," he said.
"No man has ever seen its peer."
"I am amazed by what I hear,"
the Guiromelant replied, "God's sight!
it is a pleasure and delight
to listen to the lies you tell!
No storyteller does as well.
You are a minstrel, I can see,
and I thought you were telling me   8680
you were a knight of some renown
who did some brave deed at the town.
Still I would like to be informed
about the bold deeds you performed,
and what you saw in there," he said.
"Sir, when I sat upon the bed,
A great commotion reigned throughout
the palace, which you must not doubt.
Do not believe I tell a lie:
the bed cords first let out a cry,   8690
and then the little bells which hang
upon the bed cords loudly rang.
The windows, which were closed and fast,
flung themselves open. Arrows passed,
both great and lesser ones, which hit
my shield, and many stuck in it.
A lion, with a heavy mane,
huge and ferocious, on a chain,
kept in a vault for very long,
was loosed, and then the lion strong   8700
thrust all his claws straight through my shield.
The lion struck me," he revealed,
"because a peasant let him go.
He flung himself on me; the blow
he struck my shield upon that leap
drove all his claws in it, so deep
the lion could not pull them out.

If you are still in any doubt,
look here, you still can see the claws.
Thank God I severed head and paws 8710
together! After these events,
what think you of this evidence?"
At these words the Guiromelant
dismounted quickly. Suppliant
he came, and knelt down, and implored,
hands clasped together, that the lord
Gawain accept his deep remorse.
"We'll call it quits; remount your horse."
The knight remounted, much ashamed
about the way that he had blamed 8720
the lord Gawain. "Sir, God keep me,
I did not think that there could be
in near or far lands, anyone
who had the honor you have won.
Now tell me, sir, if you have seen
or ever met the white-haired queen,
and if you asked to learn her name,
or to find out from where she came."*
"Not that I can remember, sir,
but I saw her and spoke with her." 8730
The knight said, "I will tell you, brother:
that queen is good King Arthur's mother."
"Now, by the great faith which I owe
Almighty God, sir, years ago
King Arthur lost his mother, more
than sixty long years or before,*
so I believed, and so I heard."
"Yet it is true," the knight averred,
"she is his mother, he her son,
because when Uther Pendragon, 8740
King Arthur's father, was interred,

v. 8728. Haidu notes (*Aesthetic Distance*, p. 247) that, like Perceval, Gawain fails to ask an important question ("Who is the white-haired queen and where is she from?") that would have led to the discovery that members of his mother's family were in the castle.

v. 8736. Félix Lecoy notes that Perceval was about two years old at the time of his father's death, which occurred shortly after the death of Uther Pendragon (King Arthur's father) and Queen Ygerne's retirement to the castle. Perceval himself must be in his early 20s, and the statement that events linked with his father's death occurred 60 years ago is another troublesome inconsistency in the text ("Review," *Romania 78* [1957]: p. 411).

the Queen Ygerne, as it occurred,
came to this land with all her stock
of treasure, and upon that rock
she built that castle and the rich
and beautifully made palace which
you've just described. You must have seen
within its walls another queen,
the lady beautiful and great,
who once was married to the late   8750
King Lot and mother of the man
to whom I wish all ill I can,
the mother of Gawain." "Do tell.
I know Gawain extremely well.
He lost his mother, sir, I know,
and over twenty years ago."
"It's she; you must not doubt it, brother.
She came to stay here with her mother,
since she was carrying a baby,
the maiden who's become my lady,   8760
the tall and lovely maid I love
and, not to hide it, sister of
the very man whom God confound,
who would not tote his head around,
if only I had him as near
as I have you beside me here.
I'd cut his head off on the spot;
his sister's help would come to naught.
With my two hands I'd tear and wrest
his beating heart out of his chest;   8770
I feel such hatred and disdain."
"Upon my soul," said Sir Gawain,
"you do not love the way I do.
If I loved maid or lady true,
for the great love I bore therein,
I'd love and serve all of her kin."
"I do agree that you are right,
but may no good befall that knight.
His father killed my father, and
Gawain himself, with his own hand,   8780
killed one of my first cousins, too,
a gallant warrior, brave and true.
There was no way that I could find
to pay his slayer back in kind.

Do me a favor now and bring
the lady whom I love this ring.
Go on back to that castle, sir,
and give this finger ring to her
on my behalf, and then you must
tell her I love her and so trust 8790
the love we feel for one another,
that she would rather have her brother
Gawain a painful death to die,
before she saw the day that I
was scratched upon my little toe.
Greet her for me, and then bestow
this ring upon her for my part.
I love that maid with all my heart."
He gave the lord the ring to slip
over his little finger tip. 8800
"My word," he said, "sir, I contend
you have a wise and courteous friend,
a noblewoman of high birth,
both beautiful, and of great worth,
if she is willing to agree
to all you have been telling me."
"You'll do me a great kindness, sir,
if you will take the ring to her
and make to her a present of
this ring, in token of my love. 8810
I will repay you this good turn.
I'll tell you what you wish to learn
about the castle, for you came
and asked me what might be its name,
and in exchange I'll tell you so.
The castle, since you do not know,
is named the Rock of Canguin, where*
they weave expensive cloth and fair,
red, green, and much fine wool as well,
in large amounts they buy and sell. 8820
Now I have told, and you have heard;
I've not lied by a single word,

v. 8817. The Rock of Canguin, noted for its fine fabrics and occupied by 500 beauti-
fully dressed maidens, is the opposite of the Castle of Evil Adventure in *Yvain*, which was
occupied by 300 captive and malnourished maidens weaving fabric in a sweatshop oper-
ation.

and you have carried out your task.
Now, have you something more to ask?"
"No, sir, except leave to depart."
"Good sir, before I let you start,"
the knight said, "would you be so kind
to tell your name, if you don't mind."
"Sir knight," the lord Gawain replied,
"so help me God, I will not hide   8830
my name from you. I am the man
you hate as deeply as you can.
I am Gawain." "You are Gawain?"
"King Arthur's nephew, once again."
"Upon my word, you're overbold
or overfoolish to have told.
I feel for you a deadly hatred,
and now I am infuriated
I do not have my helmet laced
upon my head, or my shield placed   8840
upon my neck and well attached.
If I were armed, and we were matched
for even combat, sir, I vow
I'd cut your head off here and now,
and nothing would reduce my hate.
If you are brave enough to wait,
I'll fetch the weapons I conserve
and three or four men to observe
our combat, or, if you would rather,
you may go someplace even farther,   8850
and we will wait for one week's space.
Then we will come back to this place
in seven days with weapons keen.
You will send for the king and queen
and all the courtiers: knight and peer;
my army will assemble here
from everyplace throughout my land.
Our fight would not be underhand;
all who are present would have seen
and witnessed it: a fight between   8860
such brave men as we're thought to be
should not be held in secrecy.
There should be witnesses, by rights,
both ladies of the court and knights.
When one of us is forced to quit,

and everybody knows of it,
the winner will be honored one
thousand times more, because he won,
than he would be if no one knew
about the fight except the two."   8870
The lord Gawain said, "I confess
that I would settle for much less:
because, if you were willing, sir,
instead of fighting, I'd prefer,
if I wronged you, to make amends
determined by our sets of friends,
as they thought reasonable and right."
"I cannot think," replied the knight,
"what other reason there could be,
except you dare not fight with me,   8880
for the proposal that you give.
You may choose one alternative,
for I have offered you a pair:
you may wait for me, if you dare,
and I shall fetch my weapons, or
you may send word to your land for
a week from now, as best you can.
I've heard about King Arthur's plan
at Pentecost to hold his court*
at Orkney, and the journey's short;   8890
just two full days of traveling.
Your messengers would find the king
and court assembled. It seems wise
to choose the plan that I advise
and send to Orkney, for they've found*
each day of respite worth a pound."
The lord Gawain said, "God save me,

v. 8889. This is the second celebration of the feast of Pentecost within Gawain's year of adventures (the first was when Anguingueron and Clamadeu went to King Arthur's court with a message from Perceval). Frappier's explanation of this inconsistency is that in stories of the Round Table, when King Arthur assembled his court, it was almost automatically said to be at Pentecost (Frappier, "Note Complémentaire," p. 314). Hilka notes that the geography is a little fantastic, for the Orkneys are islands, not a city. (*Der Percevalroman*, p. 766).

v. 8895. Hilka notes (*Der Percevalroman*, p. 768) that among other references, this proverb is listed in Morawski, *Proverbes français* no. 2451: "Un jour de respit cent souz vaut."

the court is there assuredly,
you know the truth, and as you've planned,
I pledge to you by my own hand   8900
I shall send word, as you advise,
tomorrow or not shut my eyes."
"I'll lead you to the best bridge found
in any place the world around.
The river is too swift and deep.
No living thing can ford or leap
the river to the other side."
In answer, Sir Gawain replied,
"I'll seek no other bridge or ford,
whatever may be my reward.   8910
The wicked maid has challenged me,
and she would think me cowardly,
so I intend to keep my word
and go straight back to her." He spurred,
and then his horse, which was not slow,
leapt lightly over the stream below
without a bit of hesitating.
The maiden who had been berating
and scolding him, saw Sir Gawain;
she tied her palfrey by the rein   8920
tight to a tree, and much subdued,
walked over in a different mood.
The maiden spoke a humble greeting,
and said she came to him entreating
her mercy for the great amount
of suffering caused on her account.
"Please listen, sir," the maiden told,
"to why I was so harsh and cold
to all the knights who made me ride
with them and traveled by my side,   8930
if you will let me be so frank.
That knight upon the other bank
who spoke with you, and cursed be he,
misplaced his love by choosing me.
I hated him for the heartache
he caused by killing for my sake
the one who's lady-love I was.
I realize he thought, because
of all the courtesies he'd shown,
to win my love to be his own,   8940

but in that hope he was deluded.
When first a chance came, I eluded
that first knight to accompany
the knight you took away from me,
although that's not worth speaking of.
But on account of my first love,
whose death has parted him from me,
I have behaved so foolishly,
and spoken cutting words so long,
and been so wicked and so wrong,   8950
I did not care whom I offended
deliberately, for I intended
to make some warrier thereby
so very angry, he would fly
into a rage at my caprices
and tear me into little pieces,
for I have long wished I were dead.
Now please, dear sir," the maiden said,
"put me to death in such a way,
no maiden ever dares to say   8960
cross words or speak insultingly
to knights, once she has heard of me."
The lord Gawain said, "Maiden fair,"
do you imagine that I care
to kill you as a punishment?
May God's Son never be content
to have me hurt you any way.
Come, mount your palfrey, don't delay,
and we shall cross to that strong town.
Look at the boatman, waiting down   8970
beside the seaport, as before,
to take us to the other shore."
"Sir, I'll do anything at all."
The maid got on her palfrey small
with a long mane, and then the pair
rode to the boatman waiting there
to take the two across the stream,
an effort not at all extreme.
The ladies saw, by looking down,
the knight returning to the town.   8980
The men and women who had kept
lamenting for him, and had wept,
and been beside themselves with grief,

saw Sir Gawain with deep relief,
and everyone rejoiced far more
than anybody had before.
The queen, outside the palace, sat
and waited for him, ordering that
her maids join hands in dances, showing
their happiness was overflowing.   8990
They danced round dances, sang their song,
and Sir Gawain rode in the throng,
where he dismounted. As they faced him,
the ladies, maids, and queens embraced him
and showed their joy that he had come.
With joy they took his armor from
his legs and arms and chest and head.
The maiden Sir Gawain had led
they welcomed joyfully, and paid
every attention to the maid   9000
for his sake, but they would have shown
no welcome to the maid alone.
Into the palace, one and all,
they went and sat within the hall,
and Sir Gawain, amidst this stir,
sought out his sister, seated her
beside him on the Wondrous Bed,
and then, in a low voice, he said,
"Maid, from the other bank I bring
a very pretty emerald ring,   9010
a bright green jewel set in gold.
The knight who sent it to you told
that I must greet you, for his part;
you are the lady of his heart."
"Sir, I believe that in this instance,
I'd have to love him at a distance,
if I loved him, for certainly
he's never laid his eyes on me
except across the river bed.
But I thank him, for he has said   9020
he loved me many times before,
but not crossed over to my shore.
His messengers have begged me so,
I promised him my love, although
I'm only his to the extent
of those few messages we've sent."

"Oh, but his boasts are nothing other
than you would rather your own brother
the lord Gawain were dead, than know
he had a scratch on his big toe."   9030
"Oh, it's astonishing to me
that he could speak so foolishly!
Good Heavens, I did not suppose
that he would say such things as those!
How very foolish he must be
to send such messages to me!
My brother does not know I live;
I've never seen my relative,
yet the Guiromelant is wrong!
Upon my soul, I no more long   9040
for suffering or injury
for Sir Gawain than I do me."
While the two talked, the ladies waited.
The white-haired queen interrogated
the queen her daughter at her side.
"Dear daughter, will you not confide
your view of that lord by your daughter
and my granddaughter, for he sought her
in private talk some time ago.
Why I am pleased I do not know   9050
nor know a reason to object.
He is so noble, I expect
it is the reason why he chose
the fairest, wisest maid of those
within the palace; he is right.
Would it please Heaven that the knight
would wed and love her all his life*
the way Aeneas loved his wife
Lavinia." "Oh, yes," replied*
the other queen, "may Heaven guide   9060
his heart so that they love each other
so dearly, they're like sister and brother,
so that their loving hearts would mesh,

v.9057. The queen's comment echoes the crowd's comment when Blancheflor and
Perceval sat together: "God made them each for the other" (v. 1872).

v. 9059. This passage refers to Aeneas's marriage to Lavinia, the daughter of King
Latinus, in the *Eneas*. Lavinia was a symbol of virtuous love in the Middle Ages, whereas
Dido was a symbol of sensual love.

and that the two would be one flesh."
The thoughts behind her prayers were
that he love her and marry her.
She did not recognize her son.
Because, when all was said and done,
they would be like a sister and brother;
so would the couple love each other   9070
once they had learned they were related.
The mother would be much elated
and very joyful, in another
way than she spoke of with her mother.
When Sir Gawain had talked for long
with his fair sister, from the throng
he called a young man whom the knight
had noticed standing at his right.
The youth had seemed more diligent,
brave, willing, and intelligent,   9080
than all the youths within the hall.
Down to a lesser room and small
the lord Gawain went on his own;
the young man followed him alone.
"Young man," the lord said, "from the start
I thought that you were brave and smart.
I have a secret I must tell;
be certain that you keep it well,
it would be to your benefit.
Where I shall send you for a bit   9090
you will be joyfully received."
"My lord, I would not be so grieved
to have my tongue torn from my throat
than have one word in secret float
out of my mouth." "Then, brother, go
to find King Arthur, for you know
I am his nephew, I'm Gawain.
It can be done with little strain;
indeed, the journey should be short,
because the king is holding court   9100
in Orkney town for Pentecost.
Now if the journey's high in cost,
then I will have you reembursed.
When you come to King Arthur, first
he will be full of rage and woe,
but I am certain, and I know

when you greet him on my behalf,
he will rejoice, and smile, and laugh.
The whole court will rejoice again
at news of me," said Sir Gawain.   9110
"Then you must tell the king my plan;
he is my lord and I his man,
that by sworn faith and mutual trust,
he must not fail me, and he must
come to me and be here at least
five full days after the great feast,
camped on this field beneath the tower,
and he must do all in his power
to bring his whole court here in state,
the lesser people and the great,   9120
for I have pledged my word to fight
with the Guiromelant, a knight
who does not think the king or I
of any merit nor deny
his deadly hatred for the king.
Then tell the queen the selfsame thing,
to come, by the great faith between
her and myself, because the queen
is both my lady and my friend.
She will not fail me when I send   9130
for her to come and bring with her
the ladies and the maids who were
at court that day, for love of me.
One thing I fear tremendously:
you may not have a hunter strong
to keep your trip from being long."
The youth replied there was a large,
strong, good horse, which was in his charge
and instantly at his disposal.
"I am well pleased by your proposal."   9140
And so at once the youth was able
to lead his master to a stable.
He fetched the hunters to perform
for Sir Gawain, in splendid form.
One was already fit to use
for travel, since he had new shoes
and saddle, bridle, bit and rein.
"My word," exclaimed the lord Gawain,
"lad, you have everything you need!

Go! May the King of kings both speed   9150
your travels, and may He not fail
to keep your horse on the right trail
and help you as you go and come."
And so he sent the young man from
the town and kept him company for
the walk down to the river shore.
Once more he told the ferryman
to row across the water's span.
The boatman took the youth across
and certainly was at no loss,   9160
for he had many rowers rowing.
The young man crossed the river flowing,
and then he took the right road straight
to Orkney and the city gate.
The man who learns to ask directions
can travel round the world in sections.
Meanwhile the lord Gawain returned
to his new palace and sojourned
with greatest joy and with delight,
for everybody loved the knight   9170
and waited on him hand and foot.
The queen had water warmed and put
in bathrooms in five hundred tubs,
and made the youths have baths and scrubs.
Next, after the young men were clean
and had come from the baths, the queen
had told her household to prepare
fine garments for the youths to wear,
of cloth with golden threads entwining
and ermine fur for every lining.   9180
The youths kept watch in church all night
till after matins and daylight,
not kneeling even once, but standing.
Next morning Sir Gawain was handing
the right spurs out to the young lords,
affixing them, and buckling swords,
and giving them the accolade.
There were five hundred knights new-made.
The messenger kept galloping
and came to Orkney, where the king   9190
was holding, as appropriate
for Pentecost, a court in state.

The mangy, crippled, ill, and lamed,
who saw the youth pass by, proclaimed,
"Yes, certainly, the man must bring
some message for the court and king,
from far off places whence he's come.
He'll find King Arthur deaf and dumb,
no matter what he has to tell.
The king is angry, grieved as well,   9200
and who is there to give a word
of good advice, once he has heard
what news the messenger may bear?"
"Go to, it's none of your affair,*
who cares what plans the king has made?"
said others. "You should be afraid,
despairing, lost, and woebegone.
The man who gave us alms is gone.
He gave his gifts to you and me
for love of God and charity.   9210
He's lost to us, which is a pity."
And so the poor throughout the city,
who greatly loved the lord Gawain,
regretted he was gone again.
The youth continued on his way
to court upon the holiday,
and in the palace hall he found
King Arthur seated. All around
there sat one hundred counts palatine,
one hundred seated kings to dine,   9220
one hundred dukes, but not a trace
of Sir Gawain. King Arthur's face
was sorrowful and filled with care
because his nephew was not there.
He fell down in a faint at court,
and everyone ran to support
the king and raised him instantly.
From her seat on the balcony
the lady Lore saw them all,*

v. 9204 ff. The lament of the poor for the generous Gawain is similar to the poor
ladies' lament for Lunete in *Yvain*, vs. 4353-4378 (Roques edition).

v. 9229 (9227, Roach edition). Hilka notes that Lady Lore was not a common name,
and cites references to a Lore de Branlant and a Lore de Carduel (*Der Percevalroman*,
p. 770).

and the commotion in the hall.　　　　　　　　　　9230
She sped downstairs and sought the queen,
upset and shocked by what she'd seen.
The queen, who saw her come along,
asked lady Lore what was wrong.

BIBLIOGRAPHY

This bibliography contains only the references used in the preparation of the translation. The reader is referred to Douglas Kelly's *Chrétien de Troyes, An Analytic Bibliography*, London: Grant and Cutler Ltd., 1976 (pub. 1977), which contains a comprehensive survey of the literature on the *Story of the Grail*.

Anitchkof, E. "Le Saint Graal et les rites eucharistiques." *Romania 55* (1929): 174–194.

Bezzola, Reto R. *Le Sens de l'Aventure et de l'Amour (Chrétien de Troyes)*. Paris: Editions Champion, 1968.

Brown, A. C. L. *The Origin of the Grail Legend*. New York, Russell & Russell, 1966.

Bruce, J. D. *The Evolution of Arthurian Romance*. 2 vols. 2nd ed. Baltimore: Johns Hopkins University Press, 1928.

Bullock-Davies, Constance. *Professional Interpreters and the Matter of Britain*. Cardiff: University of Wales Press, 1966.

Chrétien de Troyes. *Cligès*. Edited by Alexandre Micha. Paris: Editions Champion, 1957.

Chrétien de Troyes. *Erec et Enide*. Edited by Mario Roques. Paris: Editions Champion, 1953.

Chrétien de Troyes. *Lancelot (Le Chevalier de la Charrette)*. Edited by Mario Roques. Paris: Editions Champion, 1958.

Chrétien de Troyes. *Le Conte du Graal (Perceval)*. Translated by Jacques Ribard. Paris, Editions Champion, 1979.

Chrétien de Troyes. *Perceval le Gallois ou le Conte du Graal*. Translated by Lucien Foulet. Preface by Mario Roques. Paris: Editions Stock, 1947.

Chrétien de Troyes. *Perceval (Li Contes del Graal)*. Edited by Félix Lecoy. 2 vols. CFMA vols. 100 and 103. Paris: Editions Champion, 1973 and 1975.

Chrétien de Troyes. "Perceval or the Story of the Grail." Translated by Roger Sherman Loomis and Laura Hibbard Loomis. In *Medieval Romances*. New York: Random House, Modern Library, 1957.

Chrétien de Troyes. *Perceval ou le Roman du Graal*. Translated by Jean-Pierre Foucher and André Ortais. Paris: Editions Gallimard, 1974.

Chrétien de Troyes. *Der Percevalroman (Li Contes del Graal)*. Edited by Alfons Hilka ("Christian von Troyes sämtliche erhaltene Werke," ed. Wendelin Foerster, Vol. 5). Halle (Salle): Max Niemeyer Verlag, 1932.

Chrétien de Troyes. *Le Roman de Perceval ou le Conte du Graal*. Edited by William Roach. 2nd ed. Geneva: Droz, 1959.

Chrétien de Troyes. *Le Roman de Perceval ou le Conte du Graal*. Translated by Henri de Briel. Paris: C. Klincksieck, 1971.

Chrétien de Troyes. *Yvain (Le Chevalier au Lion)*. Edited by Mario Roques. Paris: Editions Champion, 1960.

Chrétien de Troyes. *Yvain: or, the Knight with the Lion*. Translated by Ruth Harwood Cline. Athens, Georgia: University of Georgia Press, 1975.

Delbouille, Maurice. "Le Témoinage de Wace sur la légende Arthurienne." *Romania 74* (1953): 172–199.

Frappier, Jean. *Chrétien de Troyes*. Paris: Hatier, 1968.

Frappier, Jean. *Chrétien de Troyes et le Mythe du Graal*. Paris: Sociéte d'Edition d'Enseignement Supérieur, 1972.

Frappier, Jean. "*Le Conte du Graal* est-il une allégorie judéo-chrétienne?" *Romance Philology 16* (1962–1963): 179–213, and *20* (1966): 1–31.

Frappier, Jean. "Du 'graal trestot descovert' à la forme du graal chez Chrétien de Troyes." *Romania 73* (1952): 82–92.

Frappier, Jean. "Note complémentaire sur la composition du *Conte du Graal*." *Romania 81* (1960): 308–337.

Guyer, Foster E. "The influence of Ovid on Chrétien de Troyes." *Romanic Review 12*, no. 2-3 (1921): 126–131, 216–232.

Haidu, Peter. *Aesthetic Distance in Chrétien de Troyes*. Geneva: Droz, 1968.

Hoggan, David G. "Le Péché de Perceval: Pour l'authenticité de l'épisode de l'ermite dans le *Conte du Graal* de Chrétien de Troyes." *Romania 93* (1972): 50–76, 244–275.

Holmes, Urban T., Jr. *Chrétien de Troyes*. New York: Twayne Publishers, 1970.

Klenke, Sister M. Amelia, O. P. "Chrétien's Symbolism and Cathedral Art." *PMLA 70* (1955):223–243.

Laurie, Helen C. R. "Chrétien and the English Court." *Romania 93* (1972): 85–86.

Laurie, Helen C. R. "Towards an Interpretation of the *Conte du Graal*." *Modern Language Review 66* (1971): 775–785.

Lecoy, Felix. Review of "La Composicion de *Li Contes del Graal* y el 'Guiromelant'" by Martin de Riquer. *Romania 80* (1959): 268–274.

Lecoy, Felix. Review of "La Lanza de Pellés," "Perceval y las gotas de sangre en la nieve," "Perceval y Gauvain en *Li Contes del Graal*" by Martin de Riquer. *Romania 78* (1957): 408–412.

Lejeune, Rita. "La date du *Conte du Graal* de Chrétien de Troyes." *Le Moyen Age 60* (1954): 51–79.

Loomis, Roger Sherman, ed. *Arthurian Literature in the Middle Ages*. London: Oxford University Press, 1969.

Loomis, Roger Sherman. *Arthurian Tradition and Chrétien de Troyes*. New York: Columbia University Press, 1949.

Loomis, Roger Sherman. *The Development of Arthurian Romance*. London: Hutchinson University Library, 1963.

Loomis, Roger Sherman. *The Grail: From Celtic Myth to Christian Symbol*. New York: Columbia University Press, 1963.

Loomis, Roger Sherman. "Grail Problems." *Romanic Review 45* (1954): 12–17.

Loomis, Roger Sherman. "The Grail Story of Chrétien de Troyes as Ritual and Symbolism." *PMLA 71* (1956): 840–852.

Lot-Borodine, Myrrha. "*Le Conte del Graal* de Chrétien de Troyes et sa présentation symbolique." *Romania 77* (1956): 235–288.

Micha, Alexandre. "Deux études sur le Graal: I, Le Graal et la lance." *Romania 73* (1952): 462–479.

Micha, Alexandre. *La Tradition manuscrite des romans de Chrétien de Troyes.* Paris: Droz, 1939.

Nitze, William A. and Williams, Harry F. *Arthurian Names in the Perceval of Chrétien de Troyes.* University of California Publications in Modern Philology, vol. 38, no. 33. Berkeley and Los Angeles: University of California Press, 1955, pp. 265–292.

Nitze, William A. "Le 'Bruiden' celtique et le château du Graal," and "Le 'Bruiden' et la Lance-qui-saigne." *Romania 75* (1954): 231–240, 512–520.

Nitze, William A. "The Fisher King and the Grail in Retrospect." *Romance Philology 6* (1952–1953): 14–22.

Nitze, William, A. *Perceval and the Holy Grail.* University of California Publications in Modern Philology, vol. 28, no. 5. Berkeley and Los Angeles: University of California Press, 1949.

Nykrog, Per. "Two Creators of Narrative Form in Twelfth Century France: Gautier d'Arras—Chrétien de Troyes." *Speculum 48* (1973): 258–276.

Ovid. *The Metamorphoses.* Translated by Horace Gregory. New York: Viking, 1958.

Roques, Mario. "Le Graal de Chrétien et la demoiselle au Graal." *Romania 76* (1955): 1–27.

Roques, Mario. "Le Manuscrit fr. 794 de la Bibliothèque Nationale et le scribe Guiot." *Romania 73* (1952): 177–199.

Spensley, Ronald M. "Gauvain's Castle of Marvellous Adventure in the *Conte del Graal.*" *Medium Aevum 42* (1973): 32–37.

Virgil. *The Aeneid.* Translated by Rolfe Humphries. New York: Charles Scribner's Sons. The Scribner Library, 1951.